Imagery from *Genesis*
in Holocaust Memoirs

Imagery from *Genesis* in Holocaust Memoirs
A Critical Study

DEBORAH LEE PRESCOTT

McFarland & Company, Inc., Publishers
Jefferson, North Carolina, and London

LIBRARY OF CONGRESS CATALOGUING-IN-PUBLICATION DATA

Prescott, Deborah Lee, 1954–
    Imagery from Genesis in Holocaust memoirs : a critical study / Deborah Lee Prescott.
        p.   cm.
    Includes bibliographical references and index.

    ISBN 978-0-7864-4817-3
    softcover : 50# alkaline paper ∞

    1. Holocaust, Jewish (1939–1945) — Personal narratives — History and criticism. 2. Holocaust survivors — Biography — History and criticism. 3. Bible. O.T. Genesis — Influence.
4. Bible. O.T. Genesis — Criticism, interpretation, etc.
5. Rabbinical literature — History and criticism. 6. Allusions.
I. Title.
D804.348.P74   2010
940.53'180922 — dc22   2010009825

British Library cataloguing data are available

©2010 Deborah Lee Prescott. All rights reserved

No part of this book may be reproduced or transmitted in any form or by any means, electronic or mechanical, including photocopying or recording, or by any information storage and retrieval system, without permission in writing from the publisher.

Front cover: *The Sacrifice of Isaac*, 1625 (Pictures Now); background ©2010 Shutterstock

Manufactured in the United States of America

McFarland & Company, Inc., Publishers
  Box 611, Jefferson, North Carolina 28640
    www.mcfarlandpub.com

To the memory of Larry and Betty Nix
and Mary Wood

With gratitude for all Holocaust survivors
who have told the stories of their lives

Acknowledgments

A friend from graduate school once told me that he never reads the Acknowledgments section of a book because he thought it revealed the author to be self-serving and self-congratulatory. I disagreed with this friend then as I do now. I enjoy reading authors' acknowledgments because the words pay tribute to those who contributed to the authors' thoughts and insights. In my own writing, I am made richer in my academic pursuits because of the scholarship of others, many of whom are mentioned by name in the preface.

In bringing this specific book to fruition, I have many people to thank, but here I will name only a few. I am fortunate to have many friends who have encouraged me over the years to keep my focus on the book. I am grateful for Ellen Felman, who has been tireless in her support of my interest in the Shoah and in Jewish studies. I am thankful for the training in autobiographical studies that I received from several professors, particularly Elizabeth Grubgeld, who is a fine critic of my writing. My deep gratitude goes to Kathleen Anderson, whose editorial suggestions gave me invaluable assistance.

Table of Contents

Acknowledgments — vi
Preface — 1
Introduction: Genesis and Genocide—The Holocaust, Autobiography, and Midrash — 5

One. Paradise Lost, Innocence Lost — 31
Two. God's Ark and Hitler's Cattle Car — 51
Three. The Babel of Extermination — 79
Four. *Akeda*: The Perversity of Silence — 100
Five. Israel in Auschwitz: A Malediction Forbidding Mourning — 131
Six. Fratricide — 166

Epilogue — 181
Bibliography — 185
Index — 193

Preface

In the following pages, I examine autobiographies written by Jewish Holocaust survivors who find in the Biblical book of Genesis the exact story or image by which to explicate their all but unimaginable experience. Such intertextuality creates a dynamic text with fresh insights into the Holocaust ordeal and surprising repercussions back to the Hebrew Scriptures. I demonstrate the ways in which the allusions shed light on both the Genesis text and the historical event of the Nazi genocide.

Devout Jews, nominally observant Jews, and Jews who had no interest in Judaism all fell under a death sentence if they were within the reach of Hitler's Third Reich. Piety and spiritual practice meant nothing to the Nazis in singling out the Jews; regardless of religious observation, a Jew was defined by a Nazi-invented bloodline chart and the Nuremberg race laws of 1935. I must acknowledge that millions of others were persecuted and killed by the Nazis, but as Elie Wiesel frequently notes, not all of the Nazis' victims were Jews, but all Jews were victims. Hitler and his supporters singled out the Jews for complete destruction, and as such, the Nazi destruction of the Jews was an ontological attack that makes it different from the assaults on other groups.

I explore in the upcoming pages the often surprising use of Scripture in the autobiographies of Jewish Holocaust survivors, most of whom would not consider themselves pious; yet as they turn to Genesis, the lifewriters read it not as an ancient fable but instead as relevant, modern commentary. The intersection of history, autobiography, and theology has fascinated me for years; for all of the vast number of texts on each of those subjects, mine is the first, to my knowledge, to examine in-depth the theological importance of Scriptural allusions made by Holocaust autobiographers. To appreciate the impact the memoirists' allusions make, three key elements need to be considered: the Holocaust, autobiography, and Midrash. After establishing important aspects of those key elements in the introduction, each subsequent chapter will examine a specific Biblical allusion. I situate the historical dynamics of Jewish suffering during the Second World War, examine the literary nature of the Scriptural allusion made by the autobiographer, and consider relevant rabbinic commentary known as Midrash.

Holocaust studies was at one time a step-child of Second World War studies; now it exists as a discipline of its own, interdisciplinary as it must be. My knowledge of the Holocaust has come through the rigorous and meticulous labor of many scholars; I am indebted to such writers as Alan L. Berger, Lucy S. Dawidowicz, Emil Fackenheim, Saul Friedländer, Harold Kaplan, and Alvin H. Rosenberg, to name only a few. One cannot study the Holocaust without studying Hitler and Nazism: Joachim C. Fest, Richard Grunberger, Konrad Heiden, George L. Mosse, and John Toland's work have helped me immensely.

Just as the Holocaust as an academic discipline once existed as a subset of a specific war, the same status was once assigned to the literary study of autobiography. Fortunately for literary scholars interested in autobiography, the pioneering theoretical work in the mid-twentieth century by such critics as Georges Gusdorf, James Olney, Louis Renza, and Roy Pascal established the groundwork for critical legitimacy. Later their analyses were challenged, expanded upon, and re-examined by such scholars as Sidonie Smith, Estelle Jelinek, Elizabeth Bruss, and John Paul Eakin, as autobiography's status in the academy gradually gained respectability. Today the literary study of autobiography is a flourishing field in which to work.

Jewish studies is a vast area, and as I specifically look at what Midrash is and how the Holocaust autobiographers participate in it (even if unintentionally), I draw from the wisdom and intellectual conclusions of many men and women. All Scriptural quotes are from *The Torah: A Modern Commentary*, edited by W. Gunther Plaut, published by the Union of American Hebrew Congregations; that particular edition is filled with extraordinarily insightful Biblical exegesis from thinkers throughout the centuries. Help with understanding Jewish history, Biblical interpretations, and Midrash comes from such writers as Robert Alter, Martin Buber,

Preface

Andrew Vogel Ettin, Emil Fackenheim, Saul Friedländer, Edwin C. Goldberg, Abraham Joshua Heschel, Jacob Neusner, Nahum M. Sarna, and Joseph Telushkin.

Examining the literature that has emerged out of the ashes of the Holocaust is a daunting task but one that has preoccupied me personally all my life and professionally for well over a decade. I could not have produced my analysis of Biblical allusions in Holocaust survivors' autobiographies without the survivors themselves having had the courage to write their memoirs. Moreover, I could not have had the literary, historical, and theological ability to analyze those memoirs without the invaluable contributions provided by the following writers: M.M. Bakhtin, Arthur Cohen, Terrence Des Pres, T.S. Eliot, Geoffrey H. Hartman, Barry W. Holtz, Irving Howe, Lawrence L. Langer, Philippe Lejeune, André Neher, David Patterson, and George Steiner.

For all of the writers, thinkers, and scholars whom I have just mentioned, I give my deepest thanks, for it is on their work that mine has been built. Many more scholars' insights will appear throughout the upcoming pages; for them too I am grateful.

My fascination — some would call it an obsession — with the Holocaust and the first-person accounts it generated began when I was about 12-years-old. My mother, may her memory be blessed, handed me a copy of Anne Frank's *The Diary of a Young Girl* and recommended that I read it. That book changed my life. Some people dismiss Frank's diary as juvenilia or precocious or over-praised; all I can say is that once I read it, I could not understand how the Holocaust had happened, nor could I comprehend how the world continued on, seemingly normally, after the Holocaust was over. My book will, I hope, honor the Jews who suffered so terribly under the hand of the Third Reich and contribute to the scholarship that their written texts so richly deserve.

Introduction
Genesis and Genocide — The Holocaust, Autobiography, and Midrash

> He told me his story, and today I have forgotten it, but it was certainly a sorrowful, cruel and moving story; because so are all our stories, hundreds of thousands of stories, all different and all full of a tragic, disturbing necessity.
>
> We tell them to each other in the evening, and they take place in Norway, Italy, Algeria, the Ukraine, and are simple and incomprehensible like the stories in the Bible. But are they not themselves stories of a new Bible?
>
> — Primo Levi

Primo Levi asserts a startling proposition in the epigraph above: The tales told by Holocaust victims comprise a "new Bible." Although not all would agree with Levi's evaluation that Biblical stories are "simple and incomprehensible," most readers of Scripture would concede that many of the narratives defy a simplistic interpretation. Certainly the Bible is filled with "sorrowful, cruel, and moving" stories, albeit not exclusively tragic ones. In just those few sentences from his first and best-known Holocaust account, *Survival in Auschwitz*, Levi positions victims' stories within an elevated canon. Whether or not readers would concur with Levi's proposition that the stories told by those who experienced the Holocaust comprise "a new Bible," many would agree that those tales are fascinating, recounting the best and worst of human behavior. Many autobiographers grapple not only with the inexplicable actions of human beings but also the mysterious actions (and inaction) of God, even if the individual writer may not believe in a deity. Some of those autobiographers turn to the book of Genesis to explain or contextualize the Holocaust ordeal they experienced.

Introduction

Literary citations abound in survivors' writings — to Shakespeare, Goëthe, Kafka, Dante, national poets, and regional playwrights — but within Jewish writers' texts, Biblical allusions shed a particular light on the Holocaust. Throughout the upcoming chapters, I will focus upon references made to Genesis. The Genesis allusions studied herein were made by survivors in their memoirs that were either written in English or were translated into English, and all of the autobiographers were laypeople. While some rabbis lived through the Holocaust (historians estimate that the Nazis murdered approximately 80 percent of the world's Torah scholars) and a few surviving rabbis wrote their memoirs, those works are not included in this study because it seems natural that a rabbi would find the Bible useful in communicating his ordeal. The masculine pronoun is necessary here, as all rabbis during the Second World War were men. A rabbi is necessarily a student of the Bible, but what does it mean that a layperson, who may or may not know Scripture well, finds in that ancient text the exact image by which a collision with Nazism may be effectively communicated?

The Nazis lashed out at any individual or group who did not meet their imaginary criteria of Aryan breeding or who did not support the party's ideology. As such, millions were attacked, persecuted, and killed because of who they were and what they believed. The Nazis routinely attacked such groups as homosexuals, Communists, clergy, Jehovah's Witnesses, the mentally or physically disabled, Russian prisoners of war, Slavic people, Roma and Sinti (gypsies), to name only a few, as well as any individual who challenged the Nazis' power. The Nazis killed Roma and Sinti with almost as much single-minded determination as they killed Jews. Slavs were considered by the Nazis to be a lower life-form; during the war, the Nazis were content to enslave the Slavic people and work them to death. The most pressing concern for Hitler and his collaborators as they sought to establish their Thousand Year Reich globally was the elimination of the Jews. As Elie Wiesel has said frequently, not all of the Nazis' victims were Jews, but all Jews were victims. The Nazis' hate recognized no limits, and any person who ran afoul of the Third Reich was subject to torture, imprisonment, or death. The history of the Second World War has moments of heroic defiance of Nazism — not as many as one would hope for, but those potentially lethal examples of conscience that did occur

Introduction

deserve to be honored. Many individuals whom the Nazis targeted had a chance to live, if only they would renounce their principles. Not so for the Jews of the Third Reich.

In his memoir of being a slave within Auschwitz's crematoria, Filip Müller records a thoughtful speech given by a prisoner, the Dajan, who served as the *de facto* spiritual leader of Orthodox men. The Dajan reminded his fellow prisoners that a "'pious Jew does not read the Bible like a legend, but applies its content to the present'" (p. 67). His insight transcends time and space. Hebrew Scriptures can and could be read "like a legend"; however, the "pious Jew" understands that universal truths are contained in it. Amidst the spiritual inspiration inherent within the Bible, Jews (and Christians) find in the Bible archetypal patterns. Müller recalls the Dajan saying: "'A few years ago when I read in the synagogue from the Book of Esther, which describes the cruel annihilation of the defenseless Jewish people, I had the same feeling as now'" (p. 67). The annihilation that threatened the Jews at the hands of Haman, as recorded in the Biblical text of Esther, was being accomplished "now," at the hands of Hitler. There were Jews, as Müller shows, who believed that Hitler would meet the same fate as Haman, who not only failed in his attempt to kill the Jews but who was executed for his treachery. However, there were also Jews whose autobiographical writings explore their belief that, out of all the promises ever made to the Jews, only Hitler seemed to keep his vow: the vow to make Europe *Judenfrei*, free of Jews, and *Judenrein*, cleansed of Jews.

Adolf Hitler never made his contempt of the Jews a secret. Virtually every page of his 1925 manifesto, *Mein Kampf*, drips with his all-consuming hatred. In the second chapter of *Mein Kampf*, he makes his first mention of the "two menaces" that preoccupy him — the Marxists and the Jews (p. 21), but overwhelmingly does he return to his obsession with the Jews. For instance, he muses early in his book that the Jews of Linz had, throughout the centuries, "taken on a human look" (p. 52) and he equates the Jewish people with "pestilence" (p. 58). His agenda against the Jews should have come as no surprise because he states emphatically: "*Only a knowledge of the Jews provides the key with which to comprehend the inner, and consequently real, aims of Social Democracy* [Nazism]" (p. 51, italics in text). Although the trajectory of discrimination leading to extermination will be examined throughout the upcoming chapters, here it is sufficient to remind

Introduction

readers that when Hitler took control of the German government in January 1933, he immediately began systematic means within the legal system to isolate Jews. Each year of the intended Thousand Year Reich brought greater hardships to the Jews, and by the time the war began, Jews under Hitler were suffering from a long list of legal humiliations. Although citizens of the United States commonly think of World War II lasting from 1941 to 1945, as late 1941 saw the U.S.'s entry into the war, Europeans will remember that the war actually began when Hitler marched into Poland on September 1, 1939. The discrimination against the Jews culminated in the Final Solution, the plan engineered by the Nazis to kill all the Jews of Europe. Historian Lucy Dawidowicz memorably identified the Holocaust as "the war against the Jews."

Naming the "war against the Jews" has presented multiple challenges to history. Given the magnitude of the slaughter and the moral questions that consequently arise, we should not be surprised that words fail. The most common term is *Holocaust*. The word is understood to mean the Nazi genocide perpetrated ruthlessly and primarily upon the Jews, knowing that millions of people in other groups were killed and certain groups were targeted by the Nazis for eventual elimination, including the Slavic people as well as the Roma and Sinti (gypsies). In context of the Reich's determined annihilation of such groups, the word *Holocaust* is capitalized so as to distinguish the Nazi endeavor from other destructive acts, such as nuclear holocaust. I share in the widespread regret that *Holocaust* has become the most familiar term because the word itself is problematic. *Holocaust* is a word of Greek derivation that, when used in Biblical translations from the Hebrew, means "a sacrifice wholly burnt." Thus, when used in the Bible, the Greek term connotes a wholly burned sacrifice demanded by God, who makes holy that which has been burnt (Ezrahi p. 2). In connection with the Final Solution, many people find the term *Holocaust* repugnant because of the religious implications of God's demand for, and approval of, a burnt sacrifice. Some credit Wiesel for popularizing the term; whether he did or did not, he defended the word *Holocaust* in a 1990 interview by observing: "Fire was the dominant image in this tragedy" (*Evil* p. 39). Still, he avers that he no longer uses the word because "it has been so trivialized and commercialized" (p. 39). Indeed, the word makes many scholars and students of this time period uncomfortable.

Introduction

Some scholars of "the war against the Jews" prefer *Shoah*, which implies global disaster. The etymology of that word stresses, however, natural disaster and does not necessarily connect the twentieth century calamity with others in Jewish history. A few use the term the *Event*, with the capital *E* symbolizing its primal place in humanity's recent history, while others use *whirlwind* to convey the violent, exterior force that swept away so many. Still others employ *Night and Fog*, a reference to the official Nazi euphemism for the Final Solution that conjures the era's dark, oblique nature. Less well known to non–Jewish readers is the term *hurban*, which can also be transliterated as *churban* or *hurbn*, with its connotation of violation and destruction. Andrew Vogel Ettin points out that *hurban* "places the destruction of European Jewry within a historical pattern including the destruction of the First and Second Temples" (p. 187). The connotations and denotations for the terms have strengths and weaknesses; I acknowledge that fact but will use the terms interchangeably.

A remnant of European Jewry emerged from the ashes of the Final Solution. Liberated from the nightmare world created by Hitler, they faced a shattered Europe and a public who, by and large, did not want to hear about what they had experienced. Even the youngest survivors of Hitler are now elderly, and time is running out for survivors to share with the world what they endured. Their memories are important, and we who came after them need to learn from them. It is true that we live in a world that still has Holocaust deniers, yet such people would not be convinced by any appeals to facts, logic, or history. Rather, for those who study history and know the reality of the Event, a deeper understanding can be gained from first-person accounts. Only a small number of survivors have written their recollections, and a smaller percentage has had those writings published. In recent years, there has been an organized effort to record survivors' memories; thankfully, several institutions, such as University of Southern California and Yale University, and a few individuals, including Steven Spielberg, have provided the resources for survivors to preserve their testimonies in oral and visual form. The importance of such Shoah foundations cannot be overstated; the possibility of survivors' accounts finding a worldwide audience is vast, due to the Internet. The written memoir, though, still has a place, even within contemporary society's love of YouTube. A thoughtfully written autobiography can go into greater

Introduction

depth, into deeper consideration of the events of the author's life. When a survivor writes down the story of his or her life, that autobiography becomes more than a simple recounting of one individual's life; the text plunges the reader into a place and time where individuals were under a death sentence simply because they existed.

To be at risk of being killed simply because one exists creates ontological and philosophical questions. I am not alone in seeing the Holocaust as a philosophical conundrum. How could such an Event happen? How could humanity have permitted it to happen? If there is a God and if that God is omnipotent, then is it possible that such a God would have become an impassive bystander while millions were annihilated? As Wiesel asserts throughout his work, Auschwitz is neither conceivable with God nor is it conceivable without God. The philosophical paradoxes and conundrums raised by artistic renderings of the Holocaust, such as plays, poems, and movies, are all the more present in autobiographies. Lifewriters expose the "choiceless choices," to use Lawrence Langer's term, itself inspired by Levi's concept of the "Gray Zone." Both phrases hint at the lack of clarity, the absence of absolutes, the inability to make reasoned decisions due to insufficient information. In the alternate world of the Holocaust Kingdom, as survivor Alexander Donat calls it, normal life experiences could not help a prisoner know what to do. Trapped within a world devoted to death, there were relatively few decisions to make, but such choices that could be made often had fatal consequences. Sometimes, those instant, uncertain choices included: Which line leads to life or to death? Should one volunteer for special work duty or try to remain invisible? If one is ill, is there a better chance of living by reporting to work or — here, a Nazi insanity — to the concentration camp hospital? Is it better to be killed than to kill? As the war's end appeared to draw close, should one stay in the camp, hoping that the liberators will soon arrive, or join the march out of camp, trusting that the prisoners are walking towards freedom?

The act of writing one's life story engages ontological decisions, choices that challenge the memoirist. The writer seeks to convey the inexpressible, to describe an Event that defies comprehension. Most survivors were shushed into silence after liberation, as will be shown in Chapter 5; the impulse to tell the truth to a world that does not want to know the

Introduction

truth engages the lifewriter in a metaphysical wrestling match. Many survivors have chosen to keep silent; that is a legitimate decision, given the magnitude of the event and the depth of evil. Those who have written or recorded their memories speak out in order to tell the world, to confront that world which remained silent, and thereby honor those who no longer have a voice.

A handful — not enough — of survivors have written their autobiographies; they felt that the world must know what they went through and what was experienced by those who did not live through the ordeal. Autobiography, also called lifewriting, was once considered a minor subset of the more legitimate historical document of biography. Granted, an autobiography by a known writer might gain some critical regard, but for many years, first-person nonfiction writing was considered anyone's domain. Because anyone could write an autobiography, the genre itself was not literary, and therefore, it was not considered worthy of literary study. Throughout the twentieth century, literary scholars paved the way for legitimate study of autobiography; some of the most influential scholars are acknowledged in the preface. Within the academic study of first-person accounts, a difference may be distinguished between the terms *autobiography* and *memoir*. Technically, *autobiography* is the story of the individual's life as written by that individual; whereas *memoir* implies that the author constrains himself or herself to a specific time, event, or relationship. *Lifewriting* implies that an individual has self-selected particular moments of that life to textualize. All of the works considered in *Imagery from* Genesis *in Holocaust Memoirs* are first-person, nonfiction accounts of the author's Holocaust experience; within these pages, I use interchangeably the terms *autobiography, memoir, lifewriting,* and *first-person account*.

All of the autobiographies examined herein contain allusions to Genesis, and I argue that such intertextuality creates a dynamic dialogue between the contemporary text and the ancient Hebraic work. Allusions to the Bible raise religious questions; allusions as a literary device point to authorial decisions. Peter J. Rabinowitz goes so far as to declare that "any intertextual connection whatsoever is significant" (p. 142) and "any intertextual connection is interpretively relevant" (p. 143). Rabinowitz's assertion may be hyperbolic; nevertheless, it raises the stakes for intertextual

Introduction

connection. Robert McMahon maintains that "a highly literate autobiography will contain explicit references to literary works, allusions, and perhaps more subtle intertextual patterns" (p. 338); such literary devices are ripe for interpretation. McMahon expresses his surprise that literary theorists of autobiography have, by and large, failed to consider the implications of such intertextual resonance (p. 337). Some readers of autobiography believe that the lifewriter simply writes, usually in a straightforward, linear fashion, the story of the life lived thus far. Complications arise as literary theorists wonder about how well the lifewriter knows himself or herself, given the human proclivity towards self-deception; theorists also study how the lifewriter presents the actual or perceived self as a textualized self. McMahon points out that while scholars have been preoccupied with "the dynamic engagement of the writer's self with the work-being-written," such a focus ignores "the dynamic engagement of the writer with other works and literary traditions" within the autobiography itself (p. 337). McMahon's critique is a pertinent one because he grounds his study of Augustine's *Confessions* in light of its literary allusions. *Confessions* is considered the West's first autobiography, and apparently Augustine believed that his text and his authorial self-presentation would be deepened by the intertextual discourse of literary references. That same belief is present in the Holocaust lifewritings wherein literary and Biblical references are made. By examining the intertextual connections between autobiography and the Bible, I hope to rectify, at least in part, this subject's relative lack of critical attention.

Any consideration of intertextuality will benefit from Mikhail Bakhtin's theories on heteroglossia, a term which includes, but is not limited to, literary allusions. Heteroglossia denotes a full range of literary devices by which multiple voices are introduced through quotations, dialogue, references to existing texts, and other novelistic techniques. When authors synthesize dialogic interaction from conversations, literary references, and other languages, Bakhtin theorizes that the text pulsates with more authentic life. He defines heteroglossia as *"another's speech in another's language.* Such speech constitutes a special type of double-voiced discourse. It serves two speakers at the same time" ("Discourse" p. 324). In the case of intertextual allusions, those "two speakers" are the existing work and the newly created work, with meaning subsequently resonating

Introduction

between the two. Bakhtin asserts that the creation of multiple voices gives life to the text; it becomes energetic, a vital organism, a work that is simultaneously more lifelike and more literary.

Bakhtin understands heteroglossic discourse to endow a text with life since human beings can scarcely make it through a day without quoting someone else. We repeat things we heard or read from a book, television, newspaper, radio, or the Internet; we quote our friends, our loved ones, and even our enemies. Quoting others connects us to the broader world; Bakhtin suggests that heteroglossia underscores our very need for connectedness. We do not exist in isolation, and our quotations prove it, both in our speech and in our writing. McMahon observes that intertextuality "represents reading as well as writing, an interpretation of the earlier work as well as a critical response to it" (p. 338). The fusion of reading/writing, of past/present, and of interpretation/recreation invigorates the text. Within the works of Shoah lifewriters, literary allusions abound. Allusions should not be surprising, given the classical education so many authors received and the multicultural world in which they lived. For instance, apt references to such ancient figures as Damocles, Sisyphus, and Niobe appear; concepts familiar in Jewish thought, such as Moloch and the golem, also occur. Holocaust autobiographers frequently refer to beloved regional and national poets; furthermore, references to Shakespeare, Goëthe, and Dante are common. Dante surfaces in many autobiographies; surely no other author could be more appropriate. Dante too described hell, but, over and over again, survivors insist that even Dante's imagination failed to envision the Nazi inferno.

If quoting from a literary work brings the contemporary writing to dialogic life, creating resonance between two texts, the possibilities are arguably greater when the existing text is the Bible. Rabbi Abraham Joshua Heschel believes that the Bible is inherently a dialogic entity. "The Bible has shattered our illusion of being alone," he says, for it teaches that "life is a response, not a soliloquy" (*God in Search* p. 238). The Bible's existence implies an I-Thou relationship, to use Martin Buber's terminology, because the Bible is an account of the interaction between God and humanity. An allusion to it, therefore, asserts a dialogic continuity with humanity's past, at least, and, at most, with the Creator. When autobiographers select words and images from the Bible, they create a heteroglossic work.

Introduction

The allusions by Shoah lifewriters provide vivid intertextual dynamics as they comment upon the Bible while, at the same time, they explicate Nazi oppression. In subsequent chapters, we shall see the manner in which the Nazis inverted, no doubt unconsciously, the action or theme of a particular Biblical story. I have found in the course of working with this material that I can no longer read about such figures as Noah, Abraham, Isaac, and Jacob or such events as the Flood and Babel without the specter of the Holocaust implications reverberating back to the text.

Artistic intertextual meanings can and will work retroactively, as T.S. Eliot proposes in "Tradition and the Individual Talent." He argues that "the past should be altered by the present as much as the present is directed by the past" (p. 467). Eliot asserts that while art may never improve, it is nonetheless dynamic:

> ...what happens when a new work of art is created is something that happens simultaneously to all the works of art which preceded it. The existing monuments form an ideal order among themselves, which is modified by the introduction of the new (the really new) work of art among them. The existing order is complete before the new work arrives; for order to persist after the supervention of novelty, the whole existing order must be, if ever so slightly, altered; and so the relations, proportions, values of each work of art toward the whole are readjusted; and this is conformity between the old and the new [467].

An allusion is a form of heteroglossia which moves across time but not in one direction only, as the new retroactively invigorates the old. As Eliot suggests, former meanings can deepen, grow, or change because of their contact with the present. In this book, we will consider the ways in which the Bible and the Holocaust readjust in light of survivors' words.

At this juncture, I assert the primacy of written memories over Lawrence Langer's preference for oral history. Langer's thesis, as he presents it in *Holocaust Testimonies: The Ruins of Memory*, is that oral history represents the most immediate and honest presentation of survivors' accounts because speech is not artfully filtered or cleverly composed. Both written and oral accounts have their valuable places, but, as Wiesel observes: "The spoken word and the written word do not reflect the same experience" (*All Rivers* p. 150). The spoken word can be heard by a hearer in the speaker's presence, or it can be recorded. A survivor speaking forth his or her experience for a listener — be it a solitary hearer or an audience in a lecture hall or a person anywhere in the world sitting in front of a

Introduction

computer — gives immediacy to the Holocaust experience as the speaker embodies it. Of course, oral accounts can be written down, as in a transcript from a television show or a trial. However, a problem can arise when a listener finds the survivor's testimony distressing. The listener may be too disturbed by hearing what the survivor endured to listen well. If the survivor speaks in response to an interviewer's question, potential problems exist. Scientists are not the only group to know that observation can change what is being observed. Certain studies have been weakened by an interviewer too overcome to ask follow-up questions or to press for details.

The written autobiography represents the words chosen by the author to create a textual world. The Holocaust autobiography is a form of testifying in which the author conveys his or her experience without having to negotiate the immediate response of an interviewer or an audience. Written accounts are valuable because they are potentially capable of wider distribution and a larger audience than an oral account. Langer confesses his fear that the written word, or even a speaker's reliance upon any literary conventions, such as metaphor or simile, creates situations wherein the "literary *transform*[s] the real in a way that obscures even as it seeks to enlighten" (*Holocaust Testimonies* p. 19, italics in text). Lifewriting has the capability to be more artful than the spoken word, but that does not undermine its authenticity, particularly when the writer conveys testimony or trauma. Art does not necessarily make the survivor's story more obscure; its artfulness can potentially bring forth enlightenment all the more powerfully.

The Shoah lifewriters who dialogically interact with Scripture place themselves within Levi's assessment that the stories told comprise a new Bible. The Bible records God's interaction, or lack thereof, with humanity; it also raises questions about who this God is. Shoah autobiographers grapple with the day-to-day questions that confronted them as well as the overarching philosophical and spiritual questions raised by the Event. Challenged as to God's whereabouts during the Shoah, one concentration camp survivor "responded calmly [in Yiddish], 'He was with us'" (qtd. in Carmy p. 7, brackets in text). Many lifewriters pay tribute to Jews who went to their deaths proclaiming the *Shema*, the central prayer of Judaism. However, for every confident declaration that God was present with God's chosen people, the opposite exists — an anguished or angry assertion that

Introduction

God either does not exist or that God abandoned the Jews. Some lifewriters address God in their very titles. Joseph Bau, for instance, demands, *Dear God, Have You Ever Gone Hungry?* The title of Alfred Dube's unpublished autobiography, held in the United States Holocaust Memorial Museum's archives, implores, "And Where Was God?" Those titular questions lead to more questions: If there is a God, should God be blamed for the destruction? Or does the guilt fall exclusively upon the human beings who initiated and perpetrated it? Does the prisoner's anguish prove that God was there, suffering with the victims? Or are camps in themselves proof that God was dead, absent, or ineffectual? Lucille Eichengreen recalls preparing to say the *Kaddish* for her father: "I wondered if I should recite the Kaddish, the Hebrew prayer for the dead. Its words glorify God and his mercy, but after Auschwitz, I had stopped believing in either one" (p. 198). The Jews have long had a concept of being the chosen people. Many memoirists and essayists contemplate what it means to be chosen, whether by God or by the Nazis.

As survivors grapple with writing their experiences, some turn to Scripture to assist them. While heteroglossia, allusions, and rereading the past in light of the present are often credited as gifts of literary modernism, rabbis have long incorporated other voices dialogically in their contemplations. Rabbis, in particular, have necessarily grounded their written and oral pronouncements concerning Judaism upon their Scriptural interpretations, although many prefer the Hebrew appellation *TaNaKH* to the Greek-derived word *Bible*. Naomi M. Hyman explains to those unfamiliar with the term that "TaNaKH [is] a word made up of the first letters of the Hebrew names of the three sections that make up the Bible. Those three sections are the Torah, or Teaching; Nevi'im, or Prophets; and Ketuvim, or Writings" (p. xxi). I will use the terms *Bible*, *Scripture*, *Hebrew Scriptures*, and *TaNaKH* as synonyms, and I will use the Hebrew term for the Bible's first book, *Bereshit*, as a synonym for *Genesis*. When exploring what the rabbis have to say about Scripture, one must turn to rabbinical literature. Such a collection may be classified broadly into three traditions: the legal questions that are addressed in the *halakha*, the non-legal issues that are contained within the *aggada*, and the hypothetical exegeses which are collected under the rubric of *Midrash*.

Midrash is a form of rabbinic literature wherein commentators engage

Introduction

in exegetical, philological, and hermeneutical interpretations of a Bible story. The rabbis might concentrate upon a short passage, a line, an individual word, or even the shape of the Hebrew letter that forms the word, as every element is worthy of scrutiny. The term *Midrash* is derived from the word *search* in Hebrew, a connotation which it maintains (Neusner *Introduction* p. ix). Appropriately, the Midrash records the rabbis' search for meaning within Scripture, and the compilation of rabbinic insights preserves disagreements, elaborations, and speculations over any given Biblical passage or phrase. While today's computer enthusiasts revel in the Internet's hypertext and the links it can generate, they may be unaware that Midrash exists as an ancient form of hypertext. Midrash contains dialogic interaction that moves across millennia. A word, an idea, an insight: any of these may form links and inspire insights that cross continents, interpretations, and time.

Midrash is a compilation of rabbinical exegeses, so a reader may go to the bookshelf and pull out *Genesis Rabbah*, the Midrashic commentary on Genesis, or examine the Midrash on Exodus, Deuteronomy, and so on. However, Midrash is by no means limited to that singular denotation. In *Midrash for Beginners*, Edwin C. Goldberg explains that while Midrash is "a specific body of classical rabbinic commentary on the Bible, edited from approximately the year 200 of the Common Era (C.E.) to the ninth century" (p. xii), it is more than that because "any comment which is directly or indirectly related to the Bible is [M]idrashic" (p. xi–xii). In his guide *What is Midrash?* Jacob Neusner offers a three-fold definition. When people announce that the Midrash asserts a particular point about a Biblical story, they could be describing "*a concrete unit* of scriptural exegesis" or "*a compilation* of the results of that process" or "*a process* of interpretation" (p. i, emphasis in text). Neusner consequently identifies three Midrashic attributes: paraphrase, prophecy, and parable (p. 7). As paraphrase, Midrash may bring "fresh meanings" to Scripture (p. 7). As prophecy, it "addresses contemporary times as a guide to what is happening even now" (p. 7). As parable, the final component in Neusner's triad, Midrash finds "the exegete read[ing] Scripture in terms other than those in which the scriptural writer speaks" (p. 8). Midrash, then, serves multiple functions: It speculates about the literary text of the Bible; it records how rabbis throughout the centuries have interpreted Scripture; and it contains insights into how existing text can be retroactively charged by contemporary reading in the dynamic, dialogic manner Eliot described.

In upcoming chapters, we will see how Holocaust survivors engage in the Midrashic tradition when they turn to Genesis to elucidate their ordeal. Their references participate in such Midrashic aspects as interpreting ancient understanding for contemporary situations and inviting a new perspective on Scriptural narrative. Walter J. Houston explains that Midrash is firmly rooted in a fundamental "rabbinic principle" of "difference is more fruitful than similarity" (p. 344). It bears lively proof that a text may render radically different interpretations as rabbis speculate upon a Biblical passage and wonder about the story behind the story, about the words used and the words not used, and about the letters that create the words. Yet for all its lack of consensus and its celebration of argument, Midrash always keeps the Jewish people in its heart of hearts. Midrash, says Gary G. Porter, "is a term given to a Jewish activity which finds its locus in the religious life of the Jewish community" (p. 62). Emil Fackenheim asserts that Midrash "reflects upon the root experience of Judaism" and that time is transcended because Midrash looks upon the Biblical passage as both a past and present event (*God's Presence* 20). If a Midrashic quality is to express a central experience of Judaism, then Jewish lifewriters of the Shoah participate in Midrash because their use of Scripture explicates a "root" phenomenon of European Jewry of the 1930s and 1940s, with all its lingering effect.

To read Scripture, to comment, to wonder, to question, to argue, to let the past have meaning for today and today have meaning for the past: all are aspects of Midrash. Byron L. Sherwin also emphasizes community when he says that Midrash provides "a means by which our story may become incorporated into the continuing story of Jewish experience. Midrash ensures a relationship between an ancient text and a modern problem, between ancient events and contemporary experiences" (p. 117). When the Bible is used to explicate Nazism's impact upon the Jewish community, there is Midrash, that is, the nexus of "an ancient text and a modern problem," to use Sherwin's words. Scriptural allusions used by Shoah autobiographers may be understood to be Midrashic. As we have seen, Midrash is more than a bound compilation of rabbinic commentary. Rabbi Joseph Telushkin believes that Midrash "continues to be created" (p. 157);

Introduction

similarly, Rabbi A. David Packman argues that "Midrash is ongoing" (personal interview). Although not rabbis, the *hurban* lifewriters join in the ongoing creation of Scriptural exegesis; although not formal Midrash, their reflections participate in the heteroglossic, intertextual dialogue created between contemporary autobiography and Hebrew Scriptures. When Shoah survivors draw upon Scripture to mediate their experience, their allusions become commentary.

Both Midrash and intertextuality necessarily involve the activity of reading. Judaism celebrates reading and studying, and throughout Jewish history, the Bible has influenced, inspired, and puzzled ordinary reader and rabbi alike. Rabbis have naturally read the Hebrew Scriptures deeply and actively. Geoffrey H. Hartman and Sanford Budick credit the rabbinic manner of reading as the source for our modern-day close reading of literature (p. x). Hartman notes that "literary criticism and [M]idrashic modes" have begun "to blend into each other" ("Struggle" p. 12). Barry W. Holtz argues that many people "think of reading as a passive occupation," but not so in the Jewish tradition (p. 16). "Reading was a passionate and active grappling with God's living word" (p. 16). As "living word," the text is dynamic, making claims and demanding responses. Calling the Bible "the perpetual motion of the spirit," Heschel asks us to think of the Bible as ever-new, continually creating itself energetically each time it is read or heard (*God in Search* p. 241). It transcends time and the static imprint of the letter. Buber believes that if the Bible is patronized "as merely religious writing," that is, if it is respected as an ancient mythological text or even as a spiritual guide, "it will fail us," and, reciprocally, we also "fail it"; however, if "we seize upon it as the expression of a reality that comprises all of life, we really grasp it, and it grasps hold of us" (*On the Bible* p. 4). Hebrew Scripture, in such a view, is life-giving and life-enhancing. Many Holocaust lifewriters find in it a clear expression of a reality that, prior to the mid-twentieth century, could not have been imagined.

Hebrew Scripture records Jewish history; Jews are asked to remember their history and to make it a living presence, both in daily life and when holidays, such as Passover, are celebrated. Heschel succinctly states how important memory is in Judaism: "The Jew says, 'I believe,' and is told, 'Remember!'" (*God in Search* p. 21). Essential to the core of the faith is the injunction to remember: Remember that you were slaves in Egypt;

Introduction

remember to keep the Sabbath a holy day; remember when you see the tassels on your prayer garments to follow the Lord. Such exhortations are but a few of the nearly 70 injunctions to "remember" in the Hebrew Scriptures. A cognate of "memory" is "not to forget" and that, too, has its place in Scripture. When Jews were led into Babylonian captivity, the psalmist urges memory: "If I forget Thee, O Jerusalem! Let my right hand wither! Let my tongue cleave to the roof of my mouth, if I do not remember you...." That pivotal text from Psalm 137 eventually became the rallying cry during the early phase of Zionism, a philosophical and political movement with which many Shoah memoirists were involved. Remembering is the reason some lifewriters, if not most, write. Honoring the injunctions to remember is what propels some autobiographers to face excruciating memories, if for no other reason than to perform a literary *kaddish*, the prayer for the dead.

Although Judaism has no prescribed dogma to which all believers must adhere, there is, in fact, a central principle: the *Sh'ma*, which may also be transliterated as *Shema*. The *Shema* is the divine revelation which Moses imparted to the people in Deuteronomy 6:4 and may be transliterated as "*Shema Yisra'el, Adonai Eloheinu, Adonai Ekhad.*" "Hear, O Israel, the Lord our God, the Lord is One." The Deuteronomic passage, occurring just after the review of the Ten Commandments and other ordinances, continues with the instructions to teach one's children about God and to bind the commandments upon one's body and one's house. Shortly following the *Shema* comes the cautionary "...take heed lest you forget the LORD, who brought you out of the land of Egypt, out of the house of bondage." Judaism, then, requires remembering agonizing times as a necessary component of understanding one's self, one's community, and one's God. Although Freud has received modern credit for discovering how unresolved traumas affect a person's behavior, the Jewish faith has, for millennia, recognized the desire to suppress such memories while urging people to face them in order that their lives may be whole.

In the spirit of the command to remember, the community of Jewish survivors demands: "Remember!" and "Never again!" These two admonishments call out across time's chasm, more than a half-century after the Nazis pursued with single-minded determination the annihilation of European Jewry. These two cries require that we remember a time when Hitler's

Introduction

regime almost accomplished that resolve and that we do all in our power never to allow such genocide to happen again. Only a percentage of European Jewry survived the war — and a particularly small percentage in Eastern Europe — the *sh'erit hapleita*, the saved remnant; they urge us to remember recent history. Still, we need not be labeled skeptics if we look at current events and wonder if "Never again" is a futile phrase, given the proclivities of the human heart. Ethnic cleansing took place in Cambodia, Rwanda, and Bosnia-Herzegovina, not long ago. Saying "Never again" seems meaningless when genocide is even now occurring. Rallies designed to raise awareness and outrage over the rapes and murders in the Darfur region of the Sudan have used the slogan: "Never Again Means Never Again for Anyone!" Unfortunately, the Shoah survivors' call for people to abandon their murderous ways has fallen, once again, on deaf ears.

Is the demand "Remember!" any more successful? On the one hand, survivors have found, over the 60-plus years since their liberation, an increasing interest in their stories. Whereas once only a few survivors' voices cried in the wilderness, now a plethora of books are available about the Event. Survivors who were once hushed are now asked to tell their stories to listeners in schools, civic organizations, and religious groups; some have accepted invitations to revisit the European sites they experienced during the *hurban*. On the other hand, the world did not want to know about the Holocaust when it was happening, and now, more than a half-century later, some would distrust survivors who come forward only now to share their accounts. Memory can be unreliable, and eyewitnesses to trauma can erase details, conflate facts, and misinterpret situations. Individuals who have undergone trauma may choose to forget events that are too painful to remember. Yet Judaism is a faith that has memory as its cornerstone. The Baal Shem Tov, founder of the Hasidic movement, asserted that "just as oblivion is tied to exile, so is memory tied to redemption" (qtd. in Patterson "Twilight" p. 19). The word *redemption* is an uncomfortable one to use when discussing the Holocaust, and there are those who would argue that no redemption is possible from the ashes of the *hurban*. Nevertheless, be it by God, by the Torah, or by religious leaders, Jews are told to remember.

Remembering is an essential element of autobiography. Autobiographical theorists, as a rule, warn that memory is a faulty, flimsy, and unre-

Introduction

liable thing. However, Roger Porter and Daniel Reisberg challenge those theorists in their analysis of "Autobiography and Memory." They assert that psychologists have arrived at dramatically different conclusions concerning memory's validity than have literary critics, and they argue that memory can be remarkably trustworthy. A key aspect concerning memory centers upon how important the particular event was to the person who is remembering. Using a seed metaphor, Porter and Resiberg assert that a memory plants itself by a "series of biological events" (p. 62). The seed then roots itself in "memory consolidation" (p. 62). According to a Dutch psychological survey of Holocaust survivors' recollections, specific occurrences described were verified, where possible, by camp records and the memories of others who were present; the survivors' accounts "were impressively accurate — regularly preserving both the gist of many episodes as well as a striking level of detail" (p. 62). Deeply rooted memories were, therefore, found to be reliable.

This is not to say that testimony should not be subject to scrutiny. In the collection of survivors' memories published as *Hasidic Tales of the Holocaust*, Yaffa Eliach employed historical fact-finding methods to verify survivors' accounts. One element that helped root memories was being aware of time — the month, the season, and the religious practices associated with the season. Although many former prisoners comment in their memoirs about the lack of time markers, such as calendars, newspapers, radio reports, and meaningful work, many Jews, particularly the Orthodox, were keenly aware of time. "Jewish tradition," states Eliach, "by its very nature, is time oriented. Time is classified into two major units: sacred and profane" (p. xxix). Because certain religious or devotional practices must take place at a specific time of day or season, devout Jews were trained to be cognizant of the sun, the moon, and thus the time. "Even in the skies about Auschwitz," Eliach writes, "the full moon always appeared on the fifteenth of the Jewish month. A person brought up in this tradition, where time plays such a major role, has a constant awareness of time" (p. xxix). Porter and Reisberg find that important "events are likely to be remembered more completely, more accurately, and for a longer time than unimportant events" (p. 63). Those who suffered under the Nazis found their lives filled with life-and-death events demanding to be remembered.

An autobiography written by a Jewish survivor of Nazism is valuable

Introduction

on many counts, but I wish to offer three key reasons: The autobiography is a recorded memory of an individual; it is a historical account of war; and it is a testimony concerning the history of a people. I propose that each Shoah autobiography is worthy of merit simply because it is the recorded memory of an individual, albeit some memoirists are better writers than others. Sidonie Smith and Julia Watson, among others, point out that there is a myth of autonomy and individuality pervasive throughout Western culture (pp. 6–7) and while they are not alone in critiquing the "auto" in autobiography, those distinctions falter before Shoah first-person accounts. Precisely because the Nazis strove to eliminate an entire people without regard to the individual, and precisely because the Event reckons its destruction with numbers in the millions, the Shoah autobiography is important. It matters to history and to humanity that one individual, one particular self, can speak of his or her own experience. It puts a face and a personal history on what is otherwise a numbered entity of the murdered and victimized, whose actual total will never truly be known. Our minds cannot conjure the overwhelming and bizarre statistics which emerge from the mists of *Night and Fog*, but we can sympathetically imagine what an individual experienced if that person tells us. This fact alone may explain the longevity and popularity of Anne Frank's diary. Primo Levi wonders at Frank's appeal and concludes: "a single Anne Frank excites more emotion than the myriads who suffered as she did but whose image remains in the shadows. Perhaps it is necessary that it can be so. If we had to and were able to suffer the sufferings of everyone, we could not live" (*Drowned* p. 56). On a similar note, the following axiom is appropriate: "The death of a million is a statistic, the death of one hundred is a disaster, but the death of one person is a tragedy." This saying has been attributed to a variety of persons, some with a dark connection to mass murder, but there is truth in the saying.

The second inherent value of a Shoah autobiography is its historicity. Such memoirs do more than tell the story of one life; they are valuable historical documents. Lucy Dawidowicz calls autobiography the "most direct form of history," history at its most "intimate" (*Golden* p. 6) and she approvingly cites Wilhelm Dilthey: "Autobiography is the highest and most instructive form in which the understanding of life confronts us" (qtd. in *Golden* pp. 5–6). The Shoah autobiography, then, assists the reader in imagining, however incompletely, what life was like before the Event and during it. Many memoirists honor places that no longer exist, ways of life now destroyed.

Autobiographies written by Eastern European Jews often evoke bittersweet memories of the *shtetl*, those small Jewish villages which were annihilated by the Nazis, whereas the lifewritings of their Western European counterparts frequently describe their outrage at being betrayed by their countries, the countries that had been their homes for generations. Holocaust autobiographies bear inherent historical value because they record impressions of a dramatically violent time. As historical documents in a literary genre, Shoah first-person narratives conflate autobiography and memoir; as mentioned earlier, a distinction between the two involves the common criteria suggesting that an autobiography focuses more on an individual's private life and interior development, whereas a memoir deals more with the historical time period and exterior events during which the author lived. The Shoah texts record both internal and external dynamics: Most authors present their personal lives, private thoughts, and singular ambitions even as the Final Solution raged about them. Shoah texts examine the mortal clash between the interior life and the exterior times that occurred when the private life collided with the Third Reich.

I have argued that Jewish Holocaust autobiographies are important because they contain memories of an individual and that they contribute to historical understanding of the Second World War. The third area of importance concerns the significance of Jewish autobiography as testimony of an extraordinary time. I have already quoted Wiesel's observation that although not all of Hitler's victims were Jews, all Jews were victims; therefore, the Jewish minority who survived, and those fewer still who wrote their autobiographies, testify as to what it meant to be Jewish under Hitler's regime. Each European Jew lived under a death sentence. Regardless of whether the individual Jew was religious or not or had even converted to Christianity, possessing Jewish heritage — Jewish blood, as the Nazis defined it — created a death penalty case. By narrating their ordeal, lifewriters illustrate the fate of the Jewish people. It is precisely this point that supports Levi's statement that the stories emerging out of the ruins of *Night and Fog* comprise "a new Bible" as a collective crisis generates sacred stories. Because the Jewish text overtly or implicitly acknowledges God —

Introduction

either God's presence or absence as well as the author's rejection or acceptance of God — it is a vital testimony concerning the Jews during a time when to be Jewish was a crime. David Patterson argues in his study of Shoah autobiography that "denied or embraced but not ignored, God dominates the memoir" (*Sun* p. 86). God, it seems, refuses to be divorced from Jewish history.

The *TaNaKH*, that is, the Hebrew Scriptures, recounts Jewish history. Although devout Orthodox Jews maintain that Moses wrote the Torah, the first five books of the Bible, most readers understand the book to be a collection of books, written by different authors. Those various authors, throughout the centuries, tell how a people saw their world and their God. Not every character described within the Hebrew Scriptures is a Jew or a believer in God, yet all whose stories are told are part of a larger history. One Biblical book that may serve as a paradigm for Shoah autobiographies as "a new Bible" is the book of Esther. Esther's inclusion in sacred Scripture came with controversy because of its relative lack of Jewish motifs and, more significantly, its lack of an overarching focus upon God. Nonetheless, the book of Esther is in the Hebrew Scriptures canon, and her heroic activity to save the Jewish people from the scheming anti–Semite Haman is remembered annually during the festival of Purim. The oppression of the Jews is a pattern that naturally characterizes Shoah lifewritings. There may be no mention of God in the *hurban* memoir, but, like its ancient predecessor, the text may be read as an account testifying to the collective crisis the Jewish people experienced.

Emil Fackenheim states emphatically that the Jews have become a heroic people — not just the individual survivor, but all Jews collectively — "*because the survivor is gradually becoming the paradigm for the entire Jewish people*" ("Human Condition" p. 11, italics in text). Any European Jew who lived during the period of 1933–1945 carries the weight of sacred Jewish history on his or her back, regardless of that person's own religiosity. An autobiography of a Jew under Nazi law may well be the story of every Jew, particularly every Jew who lived in that time and place. If the survivor is a paradigm for the entire Jewish people, and if the stories told constitute a new Bible, then Heschel's description of Scripture might be helpful. Heschel does not place an emphasis on heroism, as does Fackenheim, but rather he argues that the Bible is important precisely because it is not concerned with heroes. What makes Scripture important to Heschel is that is contains "the story of every [person]" (*God in Search* p. 239). Readers of the Bible may identify with characters — even those held up as God's beloved — not because they are so good, but precisely because they are not. Characters in the Bible are flawed; their faults and sins are fullblown, and they struggle with their fellow human beings and with their God. Human interaction with God and with other humans is, according to the Bible, a messy, often deadly business. Shoah texts also tell not so much about heroes but about everyday people, people who possess both weaknesses and strengths. The survivor's autobiography is surprisingly free from hagiography, given the human tendency to beatify the deceased; rather, the author presents the self and fellow individuals whose attributes and deficiencies are recognizably human. Memoirists typically describe themselves and their family members, friends, and loved ones with personal qualities and unique characteristics, yet every experience the author lived through was something any Jewish person of the time faced or might have faced.

If Fackenheim is accurate when calling the survivor a paradigm for the Jewish people, then perhaps it is only natural for the autobiographer to turn to the Bible in order to illustrate a point. Not every lifewriter alludes to Scripture or to any other text, but the autobiographers considered in the following chapters have found in Scripture an image that helps them to convey the unimaginable. Heschel states that the "Torah is not the wisdom but the destiny of Israel; not our literature but our essence" (p. 167). The Scriptural allusions employed by the lifewriters considered herein draw from the "essence" of Jewish life as their allusions participate in the threefold aspects of Midrash, which, as we have seen, are paraphrase, prophecy, and parable.

The allusions raise questions, questions about the Event and about God, questions that will be explored in the upcoming chapters. The art of asking questions is part of the Midrashic hermeneutic. The Midrash constantly asks questions of the Scriptural text. In several places in his vast work, Wiesel comments that God seems equivalent to a question. "God is in the question," he observes, as he points out that in Hebrew, the letters for God are "part of the fabric" of the letters for question (*Against* 3:297). Is the Bible a question? Some would say so, but Heschel sees it as

Introduction

an answer. "The Bible is an answer to the supreme question," Heschel insists, "*what does God demand of us?*" (p. 168, emphasis in text). Is the Shoah autobiography a question? I concur with Wiesel's consistently stated position that the Holocaust cannot be understood, grasped, or explained; it can only be a question. Therefore, a text concerned with the Shoah must itself be a question. If Shoah autobiographies create a new Bible, then what is their supreme question? From my readings, I propose that the autobiographers' question may be phrased thusly: Having endured the Holocaust when so many of our loved ones were murdered, what do we demand of humanity and of God?

Questions inspired by Holocaust texts that have been debated within the academy for some time include testimony, memory, trauma, and gender. Have we become so sensitive about the survivors' words that we fail to subject the text to scrutiny? Are survivors who are only now discussing the Event capable of remembering accurately what happened? Is gender relevant when the Nazis were completely ruthless to both men and women? Yet women had the potential to "pass" as Christian, whereas Jewish men were completely vulnerable to the marks of their circumcision. Has the bar of scholarship been set high enough in Shoah studies? Scholarship questions raged over Daniel Goldhagen's work, *Hitler's Willing Executioners*, to the extent that the popular press covered the story, a phenomenon rare within the academic community.

The literary study of Holocaust narratives is, in fact, a perilous field. Saul Friedländer states that the phenomenon of Nazism forces a "paralysis of language" (*Reflections* p. 120). The effect of this paralysis has proven to be long-lasting. In an anthology edited by Berel Lang, *Writing and the Holocaust*, the tension is explored "between the moral implications of the Holocaust and the means of its literary expression" (Lang pp. 1 2). Challenges include assessing the words authors use when describing a situation that defies comprehension and subjecting the text to the cold eye of literary or historical scrutiny. "We may begin with a suspicion that it is morally unseemly to submit Holocaust writings to fine critical discriminations," admits Irving Howe. "Yet once we speak, as we must, about ways of approaching or apprehending this subject, we find ourselves going back to a fundamental concern of literary criticism: namely, how a writer validates his [or her] material" ("Writing" p. 194, brackets mine). Howe's comment is helpful; he gives the literary critic permission to treat narrative as narrative and to evaluate how successfully the voice conveys meaning. Thus, a literary scholar may evaluate how powerfully the writing conveys the situation and how effectively the autobiographer imparts his or her story. The scholar may consider the literary devices at work and assess the author's literary techniques in textualizing the author's life.

Still, the practice of Howe's "fine critical discriminations" contains a multitude of traps. Terrence Des Pres addresses this issue head-on:

> [T]o write about terrible things in a neutral tone or with descriptions barren of subjective response tends to generate an irony so virulent as to end in either cynicism or despair. On the other hand, to allow feeling much play when speaking of atrocity is to border on hysteria and reduce the agony of millions to a moment of self-indulgence. There seemed one language left — a kind of archaic, quasi-religious vocabulary, which I have used not as a reflection of religious sentiment, but in the sense that only a language of ultimate concern can be adequate to facts such as these [p. vi].

Des Pres is right. To loosen the reins of emotion undermines the tragedy about which the lifewriter is concerned; however, not to address feelings implies the tragic events of the Shoah summon no compassion or outrage at all. Aharon Appelfeld notes the effect incurred when the writer assumes too detached a tone: "...I do wish to point out that the numbers and the facts were the murderers' own well-proven means.... They tattooed a number on his arm. Should we seek to tread that path and speak of man in the language of statistics?" ("Writing" p. 84). The Event continues to confound. Saul Friedländer, himself a survivor of the war, acknowledges that any attempt to understand Hitler or Nazism "defies all customary interpretation" (*Reflections* p. 120). As we have seen in the struggle to name the 1933–1945 war against the Jews, language fails, and the failure of words is but one battle that a scholar of that time and its literature must confront.

The challenges facing the literary scholar who examines Shoah narratives are daunting; therefore, I participate in this field aware of its many pitfalls. The systematic murder of six million Jews, one million of whom were children — and not forgetting that millions more were terrorized and killed by the Nazis — defies comprehension. Even the well-known Holocaust survivor Elie Wiesel admits in a videotaped interview that although he reads everything he can on the subject in the hope that one day he will

Introduction

finally understand it, his hope is always confounded ("Facing Hate"). Wiesel maintains that the only response to the mass murder is silence, with the paradox being, of course, that he is a prolific witness in both oral and written accounts of the ordeal. While I understand the appropriateness of silence in the aftermath of such horror and death, I concur with the majority of scholars who believe we must speak out in order for the respectful silence not to lapse into forgetfulness. The Baal Shem Tov warned that forgetfulness is tied to oblivion. "Remember!"

Remembering is at the heart of autobiography, that testimony of the self. "The self," theorizes James Olney, one of the first proponents of autobiography's worthiness to be critiqued, "expresses itself by the metaphors it creates and projects, and we know it by those metaphors" (p. 34). I suggest that we shall know the textualized self of the Shoah lifewriters considered within this study by the Biblical allusions used. The allusions skillfully work at conveying the individual's life by metaphor, at explicating historical events, and at connecting modern times to sacred history. Chapters are organized according to the chronology of events that commonly occurred to Jews under the Nazi regime: deportation from their homes; transportation to the camps; adaptation to the camps; and, for the remnant of Jewish survivors, liberation. Chapter One focuses upon pivotal stories found in Genesis 3–4 concerning Paradise, loss of innocence, and expulsion. Lifewriters refer to these stories in a number of different ways, but they have in common the expulsion from a home and a life formerly known and its accompanying loss of all that had been enjoyed. Chapter Two considers Frank Stiffel's suggestion that the inhumane conditions of the cattle cars transporting Jews to the concentration camps were a modern-day Noah's Ark. Chapter Three explores the most common Biblical allusion made in Shoah memoirs — the Tower of Babel. A primary theme of the Babel account is the confusion of languages, and although I will ground the study in Primo Levi's writings, I will show how extensive the Babel reference is throughout Shoah memoirs. Moreover, the Tower of Babel story bears connotations of slavery, and I examine Levi's reflections on Jewish slavery in the Third Reich. Chapter Four focuses on Elie Wiesel's allusion to the *Akeda*, the Hebrew term for Abraham's acquiescence to God's enigmatic command to sacrifice his son, Isaac. Chapter Five looks at liberation, primarily through the eyes of Ka-Tzetnik 135633, who is pre-

Introduction

occupied with the image of Jacob wrestling with the angel. Chapter Six returns to an earlier portion of Genesis as several lifewriters contemplate the staggering implications of fratricide, seeing in the Nazi slaughter of the Jews a parallel to Cain and Abel. I conclude the book with an epilogue reflecting upon Wiesel's haunting statement: "In the beginning was the Holocaust." In each chapter, I demonstrate the multiple levels of meaning created by the Scriptural allusions as lifewriters use them to comment upon Hebrew Scriptures and upon the Nazis' Kingdom of the Night.

André Neher states that the Bible is "the most disturbing theological document ever offered up to human reflection" (p. 136). If Neher is correct, then there may be no better source to assist our grappling with the twentieth century's most disturbing event.

CHAPTER ONE

Paradise Lost, Innocence Lost

> He pronounced "Jews" as if the word were a synonym for snake. This is exactly how he made me feel — like a snake, like the serpent in the story of Adam and Eve.
> — Sara Tuvel Bernstein

Genesis 3–4

Every story has a beginning. All cultures have tales of their beginnings — a creation myth, the story they tell to explain their origins. For those raised within or influenced by the Judeo-Christian heritage, they find in the first two chapters of Genesis their stories of beginnings. Indeed, the very word *Genesis* means "origins." The title Genesis comes from the Septuagint, the Greek translation of the Bible, whereas in Hebrew, the title may be transliterated as *Bereshit*. The first book of the Hebrew Scriptures does not presume to be a scientific report of the world's inception, but rather it offers creative interpretations of the world and humanity's origins. Interpretations must be in the plural because the first two chapters contain two different accounts of the order of creation, including different versions of how men and women came into existence.

While many people believe that the Bible contains both spiritual and scientific truths, most do not turn to the Hebrew Scriptures for a factual account of humanity's origins. Nor do all believers find in Scripture as a whole, much less its first book, one single, simple, unified declaration of faith. "The Bible does not constitute an ideological monolith," asserts Nahum Sarna (p. 1), nor does it shape a monolith of any other description. The Bible is simply too complex a work to be read or understood monolithically. Whether the issue is environmental, biological, psychological, or spiritual, the ancient text of *Bereshit* does not assert one unassailable statement but, more intriguingly, it inspires a multitude of questions.

"Whatever one may think of the Biblical account of Jewish origins — whether one takes it to be literally true or merely mythological — two facts are beyond doubt," states Emil Fackenheim. "First, even if the Biblical account is merely mythological, there is an element in it which is true; second, countless generations of Jews accepted it as true" ("Jewish Existence" p. 254). Fackenheim is a scholar of the Hebrew Scriptures; his point about truth residing even in accounts that may be mythological, in the popular use of that word, that is to say, fiction, certainly resonates to students of literature. Much of the power of fiction comes from its presentation and insights into the human condition. Moreover, Fackenheim encourages us not to dismiss Biblical stories, if for no other reason than that, through the millennia, Jews have believed in them. That point may be more challenging to support, but as we study the Biblical allusions made by Shoah survivors, who range in their commitment to Judaism, it will be helpful to remember the respect the Jewish culture has for the written word.

In her study of the lessons contained within Genesis, Naomi H. Rosenblatt summarizes the book as a "story of a people who believed in an abstract, transcendent God and embraced the concept of their creation in His image as fundamental to their identity" (p. xv). Rosenblatt grew up in the United States, yet in her neighborhood were refugees from Hitler's Germany and, later, death camp survivors. After the Holocaust, she found the Hebrew Scriptures fascinating; even though the Bible "provided no absolute answers," the text itself encouraged her "to confront tough questions about human nature" (p. xv). Biblical tales provide fodder for thinking about what is right and wrong, good and evil, just and unjust. Theological reflection is possible whether or not the stories told, particularly in the early chapters of Genesis, are literally true or historically accurate. Fackenheim acknowledges that an intelligent reader might wonder if Abraham or Moses or other important Scriptural figures ever actually lived (p. 254). Faith in the Judeo-Christian God need not be undermined if

One: Paradise Lost, Innocence Lost

Adam, Cain, Noah, and others described in the early chapters of Genesis were not real people. "But it is not possible to doubt," continues Fackenheim, "that the Biblical account of Jewish origins, however mythological, reflects something which did take place. What took place was a succession of overwhelming religious experiences," not all of which were exclusively Jewish (p. 254). Thus the writers or compilers of *Bereshit* wove stories that established a people and their God. Jewish Holocaust survivors who draw upon *Bereshit* reflect upon the Scriptural implications of the Event upon their people, the Jews. Concerning implications about God, the lifewriters come to a wide range of conclusions.

Subsequent chapters of *Imagery from* Genesis *in Holocaust Memoirs* will focus on one specific allusion to Genesis employed primarily by one particular lifewriter. The allusion anchors the Scriptural image to one main aspect of the Nazi inferno. This chapter needs to be different as several stories found in Genesis 3–4 will be examined, drawing from the foundational stories of humanity's first parents. These stories, which tell us so much about humanity's hopes and dreams, include the narratives of living in paradise, feeling shame over nakedness, and being forced to leave one's home. By grouping those stories together, with their themes of paradise, paradise lost, physical vulnerability, the loss of innocence, and exile, we will see the ways in which Shoah autobiographers unite their life experiences with their ancient ancestors.

After the first two chapters of *Bereshit*, with their magnificent accounts of God creating the universe, albeit with two different orders of creation, particularly of the man and the woman, Chapter Three opens with the first humans in a garden. The Garden of Eden is at once a symbol of paradise and an emblem for fleeting happiness. The myth of paradise is clearly important throughout human history, if judging only by its literature. Here I use the word *myth* in its theological context, to be distinguished from the word's usage in popular culture. In contemporary culture, *myth* is frequently used to imply a fantasy, an illusion, a fiction; Fackenheim drew upon such a connotation in his observation noted above. However, theologians have a different connotation for *myth*. The word itself derives from the Greek word *mythos*, which simply means a "story" in religious studies and theology, the term *myth* is used when discussing the fundamental understanding that a culture possesses about itself. According to

Sarna, myths are concerned with "the eternal problems" of humanity; they are a "vital cultural force" and "can be a vehicle for the expression of ideas that activate human behavior" (p. 6). Myths "signify a dynamic attitude to the universe and embody a vision of society" (p. 6). With the Garden of Eden myth, we see the human desire for a perfect place. The human longing for a peaceful place, full of sustenance and contentment, is wrapped up with the idea of Eden. The Hebrew expression of an Edenic paradise was different from their neighbors'. Sarna points out that the Biblical tale differs from other Middle Eastern/Near Eastern myths in two significant ways: Other cultures in the region set their paradise myth in the Garden of God, and the pivotal tree was the "tree of life" (p. 26). The Genesis text established a paradise that was the Garden of Eden, the dwelling place for the first humans, not the Garden of God. Although there is a "tree of life" that God protects, the important tree in the Eden account was the more complicated notion of a tree "of knowledge."

Paradise in Genesis is a bountiful garden, offering the first man and the first woman the delights of organic, vegetarian eating and the unique joy of being physically and spiritually close to their Creator. The final sentence of Genesis 2 depicts the harmony between the first two humans — depending on the translation, the man and the woman, or "the man and his wife" (Plaut) or "the human and his woman" (Alter). Genesis states that the humans lived together peacefully, with each other and with their God. Moreover, they were free, free to enjoy their world (save with one or two caveats) and free to enjoy their bodies; they had no physical or emotional need for covering. "The two of them were naked, the man and his wife, yet they felt no shame" (Gen 2:25, Plaut). In Robert Alter's translation and commentary on Genesis, he observes that the male is called in Hebrew ʻ*adam*, which "is a generic term for human beings, not a proper noun. It also does not automatically suggest maleness" (p. 5, footnote 26). The word ʻ*adam* puns on the Hebrew word for *soil*, ʻ*adamah* (p. 8, footnote 7), suggesting the earthiness from which humanity sprung. Thus, according to Hebrew Scripture, the first man and the first woman did not have proper names; they were typologies of our first parents; they were symbols of the human condition. How long did the man and the woman dwell in the Garden? Neither Genesis 1 nor 2 hints at a timeline, but readers in the Judeo-Christian tradition know that time in paradise is finite.

One: Paradise Lost, Innocence Lost

Many Holocaust autobiographers portray their childhood as idyllic, albeit in only a few sentences or pages. Their childhood or young adulthood established what was normal, what was real, what was reliable. The routine lives that they had known and could count upon were swept away once the Nazis gained power over the region in which the memoirists lived. Often, the memoirs open up with a dramatic rupture, the clash of Nazi abnormality destroying the authors' ordinary world. Isabella Leitner refers to her childhood home as a "cradle of love" (p. 15). Lily Gluck Lerner sums up her childhood experience in a small Hungarian town with these words: "And I was happy, and loved, and life seemed almost perfect..." (p. 18). Lifewriters often pay tribute to a loving family and to the city, town, or village that was their home. Yet life is rarely presented as absolutely perfect. Wiesel notes that many autobiographies testify to "what life was like before. The authors vividly recall their childhood"; however, he insists that "[i]t is not a paradise lost that they're mourning" (*After* p. 6). Paradise did not exist, as ordinary life was filled with its own challenges, tensions, and losses. "But in pre–Holocaust Europe, they had their parents, their friends, their lives" (p. 6). The lifewriters' pre–Nazi world was generally enjoyed peacefully, with friends, family, school, and outings.

Sara Tuvel Bernstein invokes a bucolic Garden of Eden image when she remembers the last home her parents lived in, a home and a life later shattered by the Nazis. In her autobiography, *The Seamstress: A Memoir of Survival*, Bernstein describes the Hungarian valley where her parents moved to in 1934. From the vantage point of writing about the valley a half-century later, and knowing that the Nazis would eventually force their departure from that place, she reflects: "Perhaps it would have been easier to leave a place not so beautiful, not so green and lush, that sometimes, when I lay down among the tall grasses besides the spring and watched the clouds drift, like transparent shadows, across the tree-lined ridge, I thought that the Garden of Eden could not have been fairer" (p. 43). The valley's physical beauty struck Bernstein as a type of paradise; rooted in its pristine natural setting, the place exuded an air of safety and tranquility. Her word choices of "lay down" and "watched" create a mood wherein she was safely able to do such things.

Later in her memoir, still describing that same valley in the Hungarian area of Valea Uzului, Bernstein implicitly alludes to Eden when she says that, after a rain, "[t]he world seemed freshly created at these times, the smells of earth and rain mingling with the lightness, a scud of clouds billowing across the water-blue sky" (p. 53). The newness and freshness hints at a just-made paradise. The first chapters of Genesis imagine a time when the world and all who dwell within it were new; Genesis 1 records that God, the Creator, judged these new things to be "good."

Genesis reports that the garden had within it seed-bearing trees and fruit-bearing trees; the birds flew in a sky that might well have been the color that Bernstein called "water-blue." In paradise, humans and animals lived peacefully together, without fear; humans did not eat animals, and there is no textual evidence that the animals hunted humans. Although the order of creating animals and humans differs in Genesis 1 and 2, animals are mentioned in a matter-of-fact way, neither with affection nor disdain. The situation changes in Genesis 3: The Garden of Eden is still paradise, but not for long. In the first verse of Genesis 3, the serpent appears, and life in paradise shifts irrevocably. The image of a snake would cause many people, in Biblical times and today, to react with revulsion. Alter observes that the Scriptural text conveys a "primal horror of humankind before this slithering, viscous-looking, and poisonous representative of the animal realm" (p. 13, footnote 15). Bernstein textualizes the repulsion snakes can inspire when she describes a moment from her Hungarian childhood.

As a young girl, Bernstein was eager to begin school. Christian and Jewish children attended classes together in the pre–Nazi days of the 1920s, but the Jewish students were subjected to a barrage of Christian religious education classes, as well as other studies taught through a Christian worldview. In fact, young Sara, then called Seren, was stunned when she entered her schoolroom for the first time: "Across the entire front was a raised platform, and above it, a large wooden cross with a plaster man hanging from it. He looked lifeless and barely had any clothes on. *Why do they have a dead man for us to look at?*" (p. 19, italics in text). The teacher entered; he was a priest, a severe man, barking orders at the children. School began daily with religion class, which Bernstein and the other Jewish children were required to attend but were not expected to participate (p. 20). Soon Bernstein dreaded school; the children taunted her by shouting "'Stinkin' Jew!'" and "'Dirty, stinkin' Jew'" (p. 20). In Bernstein's village, all students

One: Paradise Lost, Innocence Lost

attended school seven days a week, necessarily forcing Jewish students to be in class on Saturday, their Sabbath, and all were required to attend the Christian church on Sunday for more religious education (p. 21).

The anti–Semitic attitudes nurtured throughout Europe by various Christian denominations throughout the centuries were present, waiting to be fanned into flames only a few years later by Nazi ideology. Bernstein recounts her reaction to a sermon preached by her teacher, the priest. He focused upon a Jewish peasant woman and proclaimed:

> "Do you ever wonder why your life is so hard?" the priest would ask. "Do you ever wonder why you never seem to have enough food, why you have to sell all of your grain for very little money and live on cornmeal? ...I am sure you wonder how God can be so unmindful of you, how He can let you live in such conditions with no hope for the future. Well, let me assure you that God is blameless. He has been bountiful in His blessings. Praise ye the Lord! The blame for your sufferings can all be placed on the killers of Christ, the Jews!"
>
> He pronounced "Jews" as if the word were a synonym for snake. This is exactly how he made me feel — like a snake, like the serpent in the story of Adam and Eve. I wanted to crawl under the pew and hide there until it was time to go home [p. 22].

Acknowledging that it is unlikely that the sermon heard by an eight-year-old could have been remembered word perfect throughout the decades, surely Bernstein captured the spirit of the sermon. Likely she heard such sermons more than once; indeed, she might have heard a variation of them every day of her youth. Even had she heard those words only one time, it may have been sufficiently distressing to remember them with clarity. The venom projected in the priest's words caused young Bernstein to recoil in horror and to identify with the snake. Her desire "to crawl under the pew" to hide is reminiscent of a snake slithering into a hiding place.

The snake that appears in *Bereshit* does not hide, but rather is out in the open, and, as many commentators have noted, is strangely talkative. Immediately after the beatific vision of the couple enjoying paradise in the final verse of Genesis 2, the snake enters in Genesis 3:1:

> Now the serpent was the shrewdest of all the wild beasts that the LORD God had made. He said to the woman, "Did God really say: You shall not eat of any tree of the garden?" The woman replied to the serpent, "We may eat of the fruit of the other trees of the garden. It is only about fruit of the tree in the middle of the garden that God said: You shall not eat of it or touch it, lest you die." And the serpent said to the woman, "You are not going to die, but God knows that as soon as you eat of it your eyes will be opened and you will be like divine

Imagery from *Genesis* in Holocaust Memoirs

beings who know good and bad" [Genesis 3:1–5. All Scriptural passages quoted are from *The Torah: A Modern Commentary*, edited by W. Gunther Plaut, published by the Union of American Hebrew Congregations].

The Plaut *Commentary* glosses the snake in this way: "The association of serpents with guile is an old one. In Mesopotamian, Hurrian, and Ugaritic myths serpents oppose the will of the gods; 'snake' was already a derogatory term in an old Hittite document" (p. 35). The *Commentary* demonstrates that, culturally, the Hebrew people hearing the text would recognize the snake's pejorative associations. Sarna observes that a "reptile figures prominently in all the world's mythologies and cults" (p. 26). Humans have long been preoccupied with serpents, generally repulsed, but not exclusively so. Although Christians ascribe a satanic aspect to the snake, Jewish thinking does not. Sarna notes that in Genesis the snake "is not an independent creature; it possesses no occult powers; it is not a demoniacal being; it is not even described as evil, merely as being extraordinarily shrewd" (p. 26). The snake assumes its place in Middle Eastern ancient literature as an entity promoting action contrary to the Divine will; not surprisingly, God condemns the serpent in Genesis 3:14–15 for its part in Adam and Eve's disobedience. Alter observes that God's curse of the snake records "the first moment in which a split between man and the rest of the animal kingdom" (p. 13, footnote 15). Thus the snake represents rupture: between humans and divinity, between humans and animals.

Jewish theology does not identify the serpent with Satan, nor does it classify Eve and Adam's eating of the fruit as original sin, spilling its dire consequences to all unborn humans. Rather, many rabbis see the interaction between humanity and snake as the first step to the first lie, which shatter the truth-filled life of integrity. Eve tells the serpent that God told them not to touch the tree, which, in fact, was not part of God's admonition in Genesis 2. Rabbinical thought judges the lie not as sin itself, but as a manipulation of the truth, which thereby can open the door to sinful actions (Plaut p. 41). Such a rabbinical stance places the responsibility squarely upon the human rather than on the evil doings of the snake. In the Christian tradition, the snake is Satan disguised; the snake is the devil himself who tempts Eve, who thereby misleads her husband, Adam, into disobeying the Lord's directive. Christian thought assigns this to be the first sin, and therefore, the originator of all human sin: original sin. Belief in original sin leads directly to the Christian belief that humanity requires a savior, and that savior is Jesus. Therefore, countless Christian sermons have emphasized the need for Jesus and the dire consequences for the Jewish people who do not accept him as their Messiah. Bernstein's teacher, the priest, obviously preached from this paradigm. However, the word *sin* is not actually used in Scripture until the post-paradisiacal story of Adam and Eve's sons, Cain and Abel, found in Genesis 4.

The trauma Bernstein felt upon hearing the priest's sermon caused her to identify with the snake of Genesis 3, that creature who was participatory in, if not directly responsible for, Adam and Eve's consumption of the forbidden fruit. Prior to their disobedience, the man and woman were at ease with themselves, their bodies, and their God; after eating from the Tree of Knowledge, they were ashamed, emotionally and spiritually. The shame felt over their actions apparently was projected upon their bodies, for Scripture records their embarrassment that they were naked. "Then the eyes of both of them were opened and they perceived that they were naked; and they sewed together fig leaves and made themselves loincloths. They heard the sound of the LORD God moving about in the garden at the breezy time of day; and the man and his wife hid from the LORD God among the trees of the garden" (Gen. 3:7–8). Their shame caused them to reach for what they could put their hands on in the garden of Paradise, and so the fig leaves became humanity's first clothes. Their shame also caused them to hide from their Creator, the one with whom they previously had enjoyed an emotionally close relationship. The author of this section of Genesis puts it this way: "The LORD God called out to the man and said to him, 'Where are you?'" (Gen. 3:9). Adam answered: "'I heard the sound of You in the garden, and I was afraid because I was naked, so I hid.' Then He asked, 'Who told you that you were naked? Did you eat of the tree from which I had forbidden you to eat?'" (Gen 3:10–11).

Adam and Eve had eaten from the Tree of Knowledge. Endless is the theological debate over what constitutes knowledge; endless also is the debate concerning why God did not want the man and the woman to be initiated into it. The Plaut *Commentary* identifies at least three interpretive categories regarding knowledge: Biblical, intellectual, and sexual (pp. 38–39). Martin Buber notes in his study, *On the Bible*, that once the first parents had eaten of the Tree's fruit, they had indeed gained knowledge, and that they were consequently forced to "see themselves as they are"—not simply living without clothes, but "naked" (p. 17). Buber asserts that an existential difference between nakedness and nudity. Adam and Eve were nude without shame; it was their natural, organic state. Once "their eyes were opened," as Genesis puts it, and vision brought with it understanding, an understanding that they had been disobedient, they felt shame for the first time. More than merely being physically naked, Adam and Eve were ontologically exposed. Another feeling the text suggests that the first humans experienced for the first time, due to their budding awareness and shame, was vulnerability. Humans feel exposed and vulnerable when naked, particularly when another is watching. For Adam and Eve, that other was God; for the Jews of the Third Reich, it was the Nazis.

According to Scripture, Adam and Eve were right to feel ashamed of their actions, even though they externalized it to their bodies. Jews swept into the Nazi universe of the Final Solution were also exposed. Unlike Adam and Eve, who went from being nude to naked to clothed, the Jews were stripped of their belongings, their clothes, and ultimately, their lives. Shoah memoirs are full of accounts describing the Nazi theft of their goods: Wherever the Nazis took control, they demanded of the conquered their radios, bicycles, furs, and, in some cases, even beloved pets. The oppressed felt shame, not due to any wrongdoing on their part, but rather their emotions were due to the natural reaction to being physically vulnerable to a malevolent force. When taken to slave labor camps and concentration camps, the Nazis and their collaborators subjected their prisoners to undergo multiple humiliations that varied from camp to camp, but as they turned Jews into inmates, the overlords distributed either prison clothes or wildly inappropriate clothes culled from victims' suitcases. Jewish men and women entering Auschwitz and other camps faced more degradation: They were forced to remove their clothes and have their body hair shaved.

Male lifewriters often mention the oddity of men's appearance, shorn of all distinctive facial hair. Being shaved was traumatic, particularly so to Orthodox men, who obey Biblical teachings about their hair, side locks, and beards. Being shaved marked a person and was a type of physical assault; for Orthodox Jewish men, their beards and side locks represented a commitment to their faith. George Lucius Salton describes in his mem-

One: Paradise Lost, Innocence Lost

oir his astonishment at seeing the odd appearance of his fellow Jews at the concentration camp to which he had just been sent. Newly deported from a ghetto, Salton remembers noticing that the Jews "had no hair. Their heads had been shaved. They looked like prison inmates" (p. 85). His turn to be shaved came the next day. Mortified that he looked "like a prisoner," he says that he "felt violated and ugly" (p. 86). In the downward spiral of dishonor inflicted upon them by the Nazis, Jews were forced to bear the mark of a criminal. Legally, the Nazis judged the crime of being Jewish as a death penalty offense.

As part of the process of turning Jews into concentration camp prisoners, newly arrived inmates typically had their clothes taken away from them. Often large groups of men or women were herded into a huge room for a shower *en masse*. Many women lifewriters mention their primal embarrassment of their nudity in such a situation. Women express feeling particularly vulnerable when describing their nudity and the shaving of their hair, which included the hair on their head as well as their underarms and pubic hair. Such shaving was done mechanically, even violently, with dull scissors and razors, by fellow Jewish prisoners as the SS supervised. Newly arrived in a bitterly strange world, the women felt abased standing naked in front of supervising SS men. Some autobiographers remember their fear of men looking at them, but usually the prisoners quickly grasped that the SS did not see them as humans. In conveying their ordeal of being shaved, Judith Magyar Isaacson and Linda Rosenfeld Vago explicitly refer to Adam and Eve's shame of their nudity.

Judith Magyar Isaacson was a young Hungarian girl called Jutka when she and her mother were deported from the Kaposvár ghetto to Auschwitz. Faced with unimaginable horrors, she quickly grasped that Auschwitz was "a new world, a different planet" (p. 62), "a hostile planet" (p. 67). Isaacson describes the shearing process in her autobiography, *Seed of Sarah: Memoirs of a Survivor*: "A woman in a striped dress grabbed me by the hair and attacked me with scissors. Another drove a razor around my crown. I stood in a heap of my own hair, fingering my scalp; the stubble was foreign to touch. A shove in the buttocks propelled me along the assembly line" (p. 66). Orders given in German commanded her to lift her arms and to spread her legs. "A razor moved into my crotch. A shower of disinfectant hit my armpits and scalp. A sudden spray scorched my vulva. An attendant shoved me from behind" (p. 67). Isaacson captures the violence contained in the shaving ceremony with such vivid verbs as "grabbed," "drove," "propelled," "hit," "scorched," and "shoved." This was no cosmetic grooming, but rather the first of many physical assaults.

Sent to "Mexico," the poorest, least monitored part of planet Auschwitz, a term lifewriters use that captures the other-worldly quality of the death camp, Isaacson and her mother had little hope that they would live. "No one was meant to survive there for more than three weeks," Isaacson states. "And no one did" (p. 68). Faced with imminent death, the women of "Mexico" spoke longingly of the things they loved, the things they no longer had: a home, family, food. "We wanted to cover our nakedness, and unlike Eve in the Garden of Eden, we had to include our nude heads" (p. 77). Eve, with her name etymologically explained in Genesis 3:20 as the "mother of all the living," was not a Jew; she and her spouse lived in a pre–Jewish time. If thinking of her as an actual woman, as Isaacson does, Eve would not have covered her head with a scarf or wig. Isaacson links her own nudity with Eve's and emphasizes that an Orthodox woman would have been all the more distressed because her bare head would have been so unusual, so culturally inappropriate.

Dwelling within the poverty of "Mexico," Isaacson soon found a barter system that allowed women to find a scrap of cloth by which to cover their head: "the going rate for a ragged kerchief soon rose to a day's ration of bread" (p. 77). The bread was foul; autobiographers often detail how they had to force themselves to eat the bread when they first arrived at the camps, but that bread was all that stood between them and death by starvation. Fortunately for young Judith, she was able to get some fabric without risking her day's allowance of bread, the only food source she had. She mused as she prepared her kerchief: "We women were a strange sex, I decided: we sustain our sanity with mere trifles. Even in hell. Yes, even in hell" (p. 77). Eve felt her shame in paradise; Isaacson and millions more felt their shame in hell.

In her essay, "One Year in the Black Hole of Our Planet Earth: A Personal Narrative," Linda Rosenfeld Vago recounts her shaving process after being sent to Auschwitz. She and the other female prisoners were forced into a large facility where women prisoners with scissors and razors awaited. "Working as if in a race against time, they rudely cut our hair, leaving us bald and clean shaven everywhere on our entire bodies," she

One: Paradise Lost, Innocence Lost

writes (p. 275). The assault was both physical and cultural: "The culture shock proceeded as our female bodies were stripped of their fig leaves and exposed to the lascivious gaze of the German soldiers" (p. 275). Vago and the other women came into the showers with, metaphorically, Eve's fig leaves. The veil of modesty ripped asunder by the presence of the guards, Vago and countless others lost not only their symbolic fig leaves; they also lost their clothes, their individuality, their names, and, for most, their families. Standing naked before the SS men, she worried that the women could be sexually victimized. "But the soldiers couldn't care less. I decided not to feel ashamed, humiliated, degraded, defeminized, or dehumanized" (p. 275). The soldiers did not see their charges as humans, but Vago still clung to her humanity. Such an act of will allowed her to reject the Nazi metaphysical assault upon her personhood; she held on to her sense of self, the only thing she had left.

Women lifewriters who describe the shaving of their body hair typically do so with a mixture of sadness, shame, and regret. Sara Tuvel Bernstein remembers the shaving process at Ravensbrück as the "sharp pull on my pubic hairs followed by a biting pain"; it was so painful and humiliating that she thought, "I would almost rather die than suffer this" (p. 198). She keenly felt the emotional assault that resulted from the physical act. "The shearing of our heads and vulvas, the stealing of our clothes and everything we had owned, took from us the last traces of who we had been," she states (p. 199). Laura Hillman states that "the dull clippers" tore at her skin; next she found blood running down her legs due to the rough treatment used when her pubic hair was shaved (p. 196). Livia E. Bitton Jackson recalls the procedure, in a dark, cold room in Auschwitz, with "over a thousand, shivering, humiliated nude bodies" of newly arrived women (p. 59). In addition to the pubic hair being shaved, losing the hair on their heads "has a startling effect on every woman's appearance. Individuals become a mass of bodies" (p. 59). Some began to laugh hysterically; others called out the names of their relatives because, without their hair, everyone looked alike. Jackson assesses the moment in a strangely positive way: "The shaving had a curious effect. A burden was lifted. The burden of individuality. Of associations. Of identity. Of the recent past" (p. 60). Jackson's response of a certain freedom in no longer being an individual might have helped her cope in a manner different from Vago's defiant resistance to being "dehumanized."

Imagery from *Genesis* in Holocaust Memoirs

In *Auschwitz: True Tales from a Grotesque Land*, Sara Nomberg-Przytyk also mentions the cruel manner in which women were shaved at Auschwitz. The "scissors [were] so dull that they tore bunches of hair out of our heads," she recalls (p. 14). "'Spread your legs,'" shouted the *kapos*, the prisoners who served as leaders (p. 14). "It did not bother [the barbers] that cutting hair close to the skin with dull scissors was excruciatingly painful. It did not bother them that we were women and that without our hair we felt totally humiliated" (p. 14). It did not disturb the barbers that the women were humiliated; sucked into the "grotesque land" of the Nazi concentration camp, *kapos* and long-term prisoners were forced to adjust to their circumstances. Being stripped and shaved initiated the new prisoners into the alternate universe of the concentration camps.

The shaving of body hair was a break with the past, just as Adam and Eve's awareness of their nudity was the break in their close relationship with God. Jackson portrays the women's entrance into Auschwitz itself, after the shaving: "Newborn creatures, we march out of the showers. Shorn and stripped, washed and uniformed, women and girls from 16 to 45, separated from mothers, fathers, husbands, sisters, brothers, and from offspring — transformed into bodies marching uniformly towards the barracks of Auschwitz. An abyss separates us from the past" (p. 61). The chasm that separated the first humans from their paradise separated the prisoners of Auschwitz from their past lives; one morning of prison processing translated into her former life having existed "eons" ago (pp. 61–62). "Our parents and families belong to the prehistoric past. Our clothes, our hair — had they been real? The homes we left only recently are in a distant land, perhaps of make-believe. Our lives of yesterday belong to a bygone era" (p. 62). The unreality of planet Auschwitz was so all-consuming that normal "lives of yesterday" themselves seemed unreal. Those shattered lives belonged to "a bygone era," a time and so completely destroyed that survivors could not return to their home unscathed. The Jews of the Third Reich were in exile from the life and the home of their past.

Before Adam and Eve were forced to leave the only life that they had known, they had witnessed God condemn the serpent and then they were told the consequences of their action. The Lord decreed that man's destiny was tied to working the land while woman's was linked to desire for her husband and subsequent pain in childbirth. Then God does some-

One: Paradise Lost, Innocence Lost

thing surprising, according to Genesis 3:21: He (the Hebrew text identifies God with the masculine pronoun) sews "garments of skin for Adam and his wife, and clothed them." The act of sewing clothes carried with it two ramifications: It was compassionate because the skins would have been softer than fig leaves, yet it bore implicit violence because this was the first time animals became a product. After sewing the clothes, the Lord casts out the first humans from Eden. "So the LORD God banished him [Adam] from the garden of Eden, to till the soil from which he was taken. He drove the man out, and stationed east of the garden of Eden the cherubim and the fiery ever-turning sword, to guard the way to the tree of life" (Gen. 3:23–24). Banished from their home, there was no chance to return, either physically or spiritually.

The cherubim guarding Paradise were no rosy-cheeked, fat-baby angels, explains Alter, knowing that such would be the contemporary iconic association. Alter says that the Hebrew implies that the cherubim were "winged beasts, probably of awesome aspect" (p. 15, footnote 24). Fiercely forbidding re-entry into the Garden with its "fiery" sword, the angel stood as a marker between the life that belonged "to a by-gone era," to use Jackson's words, and a new life, banished and in exile. Unable to return to the only life they had known, Adam and Eve had to adjust to their new and unanticipated circumstances. Restrictive measures instituted by the Nazis forced Jews from their homes. Depending on the area of Europe controlled by the Nazis and the action initiated, the forced removal from homes led Jews to ghettoes, to transport stations, to labor camps, to death camps.

Most Jews of the Third Reich lost their beloved homes as they experienced the complete disintegration of the only life they had known once the Nazis entered; if, after the war, return was physically possible, life had been irreparably changed. Because most autobiographers were children, teenagers, or young adults when the Third Reich disrupted their lives, they would naturally view their pre–Nazi years as idyllic, or nearly so. Many autobiographers speak wistfully of their childhood homes, that demi-paradise, destroyed by the *hurban*. As Wiesel suggested, survivors may not necessarily equate their youth with a lost paradise, but life had a quality of normalcy. "Tomorrow was filled with worries," Wiesel points out, "but it was also charged with promise" (*After* p. 6). The promise was shattered. When survivors look back, as they must when they write their autobiographies, most cannot help but see their pre–Nazi life as something precious that had been destroyed.

Mentioned earlier was Sara Tuvel Bernstein's description of a beautiful Hungarian valley nestled in the Carpathian Mountains where her parents had their last home, a place she explicitly characterized as a Garden of Eden. After the expulsion, Bernstein and her father were arrested; housed at the same prison, daughter and father were eventually permitted an hour's rest in the prison courtyard. She implicitly alludes to looking back to Paradise once her family had been banished from their home: "We sat there together for the rest of the hour, hand in hand, each dreaming our separate dream of home..." (p. 85). Although this is not a direct reference to Adam and Eve's banishment from the Garden of Eden, Bernstein's simple statement invites reflection. After portraying her parents' last home as a place set within a Garden of Eden, the image of father and daughter sitting together, "hand in hand" for comfort and support, dreaming of past happier days, might well raise images of Adam and Eve's longing for the home they lost. Should we allow our imagination to picture the first man and the first woman, now exiled from paradise, we might see them resting after hard labor, not talking, but reminiscing about their home, that paradise lost.

Yet there can be degrees of Paradise. Often in their autobiographies, survivors evaluate one concentration camp or slave labor camp as being paradisiacal compared to another. In some cases, the assessment is due to better living conditions: more food, less punishment. Laura Hillman recalls a fellow prisoner's evaluation of the Krásnik camp when she is transferred there, a prisoner whose "words came to mind: Krásnik is a paradise'" (p. 89). Krásnik was significantly better than where Hillman had been, if only because the physical structures appeared less like a prison. Hillman also quotes another prisoner's use of the word "paradise" later in her memoir. Close to the war's end, she was reunited with the love of her life, the man she would later marry. He promised her a gift later that evening and asked her to guess what the gift might be. He gave her a clue: "'It was first seen in paradise'" (p. 227). When he gave her the gift — an apple — he told her that it came "'from paradise'" (p. 228). In this context, Hillman uses her future-husband's words both to allude to the Genesis story (the fruit being understood in some cultures as an apple, although Scripture does not say so) and to a sense of happiness that will be regained. The Nazis' defeat was on the visible horizon as Hillman, her closest friends, and her future husband worked in comparative comfort for Oskar Schindler. There was the hope that paradise could be regained.

However, most lifewriters cite paradise ironically. As their lives grew ever harder, ever more difficult, Jews could assess what they just endured as significantly better than their current circumstances. Yes, they had been in hell, but now they had been sent to a deeper level of hell. Unlike Hillman's situation of experiencing the Krásnik camp as significantly better than her former camp, most prisoners found themselves moving from bad to worse. Mirroring the descending levels of hell in Dante's *Inferno*, many prisoners saw each move as something more terrible than the one before. Lerner assessed her arrival at the Stuttgart concentration camp as yet "another descent into hell" (p. 103). Thus, in comparison, many lifewriters could distinguish between the hell that they had been in and the one in which they were now describing.

Helen Lewis grew up in a part of Czechoslovakia that Hitler coveted because that region, the Sudetenland, was Germanic in language and heritage. Her Holocaust journey took her from her home to a small ghetto in Prague and then to Terezín, the concentration camp/transport camp/ghetto also known as Theresienstadt. In her autobiography, she reflects upon that journey: "Amid the soul-destroying restrictions and deprivations of daily life in Terezín, I had thought of home in Prague, even under German occupation, as a lost paradise.... I found myself remembering the ghetto's ugliness with something like the same nostalgia" (p. 64). The Prague ghetto, with all of its "ugliness," starvation, and deprivation, seemed like "a lost paradise" compared to the hardships of Terezín. Things would get worse for Lewis when she was sent to Auschwitz. Ruth Kluger had a similar experience to Lewis's when transported from Theresienstadt to Auschwitz. Only a child, she witnessed the barracks' leader screaming at the newly arrived prisoners. Stunned by the verbal violence and abuse, young Kluger could not take it all in. "But one sentence struck me: 'You are no longer in Theresienstadt.' She made it sound as if we had just been expelled from paradise" (p. 96).

Bertha Ferderber-Salz ironically calls Bergen-Belsen a "paradise" in her memoir. Towards the end of the war, Nazi Germany faced certain defeat as the entire Third Reich was imploding, but that did not stop them from their single-minded goal of making Europe *Judenrein*. Ferderber-Salz was transferred along with a large group of Jews in the bitterly cold January–February 1945 to Bergen-Belsen, but there was no room in the concentration camp for the new arrivals. The suffering was great as the Jews were forced to live in tents until they could be processed into the concentration camp; hunger, illness, and the weather contributed to their ordeal. "Many among us did not live to enter that 'paradise' called Bergen-Belsen," Ferderber-Salz recalls, "breathing their last in the open field and sinking into the muddy ground" (p. 142). Even the hell of Bergen-Belsen was a type of utopia compared to the exposed field that hosted the death of so many.

Going from bad to worse is a consistent theme when narrating the Holocaust journey. While at Auschwitz, Isabella Leitner and her three sisters learn that they going to be sent to an unknown concentration camp. Not satisfied with a mere earthly paradise, she compares Auschwitz to an unlikely place: heaven. "And they lead us away from this heaven. I say 'heaven' because, so far, each change we have gone through was for the worse. Perhaps the next one would make us long for what we have now" (p. 50). Such was the case for most Jews who were transferred at the whim of their Nazi overseers.

Sara Nomberg-Przytyk uses the term "paradise" when relating the Death March out of Auschwitz. "We walked through a valley of death formed by the side of the road," she remembers (p. 128); the SS shot anyone who could not keep up. Young Sara struggled to keep walking, if for no other reason than she did not want to be shot or to have one of the SS's dogs set upon her. "The skin was completely peeled from my feet," she recalls; "I could feel the blood swishing around inside my boots" (p. 129). At the point of being unable to walk, a most unusual event occurred. "Suddenly, as if by magic, a sled drawn by two horses appeared along the side of the road," (p. 130); even more magically, she was allowed to ride in the sled. However, when the SS men command the sled to stop, she thinks: "'My life in paradise is over'" (p. 130). Remarkably, the SS treat her kindly, thereby giving her the opportunity to live for one more day.

Dr. Samuel Drix alludes to Eden ironically in his account, *Witness to Annihilation*. In the chapter "Prisoner in Hell," he depicts the new inmates' arrival at the Janowska concentration camp. Some 200 men were marched

One: Paradise Lost, Innocence Lost

into Janowska and were observed by the old inmates. "For these prisoners we seemed to become objects of pity on the one hand or of interest on the other. Many of them were looking for relatives or acquaintances. We were looked upon as if through the eyes of experts in meat cattle, judging how long we might stand this garden of Eden" (p. 61). Drix's sarcasm sums up the anti-world created by the Nazis as Eden becomes hell.

Judith Dribben arguably provides the best summation of the paradise/hell situation that the victims of the Nazis experienced. She describes in her autobiography her situation — a Jewish woman living with false papers as an Aryan Christian, working for the underground resistance. She was eventually arrested, suspected not of being a Jew but rather a spy; fortunately for her, throughout her incarceration at a number of prisons and concentration camps, she managed to keep her Jewish identity a secret. She records a verbal exchange between herself and the overseer of a prison; the prison official refused to tell her where she was being transferred but warned her that she would soon pine for the prison as if it were a "lost paradise" (p. 179). Dribben defiantly challenged him: "'You're wrong. Any place under the Nazis is a piece of hell'" (p. 179). Regardless of the place, to be under Nazi rule was to be doomed to a portion of the Inferno.

Some survived the anti-world, the Kingdom of Death, as Wiesel calls the era of the Third Reich. Wiesel remembers that when he was sent to an orphanage in France after the war's conclusion, he wondered what the teachers could teach young Jewish survivors. "Poor counselors," he says of the adult workers at the Jewish orphanage, "did they think they could educate us? We who had looked death in the face knew far more than they or their teachers about the mysteries of existence and Creation, about the fragility of knowledge and the end of history" (*All Rivers* p. 111). Regardless of what age they were upon liberation, those survivors had indeed knowledge, wisdom that most of us would never want to possess, about "the mysteries of existence and Creation." Adam and Eve have taught us that "the fragility of knowledge" and the end of a life known are lessons painfully gained.

During the period of the Third Reich, and most especially during the implementation of the Final Solution, the Jews of Europe "looked death in the face." Some understood upon the Nazi consolidation of power that they were facing probable death; they believed Hitler would single-mindedly seek to accomplish his goal of making Europe free of Jews. Others were more optimistic, hoping that the war would end soon or trusting that the Nazi work camps were humane. What could scarcely have been imagined was that the Nazis, with systematic efficiency and almost religious zeal, gathered the European Jewry for destruction. Never before had census data been used for the nefarious purpose of targeting a people. Never before had the railroads been used to ship mass numbers to their deaths. In the next chapter, we will look at the ways in which the Nazis turned the railroads into a perverse version of Noah's Ark.

CHAPTER TWO

God's Ark and Hitler's Cattle Car

> Everybody hated everybody, and cursed everybody, and would have liked to survive at everybody else's expense. It wasn't a car full of Jews; it was Noah's ark all over again.
> — Frank Stiffel

Noah's Ark: Genesis 6–9

The Bible has long been a best-selling book in the United States. Beyond the book itself, the Scriptures have spawned an entire industry of art (and kitsch). While marketing strategies revolving around themes found in the New Testament appear to be endless, there are also a staggering number of commercial goods waiting to be bought that are images based upon the Hebrew Scriptures. Stores sell such items as representations of Daniel in the lion's den and wall-of-Jericho menorahs. A rock-opera based on the story of Joseph and his coat of many colors has been popular for decades. Yet, overwhelmingly, the most popular image from the *TaNaKH* is that of Noah and his ark. American consumers can scarcely think about Noah and the ark without envisioning the optimistic aura that surrounds the products. Sold in Jewish, Christian, and secular stores, the merchandise portrays a happy Noah flanked by pairs of cheerful yet incongruously placed beasts. Pairs of animals stride confidently toward a large wooden boat. They beam their happy gaze from the ship's deck, and why shouldn't they? They are riding out the storm on a boat built especially for them, according to God's specifications, no less. Noah and his animals have become embodied commerce, asking to be bought in the form of pictures, figurines, flags, gift bags, as well as other knick-knacks. Often the iconography includes a rainbow, the sign of God's promise never again to destroy the earth — at least, by water. Buyers of such objects presumably take them home to bask in the implicit reminders that God loves animals and that the Lord does keep promises.

While a community of smiling animals coexisting harmoniously under a providential rainbow possibly foreshadows Isaiah's peaceable kingdom, the popular image leaves out troubling details from the Genesis story. The sunny pictograph rejects much of the narrative's drama; indeed, Eli Wiesel calls Noah's Ark "one of the saddest and most oppressive stories in Scripture" ("Noah's Warning" p. 4). Regardless whether the story is read as fable, history, etiology, or archetype, the questions it raises are disturbing. Who is this deity who destroys what he has created? What did Noah do to cause his family and himself to be saved from destruction? If a holocaust is global destruction, then was Noah the first holocaust survivor? By examining Frank Stiffel's use of Noah's Ark as an image of transporting Jews to concentration camps, we will become aware of the resonance emerging from Biblical and Shoah themes of animalization, enclosure, and apocalyptic survival.

Many ancient cultures have a flood story in their mythic explanations of the world and their own history. Scholars of early Middle Eastern literature must contend with striking similarities found within the "Atrahsis," the "Gilgamesh," and the Noah passage, all of which portray a cataclysmic flood. Does that suggest an actual historical event, a compelling literary device, or a pertinent archetypal pattern? Most academic books on the subject of Noah's Ark consider such aspects of literary invention, Scriptural teaching, and historical anthropology.

The Genesis account of Noah and the flood that destroyed the world is not one story, but two. Genesis 6–9 gives two different accounts of how many animals were brought to the ark, what types of animals they were, and how long the ark floated upon the waters. Modern Biblical scholarship understands those discrepancies as proof that the narrative was originally two separate accounts, at least, that were woven together, rather inelegantly. Distinct writing styles, specific details, and theological interpretations suggest that there were multiple writers as well as an editor or a redactor. Reading certain Biblical stories, notably Creation and Noah's

Ark, without considering that multiple authors were involved, can cause confusion because of the contradictory elements. Two stories are told, although they are sometimes separated (as in the Creation stories told in Genesis 1 and 2) and sometimes merged (as with Noah's Ark). Thus, in the Noah tale, the lack of congruence over such points as the kinds of animals admitted into the ark and the number of days rain fell indicate that two authors, at the minimum, wrote their own stories. However, by acknowledging multiple authors and editors' mysterious ways, readers can examine the juxtaposition of different outlooks as sharpening the text's intricacies rather than rendering it unintelligible.

To appreciate the full complexity of the Noah's Ark account, readers should go to Genesis 6–9. In this chapter, I will give a truncated version, as I have eliminated many verses that repeat material. I regret doing so, as Hebraic repetition was seen as an elegant literary device, but in order to be concise, I have deleted passages which either elaborate upon the theme or repeat recently given details. Unfortunately, by sacrificing many verses of the story, I have surrendered important complexities, but, for the purposes of this chapter, we need focus only on the broad outline of the plot.

At the beginning of the Noah passage, God decides to destroy the earth but plans to save Noah, his family, and two each of all the creatures of the earth and the air. Pairs of animals, or two of "all flesh," were ordered to join Noah in the ship that God commanded him to build. Masculine pronouns referring to God are present in the original text and represent the traditional understanding of the deity.

> This is the line of Noah.—Noah was a righteous man; he was blameless in his age; Noah walked with God. Noah begat three sons: Shem, Ham, and Japheth.
> When God saw how corrupt the earth was, for all flesh had corrupted its ways on earth, God said to Noah, "I have decided to put an end to all flesh ... I am about to destroy them with the earth. Make yourself an ark of gopher wood; make it an ark with compartments.... This is how you shall make it: [specifications are given]. Make an opening for daylight in the ark...."
> "For My part, I am about to bring the Flood—waters upon the earth—to destroy all flesh under the sky in which there is breath of life; everything on earth shall perish. But I will establish My covenant with you, and you shall enter the ark, with your sons, your wife, and your sons' wives. And all that lives, of all flesh, you shall take two of each into the ark to keep alive with you; they shall be male and female...." Noah did so; just as God commanded him, he did....

Imagery from *Genesis* in Holocaust Memoirs

...In the six hundredth year of Noah's life, in the second month, on the seventeenth day of the month, on that day
All the fountains of the great deep burst apart,
And the flood-gates of the sky broke open. (The rain fell on the earth forty days and forty nights.) That same day Noah and Noah's sons, Shem, Ham, and Japheth, went into the ark, with Noah's wife and the three wives of his sons — they and all the beasts of every kind.... They came to Noah into the ark, two each of all flesh.... And the LORD shut him in.
...The waters swelled and increased greatly upon the earth.... And all flesh that stirred on the earth perished — birds, cattle, beasts, and all the things that swarmed upon the earth, and all mankind.... All existence on earth was blotted out.... Only Noah was left, and those with him in the ark.
And when the waters had swelled on the earth one hundred and fifty days, God remembered Noah and all ... that were with him in the ark.... The waters went on diminishing until ... in the tenth month.... At the end of forty days, Noah opened the window of the ark he had made and [after sending out a raven and a dove].... [Noah] waited ... [and] the dove came back to him ... and there in [the dove's] bill was a plucked-off olive leaf!
...God spoke to Noah, saying, "Come out of the ark...." ...Then Noah built an altar to the LORD and, taking of every clean animal and every clean bird, he offered burnt offerings on the altar [Genesis 6:9–8:20].

If we imaginatively place ourselves within the Flood story, events may terrify or baffle, particularly God's anger that lashed out against all but a select few. Contemporary American culture insists on the story's sunny side — animals, survival, rainbows — and while the story gives reason for optimism, not all have read it as simply a survivor's tale with a happy ending. Children in American culture are often taught the story with the moral being that God can be trusted, that all will be well. However, several *hurban* survivors specifically mention Noah's Ark when they recall their childhood religious training, and no one specific interpretation dominates.

Saul Friedländer, a child survivor who became one of the premier historians of the Event, lived his pre-war childhood years with his parents in Prague, although their ancestry was German. The Friedländer family was of Jewish heritage but did not practice the faith at all. Despite the absence of Jewish self-identification, young Saul felt humiliated when he and the other few Jewish classmates were required to leave the classroom when Christian students learned their catechism. He describes in his memoir listening vaguely as the rabbi, whom the school arranged to come, recited Bible stories: "Adam and Eve, Cain and Abel, the hapless builders of the Tower of Babel and those who *happily* escaped the Flood. I couldn't say

Two: God's Ark and Hitler's Cattle Car

whether we listened to these stories eagerly or were bored; all I remember is having heard them" (*When Memory Comes* p. 28, emphasis mine). The English adverb "happily" originally suggested "by chance," but more recent connotations imply "fortunately" or "with happiness." Friedländer hints that the rabbi might have taught the Flood story with an emphasis on the survivors' joy of overcoming tragedy; yet as Friedländer readily admits, his memory retains no visceral response to the stories.

On the other hand, Norman Salsitz characterizes his childhood as alive with the excitement of Biblical stories. Born into a Polish Hasidic family, Salsitz remembers: "How I thrilled to those tales — of creation, Adam and Eve, the tower of Babel, Noah and the flood ... and countless others. So often did we hear these stories, so much a part of our lives were they, that at times we seemed to exist suspended somewhere between the past and the present" (p. 148). For Salsitz, the Biblical tales were not fairy tales; instead, they were stories of real people, important people, whose adventures and mistakes could serve as a model — or a warning — for the lives of those who came after.

Elie Wiesel was a Jewish child, passionately in love with his faith and with his God. As a boy daydreaming of his future in the yeshiva, he read key Biblical stories with a blend of "wonder mixed with anguish" (*Messengers* p. xi). Scriptural tales threw life and death, beauty and horror, into sharp relief, particularly as they spoke of the Jewish people. Biblical stories raised questions about who God is and about God's relationship with the Jewish people. And as with any questions that would arise concerning God and the chosen ones, Wiesel recalls, his teachers would "have us read and reread the Bible"— a book that describes the "suffering," the "defiance," and the "permanent conflict" that have surrounded the Jewish people (*All Rivers* p. 19). Those stories impressed Wiesel from his youth and would later serve him as prophetic paradigms for the Nazis' actions. Wiesel comments upon how reading Noah's story affected him: "As I reread Noah, I see myself as a child ... under the watchful eye of the teacher. I see myself and the world before ... before the other deluge, the one my generation had to endure" ("Noah's Warning" p. 5, final ellipsis in text). The deluge swept away the people of Noah's time, according to the Bible; Wiesel watched as a modern-day catastrophe swept away his people.

The dark tone that Noah's story possesses, but which our own culture stubbornly ignores, was not lost on Frank Stiffel. Although his autobiography, *The Tale of the Ring: A Kaddish*, is not one of the better-known survivors' texts, his dramatic account deserves a wider readership. Stiffel describes extraordinary wartime adventures that include escaping from an infamous death camp, living as an Aryan, and trusting in a ring that seems to him to possess magic powers. He alludes to Noah's Ark when he describes the cattle car transporting him to a concentration camp: "Everybody hated everybody, and cursed everybody, and would have liked to survive at everybody else's expense. It wasn't a car full of Jews; it was Noah's ark all over again. Suddenly, these were not people but animals. Sick animals, dying animals, raging animals. The air of the slaughterhouse was all over us" (p. 69). With these words, Stiffel forces readers to put behind them the cheerful image of animals happily co-existing on a safe ship; rather, his imagery invites readers to imagine the dark, dank aspects of animals journeying in a contained space through a harrowing event destroying all that had been previously known. People were no longer people; they were animals, trapped, under the control of malevolent masters. Jews and other victims of the Nazis were treated like animals—confined, contained, deprived, and destined for slaughter. They were suffering from a systematic process of humiliation that began immediately upon the Nazi seizure of political and military power.

Once the Nazis assumed governmental control, previously unimaginable hardships were instituted immediately. The Nazi tactic of legally strong-arming their enemies was observable once Adolf Hitler became Chancellor of Germany on January 30, 1933; legal pogroms against the Jews were quickly instituted. In April of 1933, the Nazis organized a boycott of Jewish businesses. "For Jews," reports Marion A. Kaplan, "daily fear was accompanied by economic strangulation" (p. 21). One of the economic constraints was food rationing; gradually certain foods were declared "Aryan" and therefore forbidden to Jews. Only six months after Hitler's assumption of power, the German rabbis of the independent Orthodox communities wrote him in protest of the "wholly intolerable" condition of the Jewish people (qtd. in Mosse p. 59). The immediate restrictions placed upon the Jews regarding employment, combined with the Nazi boycott of Jewish-owned businesses, made it clear to the rabbis "*that the German Jew has been sentenced to a slow but certain death by starvation*"

Two: God's Ark and Hitler's Cattle Car

(qtd. in Mosse p. 60, italics in text). Not content for Jews to experience "a slow but certain death," the Nazis accelerated that process.

Soon after the Nazis overtook Poland and much of Eastern Europe, they issued decrees forcing Jews into ghettos. Best known to history are the ghettos established in Lodz, Lublin, Lvov, Vilna, and Warsaw, but nearly 50 major ghettos were created throughout Eastern Europe. Stiffel protests that words cannot convey the misery enclosed within the Warsaw Ghetto, a "shameful monument to the depravity of Western culture" (p. 50). Food was in scarce supply—indeed, almost nonexistent, although those who ran soup kitchens valiantly sought to serve the Jews of the ghetto. Because food was so rare, a thriving but risky activity developed of smuggling. Children in particular were valuable as smugglers because, being small, they were often best able to escape the ghetto walls in search of food to bring back inside. Alexander Donat records the severe physical restrictions of the Warsaw Ghetto: "The most unmistakable indication of Nazi intentions concerning the Jews was the food ration. Germans in Warsaw were allotted 2,500 calories a day and could obtain a wide variety of goods at fixed prices in special stores. The Jewish ration came to less than 200 calories a day for which Jews paid 20 times the price Germans did" (p. 7). The ever-tightening noose of the Nuremberg Laws and the creation of ghettos served its purpose: Virtually all European Jews were physically, psychologically, and spiritually broken through starvation, beatings, and emotional abuse. Literally sealed off from the rest of the world, ghetto inhabitants held on as best they could to their dignity, to their humanity. Death by starvation was rampant. Photographs show the bleak reality of the starved bodies, be they adults or children, on the ghetto pavements. Those who did not die in the ghetto were eventually rounded up for deportation to the concentration camps. The predominant mode of transportation to the camps was by train. The Nazis and their collaborators did not consider Jews worthy to sit in seats; instead, the Jews were herded into compartments that previously had transported goods or cattle.

By insisting that the cattle cars equaled Noah's Ark, Stiffel acknowledges the animality that so often surfaces in life-or-death situations; his readers may sympathize with that terrorized collection of humanity who traveled with him to the camp. The Flood signifies chaos, and chaos is inherently frightening. The "concept of the Flood as a returning to primeval chaos," explains Nahum Sarna, "has profound moral implications. For it means that in biblical theology human wickedness, the inhumanity of man to man, undermines the very foundations of society" (p. 55). All who traveled in the modern arks knew that they were buffeted not by the primeval chaos or a mysterious divinity but rather by manmade forces that had sprung up before their eyes. The "animals" that filled Stiffel's train compartment, and so many others like it, were not illustrative of the contemporary American sentimental portrayal of animals as either lovable pets or dignified fellow creatures. Rather, Stiffel captures the degraded status of an animal, especially an animal tortured by hunger, thirst, entrapment, discomfort, and fear. People are sometimes referred to as beasts or animals when they savagely grasp at something; Stiffel's allusion forces readers to consider multiple levels of the animalization metaphor. In the Nazi lexicon, bestial associations were not attached to their own clawing after power but were linked instead to the people whom they deemed inferior. An integral part of the Nazi assault on the integrity of the Jews' humanity was the Nazi propaganda that linked Jews with animals. Such an equation makes all the more apt Stiffel's observation that the Jews in the cattle cars were like animals, in their powerlessness and in their instinctual desire to survive.

In the Third Reich's hierarchy, the super-race of Germans looked with disdain upon anyone who did not meet their imaginary standard of Aryan heritage; however, their most intense fury was always unleashed upon the Jews. Even before the implementation of the Final Solution, the Nazis linked Jews with animals. Most autobiographers record a time when such degradation assaulted them. Gerda Weissmann Klein remembers the humiliation she felt when she and her father's business associate dared to walk past the factory where her father had previously been employed. "Instinctively, I looked towards the windows of my father's office. Then I heard a strange laugh from Mr. Pipersberg" (p. 26). His nervous laughter and his shaking hand caused her to look at the large sign to which he was pointing: "DOGS AND JEWS NOT ALLOWED TO ENTER" (p. 26, capitalization in text). Throughout the Third Reich, the Nazis posted signs with identical or similar wording at such public places as parks, restaurants, pools, and stores. Dr. Samuel Drix relates in his memoir a time when the Nazis summoned the Jews of his town. Significantly, the Jews were told to assemble in a stable. The SS took pleasure in the Jews' panic and in the women's sobs, and as they ridiculed their victims, the SS called them "dogs" (p. 54). Judith Magyar Isaacson recalls that because she had to pull a heavily laden wagon in a concentration camp, the Germans commanded her "about as 'Pferd—horse'" (p. 96). Sara Tuvel Bernstein describes a time when, seeking to enjoy a relaxing day by a lake, she and her friends were stunned to see the sign, "No Dogs or Jews Allowed" (p. 128). "'Now we're considered the same as dogs!'" her fiancé exclaimed; "What next? What will they decide we are next?" (p. 128). History would record what the Nazis decreed: In the Final Solution, Jews were equated with vermin.

The Nazis consistently degraded Jews by equating them with animals, at best, and with biological pathology, at worst. Although the Judeo-Christian common era history is replete with violence and oppression committed by Christians upon the Jews, throughout much of that sad litany was a theological motivation. Such a religious-based persecution was not fundamentally the root of the Nazi hatred of the Jews. Clearly the Nazis took special pleasure in mocking Jewish belief, in desecrating religious items, and in humiliating Jews in ways that ridiculed the victims' faith. To give only a few examples, the Nazis forced rabbis to spit on the Torah, pages from holy texts were used as toilet paper, synagogues were desecrated, torn prayer shawls were given to prisoners for underwear, and tombstones were converted into stepping stones. These actions were designed to torment the oppressed. Nonetheless, the Nazis did not attack Jews based on theological grounds, and most scholars do not associate the Nazis' hatred of the Jews with any religious underpinning.

One Holocaust scholar who sees the Nazi desecration as a sign of theological hatred is Michael Berenbaum, former director of the United States Holocaust Memorial Museum and co-author of the recent *Memory and Legacy: The Shoah Narrative of the Illinois Holocaust Museum*. When asked in a forum the inevitable but unanswerable question—why did the Holocaust happen?—he gave a range of potential reasons; the first reason that he mentioned was religious. "Hitler tried to establish himself as a God," Berenbaum states, and therefore Hitler "had to slaughter other Gods. The easiest way to destroy Christianity was to destroy the mother religion Judaism[,] not the daughter religion" (qtd. in Tokudome p. 30).

While an intriguing position, Berenbaum's assertion that religion was a motivating factor in Hitler's obsession is rare.

The Nazi persecution of the Jews was based on an amalgam of hatred, mixing race, economics, and fictional science; Hitler himself argues in *Mein Kampf* that Judaism is not a religion. "On this first and greatest lie," he says in a typical passage, "that the Jews are not a race but a religion, more and more lies are based in necessary consequence" (p. 307). Hitler saw Judaism as "blood" and "race," full of disease, corruption, and deceit. "The foremost connoisseurs of this truth regarding the possibilities in the use of falsehood and slander have always been the Jews; for after all, their whole existence is based on the great lie, to wit, that they are a religious community while actually they are a race — and what a race!" (p. 232). He uses a disease metaphor, establishing a paradigm that as an illness threatens a community, so does the Jew threaten the Aryan race: "The disease would have become chronic, while in the acute form of the collapse it at least became clearly and distinctly recognizable to a considerable number of people.... Exactly the same is true of diseases of national bodies" (p. 232). Edward Feld observes that the "Jews were not persecuted for religious reasons by the Nazis, though their demonic image of the Jews depended on inherited religious imagery" (p. 97). European history is filled with anti–Semitic images that Hitler's henchmen could and did draw upon, including bloated capitalists, leering sex fiends, and scampering rodents. Indeed, when Goebbels released the film of his dreams, *The Eternal Jew*, the apotheosis of anti–Semitic diatribes, he explicitly linked Jews and rats.

The animalization of the Jews that reached its ultimate point in the cattle cars had, at its basis, the fact that Hitler blamed the Jews for every calamity of his life, including the personal failure of his artistic ambitions in Vienna as well as the national shock of the Central Powers' defeat in the Great War, to name but two from a long list. As he grew in political power, Hitler created a scapegoat based primarily on two paradigms: economics and biology. When drawing upon an economics schema, Hitler accused the Jews either of being fantastically wealthy capitalists who controlled the world's wealth or of being conniving revolutionaries who planned to undermine stable governments. More deadly than the economics-based diatribe, however, was the biology paradigm.

Two: God's Ark and Hitler's Cattle Car

As Hitler's pathology of the Jew became officially sanctioned and embraced by the wider culture, the Nazis created "scientific" institutes where racial superiority and inferiority would be calibrated and analyzed. The "science" of eugenics worked hand-in-glove with the new strategy of euthanasia, which helped the Nazis dispose of those people designated as "useless eaters." "Life unworthy of living" was a term that permitted the Nazis to euthanize many, adults and children, who had mental and physical disabilities. The Christian churches protested that action, and the Nazis backed down. Tragically, the majority of Christian churches failed to protest the Nazi persecution of the Jews. Only a few Christian pastors and laypeople protested the disappearance of the Jews.

Hitler's disdain for Jews and other groups whom he considered biologically inferior was never hidden. According to Joachim Fest, whose biography of Hitler stands as one of the most important on the subject, the leader's disgust was publicly revealed as early as a 1923 radio address and was the *raison d'être* for the Wannsee Conference, that meeting of the minds who planned the Final Solution. Fest quotes from the 1923 speech at Krone Circus wherein Hitler stated: "The Jews are undoubtedly a race, but not human" (qtd. p. 212). Hitler continued: "Jewry means the racial tuberculosis of the nations" (qtd. p. 212). Fest shows how Hitler drew "from the language of parasitology: the laws of nature themselves demanded that measures be taken against the 'parasites,' the 'eternal leeches,' and the 'vampires upon other peoples'" (p. 212). Nineteen years later, Hitler's celebratory remarks concerning the plan concocted by the intellectuals and scientists at Wannsee left no room for doubt concerning the Nazi plan for the Jewish people: "The discovery of the Jewish virus is one of the greatest revolutions which has been undertaken in the world. The struggle we are waging is of the same kind as, in the past century, that of Pasteur and Koch. How many diseases can be traced back to the Jewish virus! We shall regain our health only when we exterminate the Jews" (qtd. in Fest p. 212). The Nazi mania for containing, and then eliminating, "the Jewish virus" led to the segregation of Jews into ghettos and, ultimately, to their murder in the death camps.

Noting the stereotypical German thoroughness with which the Nazis sought to decimate the Jewish people, Richard L. Rubenstein points out that gas used in the gas chambers was Zyklon B, also spelled Cyclon B, which was "chosen because it could kill large numbers quickly and efficiently. It was a variant of Cyclon A, an *insecticide*" (p. 33, italics in text). If a sign linking Jews and dogs was the beginning of the animalization process and killing with insecticide was the end, then the middle portion was, for many, the train trip to the labor and death camps in twentieth-century arks.

Helen Lewis refers to Noah's Ark when she describes being plunged into an emotional maelstrom when she and her husband were catalogued by the Nazis and sent to their fate. They were compelled to register at a large building, and as they went into the hall, she and her husband "paused for a moment to take in the scene before us. It reminded me of the Gustave Doré illustrations of the Old Testament, which I gazed at in awe when I visited my grandparents as a child" (p. 38). Doré's drawings captured the bleak horror of the Flood, a horror that she was even then experiencing: "This was a re-enactment of the Flood, the sea, disappearing under the multitude of drowning bodies, except that here the human mass was floating on top of thousands of mattresses and suitcases" (p. 38). Just as Doré invoked the image of hapless bodies surging in and out of the flood waters, so too did Lewis perceive the people within the hall as human flotsam. "Our senses were overcome by the sight of so many bodies in perpetual motion, and by the eerie and yet all too human sounds that filled the air. But there was no time for reflection, we had to find a space for ourselves, impossible as that seemed to be. When we did find it, we disappeared into the anonymous mass that opened for a moment and then swallowed us up" (p. 38). Drowning in a metaphorical flood unleashed by the Nazis caused Lewis to realize that she had lost everything. She no longer had her name, her history, her identity. That had all been swept away; now she was only a number (p. 38). The stripping of personhood was a symbolic drowning of individuality. The undulating mass of bodies reacted to the tide of fate that brought them to the deluge that was sweeping away their life. Gustave Doré's representation of Noah's Ark captures the dark, depressing tone of the story; Lewis' words do as well.

"The story of the Ark," maintain the editors of *A Rabbinic Anthology*, "was often used as the medium for inculcating kindness to animals" (Montefiore p. 42). In the Nazi transmogrification of the Genesis tale, Jews, now seen as animals, were denied any kindness or sympathy. When

Two: God's Ark and Hitler's Cattle Car

the Nazis began transporting Jews in large numbers to the numerous concentration camps spread across Europe, they did not fail to humiliate their victims even further. Since the Nazi propaganda equated Jews with animals at best and with disease at worst, Jews could not be transported in trains fit for human travel. Rather, Jews were sent to the camps in train cars previously used for transporting animals or cargo. "All God's creatures, the smallest worm had a right to live," Ruth Altbeker Cyprys says when describing the train experience, "only we had to die, for such was the will of Adolf Hitler" (p. 98). Worms had greater freedom than Jews, as Cyprys correctly noted; they were not automatically doomed for extermination.

Animals in confined conditions cannot control when they eat, drink, or eliminate; Jews transported to the camps found themselves in the same situation. Being forced into a small wooden compartment, overcrowded, and deprived of sufficient ventilation, food, water, and toilet facilities, some deportees found the journey traumatic, as traumatic as the camps themselves. Frightened, humiliated, and parched to the point of madness, those humans in the cattle cars guessed correctly that this phase of the trip was the penultimate moment of the Nazi degradation. Autobiographers who survived this torment commonly describe the harrowing nature of the ordeal. The cattle car transport's horrors included the emotional and psychological fears that seemed to rebound within the close confines of the cars' walls, as the Jews typically did not know where they were going. The torture included a large number of humans crammed into vehicles designed to carry animals or freight, so there were no seats or berths. There was usually a complete lack of food, water, and toilets, and, perhaps the worst of all, the lack of privacy when needing to relieve oneself.

The trains' overcrowded and substandard conditions initiated the "excremental assault," to use Terrence Des Pres's memorable terminology. Des Pres argues that the Nazi assault on human dignity included, but was not limited to, a lack of toilets, and the situation "began in the trains, in the locked boxcars" (p. 203). Such degradation, which would continue in the camps, was a premeditated move which forced people to wallow in urine and excrement — their own and others'. The lack of privacy and the lack of control over one's bodily functions had the effect of making a human being feel like an animal. Leon Szalet graphically describes the

Imagery from *Genesis* in Holocaust Memoirs

degradation in his autobiography, *Experiment "E": A Report from an Extermination Laboratory*, one of the first survivors' accounts, published in 1945. Primo Levi insists in *The Drowned and the Saved* that the assault's intent was twofold: It permitted the Germans to feel superior to the victims, and it caused the victims to be demoralized. Cyprys recalls the cattle car being turned into "a latrine," which in itself "deprived [us] of another bit of human dignity" (p. 96).

The deportees could scarcely feel like humans in their modern arks. Stiffel notices that the compartment he is pushed into bears the stenciled declaration of its limits from its use in the Great War: "Eight Horses, or Forty Men"; however, he counts 120 people in his car (p. 68). Seventy-five persons were packed into the cattle car that transported Isaacson from her Hungarian home to Auschwitz (p. 58). Levi remembers that there "were 12 goods wagons for 650 men; in mine we were only 45, but it was a small wagon" (*Survival* p. 16). None within the wooden confines of the train compartments knew where they were going, when they would arrive, and what would happen upon their debarkation. Most were told that they were to be resettled in the East, where they would work for the Reich; many knew the rumors of death camps, but a place designed to murder large numbers of people seemed too fantastic for many Jews to believe. How could such atrocities exist? The anxiety concerning the future was compounded by lack of essentials — air, food, water, toilets. If the boxcar had a window-like opening, it was barred. Observers from the outside can recall the faces desperately peering out from behind the bars or shouting through the wooden containers, begging for basic necessities. Packed into the cars, the deportees often desperately searched for a crack in the walls through which a gulp of air could be gasped or a drop of moisture could be swallowed.

The cattle cars that transported Jews across Europe to their deaths have become a metonym of the Holocaust. At some Holocaust museums in the United States, visitors may look at or walk through such compartments; if only for a moment in an empty cattle car, the museum guest may imagine the containment of human misery. Visitors walk through a cattle car at the United States Holocaust Memorial Museum in Washington, D.C., a liminal transition from the ghetto to the concentration camp. Guests entered the Holocaust Museum in Dallas, Texas, by walking through

Two: God's Ark and Hitler's Cattle Car

a cattle car in the museum's original design. That simple action — passing through time, as it were, via the twentieth-century ark — asks us to leave our world behind and to enter into vicarious memories. In the Illinois Holocaust Museum and Education Center, visitors walk up a ramp to the cattle car, inviting us to consider how Jews were often forced up ramps into the trains. The film *Paperclips* records Tennessee schoolchildren's efforts to bring a *hurban* cattle car to their school in order to honor and memorialize the suffering experienced long before they were born.

The victims contained within its wooden barriers had the door locked from the outside by an authority that had power over life and death. Like Noah and his animals enclosed within the ship, deportees experienced the phenomenon of enforced enclosure. Cyprys relates the sounds she heard before the train departed: "we heard dull rhythmic knocks, one, two, one, two. 'They are sealing the wagon,' somebody said. The hammer blows ceased; the nails of our coffin were in place" (p. 93). Both the inhabitants of the ark and of the cattle cars were powerless to affect their future; neither knew where they were going or how long it would take to arrive. They could control neither the storm nor their passage through it.

The trauma of enclosure was fatal for some in virtually every compartment; rarely does a Shoah lifewriter who experienced this transport describe it without mentioning those who died or went mad. Madame Schächter, a Cassandra-like figure in Wiesel's *Night*, screamed in the darkness of the cattle car that she saw fire, flames, a furnace (pp. 22–23); those in the compartment with her found her prophetic madness an exceptional strain on their own ability to control themselves, physically or emotionally. Olga Lengyel emphasizes death when she uses such charged words as "abattoir" and "gehenna" to convey the trains' conditions (p. 19). The cars were an initiation into, or a continuation of, death. For Lena Berg, who tells her story at the conclusion of her husband's autobiography, the hardship of the Warsaw Ghetto had already issued her a death blow. "We had lived our deaths in Warsaw. What survived of us now was only a cattle-car incarnation. They could destroy us, but they could no longer kill us: we were already dead" (Donat, 1st ed. p. 307). Wiesel tersely identified the transport as a death: "Life in the cattle cars was the death of my adolescence" (*All Rivers* p. 75). Cyprys recalls a person saying, "'Jews, we are in a morgue'" (p. 94). Livia E. Bitton Jackson, trapped amidst 85 people in her train compartment, tries to comfort herself with her rabbi's final words: "'God is going into exile with his people. I do not sense God in the cattle car. It is dark and chilly. And I tremble with fear.... Oh, God, I do not want to die!'" (p. 51). Such fear must have overcome every person within the trains — some felt it more strongly, or for a longer time; some lost their sanity; some died within the fear.

As the trains traveled throughout Europe, the inhabitants strove to glimpse their surroundings to ascertain where they were and thereby speculate what their destination might be. A crack in the wood or a peek through a barred window would sometimes permit the deportees to see road signs or significant scenery, helping them to determine what country they were in. Isaacson noticed signs in Polish and wished her knowledge of geography were better than it was (p. 60). Levi similarly looked for information: "Through the slit, known and unknown names of Austrian cities, Salzburg, Vienna, then Czech, finally Polish names" (*Survival* p. 18). Within the compartments' numbing crush, courtesy was not instantly abandoned, although some would fight for a certain space, with the corners being particularly coveted. But as the minutes slipped into hours and then the hours into days, the physical and psychological stress was debilitating. The situation was exacerbated by the lack of information. No one knew where they were going or what would happen when they would arrive. Levi recalls that the daytime was bearable because "the state of nervous tension made the hunger, exhaustion, and lack of sleep seem less of a torment. But the hours of darkness were nightmares without end" (p. 18). The humans, designated by the Nazis to be animals, were contained within an enclosed space, a space of both mental and physical confinement. Their future was ominous.

If readers choose to imagine what life might have been like aboard either the cattle cars or within Noah's ark, we must give our senses full play. What would we have seen? Or, in the darkness, not seen? Can we imagine the physicality of bodies crushed into other bodies? Can we smell the odors? The Genesis authors did not give readers any insight into the thoughts and fears of the ark's occupants. Presumably, the humans within Noah's ark perceived that the ark was designed for their current safety and ultimately for the saving of their own lives as all others perished; inhabitants of Hitler's cattle cars did not know their fate. Some correctly intuited that they were going into slavery and perhaps death, even though the Nazis usually told the Jews that they were being transported to a work camp. If we place ourselves within those containers riding through the apocalypse, then we must imaginatively relinquish knowing how long we will be contained. "How long, O Lord?" is a refrain found throughout Scripture, particularly in the Psalms; the question suggests that the Lord is slow to action, yet people can endure if only they know that their suffering will eventually end.

The waters continued for "forty days and forty nights"—a familiar refrain—after Noah's family and the animals entered the ark. Less well known is the Genesis declaration that the waters covered the earth for "one hundred and fifty days" (7:24). Doubtless the "forty days and forty nights" phrase is well known since that number is used throughout the Bible, even into the New Testament, to signify a long time. However, there are two periods of these "forty days and forty nights" within Noah's story: The first occurs when the flood begins (7:17), and the second is when the waters diminish (8:6). Such parallelism invites attention to the story's palistrophic structure—that is, a story whose rising action is mirrored inversely by the falling action, balanced in the middle by the climax. In the Noah palistrophe, the number of lines used to detail God's displeasure with humanity and the sending forth of the flood waters is equal roughly to the number of lines used to relate the story's conclusion. Mario DiCicco suggests that the "palistrophe is a literary figure whose essential feature is return" (p. 17). If we apply a palistrophic reading to the Genesis text, the climax may imply that God returned to Noah. The literary and religious climax of the Flood account is Genesis 8:1 with the simple line, "God remembered Noah." We have seen the importance of remembering for the Jew. But what does it mean for God to remember?

Many scholars and rabbis read "God remembered" as an emphatic underscoring of God's activity: It was not that God had forgotten Noah, but rather that the time was right for God to intervene once again in the Flood drama. The Plaut *Commentary* affirms that the expression *va-yizkor*, *God remembered*, "occurs frequently in the Bible and consistently reflects a belief in moral continuity" (p. 62). "Remember" in this context emphasizes the ongoing care that the Lord possesses for the world and suggests that, while never forgotten, an event may now take center stage. DiCicco insists that the literary form itself "highlights the fact that it was God who acted decisively to save Noah just at the moment when chaos seemed to overwhelm everything, throwing it back into its primeval state" (p. 20). The climactic "God remembered" may be understood as emphasizing the precise moment when God could dispense mercy and justice.

Nevertheless, it is difficult to read "God remembered" without holding in tension its opposite, "God forgot." In such a light, the ringing climax of the Flood story may well convey the impression that God had utterly forgotten about Noah and, by association, the global annihilation that surrounded Noah. The implications of a god who decides to exterminate all of humanity except for a few are chilling enough; the implications of God forgetting Noah, his family, and the animals are disturbing. If it is possible that God forgot about the inhabitants of the ark, then it would seem that this is a God who does not care. Is this the same God who appeared to have forgotten those who were sealed in the Nazi cattle cars?

In the Noah account, God is in the details. "Read the story," Wiesel encourages, "and you will be struck by its realism: dates, figures, measurements. One might take it for a scientific report" ("Noah's Warning" p. 4). The Lord conveys clear specifications for the height, depth, and number of levels, as well as insisting that only one entrance should be made. After Noah, his family, and the animals have entered, the entrance must be closed, and Noah is not given that particular responsibility. "They came to Noah into the ark, two each of all flesh in which there was breath of life. Thus they that entered comprised male and female of all flesh, as God had commanded him. *And the Lord shut him in*" (7:15–16, emphasis added). I have chosen to italicize the final line (Gen. 7:16b) because it is so short, so simple, that we may easily overlook its significance. We have heard the sound effects in movies when a jail door clangs shut, trapping the protagonist within a prison. Nora's slamming of the door when she leaves Torvald in Ibsen's *A Doll's House* was one of the most shocking sounds to audiences in modern drama. We ourselves might recall a time when a door literally shut upon us and upon our hopes. Genesis invites us to envision the story that the Flood narrative tells. What is the sound of God sealing in his chosen, his elect? Can we imagine how a person might feel when powerlessly hearing God's own hand sealing, from the outside, the only door? Would that person feel safely secure or hopelessly trapped?

Two: God's Ark and Hitler's Cattle Car

Carol Gilligan observes that Noah's story "is about enclosure" (Moyers p. 121). One need not be claustrophobic to imagine the uncomfortable sensation of being locked in a wooden container with no possibility of opening it. This forced enclosure raises issues of control, power, and authority, and it further summons up an image of riding out the storm, a storm surrounding first Noah and later European Jewry. When Noah emerged from the ark — that is, when God opened the door — he saw that he had survived when all others have drowned. He is, in a certain sense, the first holocaust survivor. To view the primeval flood as a holocaust is to ask questions about the goodness of God, questions that haunt the world after the twentieth-century Shoah, questions that hover over the pages of survivors' autobiographies.

God set into motion events that killed every person on earth except Noah and his family, according to Genesis, and at a certain time, God remembered Noah enduring his dark confinement. If God remembered Noah, did God remember the people at Auschwitz? In an essay entitled "A Kind of Survivor," George Steiner ponders that question. Feeling as if he, too, is a survivor — he is alive because his parents left Europe before Hitler's rise to power — Steiner wonders what sort of God permits the existence of the concentration camp. Who is this God who claims to be good and merciful and where was this God when so many millions were dying particularly heinous deaths at the Nazis' hands? In considering these questions and concluding from the evidence that God turned away from the people, Steiner finds Biblical precedence not in Noah's story, as Frank Stiffel did, but in a curious passage from Exodus. Steiner sets up the Exodus 32:22–23 story: "Moses is once more on Sinai, asking for a new set of Tablets (we have always been nagging Him, demanding justice and reason twice over)" (p. 142). God promises that Moses shall see God and God's glory, but not His face. Rather, Moses will witness God's "back parts" (p. 142). Steiner explicates Moses' odd opportunity in this way: "This may be the decisive clue: God can turn His back. There may be minutes or millennia — is our time His? — in which He does not see man, in which He is looking the *other way*. Why?" (142, italics in text). Steiner speculates that it is a design flaw of the universe that prevents the All-Mighty, the King of the Universe, to see everything "...because somewhere there is a millionth of an inch, it need be no more, out of His line of sight.

So He must turn to look there also. When God's back parts are toward man, history is Belsen" (p. 142). Perhaps Steiner's explanation is as good as any, all of which fail, regarding an omnipotent God and the reality of the death camps.

Steiner describes a God — a God, maybe, of good intentions — who simply cannot keep an eye on the entire creation all at one time. When God cannot survey the entire creation, then evil can establish a stronghold. Necessarily, this vision of God means that God can fail the creation and the people. Many Jews who believed, even passionately believed, in a loving and kind God express their anguish over God's apparent failure in their autobiographies. Stiffel concludes *The Tale of the Ring: A Kaddish* with a lament directly addressed to the Lord: "Oh, God, how could you!" (p. 327). Many other lifewriters say nothing about their religious beliefs or confess that what they saw prevented them from ever believing in the God of their childhood.

Most autobiographies emerging from Bergen-Belsen, Auschwitz, and other death sites wrestle with God's presence, God's memory, and God's absence. The authors come to different conclusions about God, God's intentions and God's whereabouts, but all must confront the questions. Wondering about God, taking God to task, arguing with God, or even putting God on trial, as Wiesel did in one of his plays — all these activities are normal in the Jewish tradition but are viewed askance in the Christian tradition. Grappling with God causes the Shoah autobiography to become part memoir, part theological reflection. Questioning God's benevolence contributes to the philosophical current contained within the survivors' stories and within Noah's story as well.

Steiner's analysis of the Exodus passage implies that God's glance must have been elsewhere during the long, dreadful years of the Final Solution. Seemingly, God has forgotten the chosen people, just as the Genesis text implies that Noah had been forgotten. "In the vocabulary of Nazism," Steiner writes, "there were elements of a vengeful parody on the Judaic claim. The theological motif of a people elected at Sinai is echoed in the pretense of the master race and its chiliastic dominion" ("A Kind of Survivor" p. 153). Steiner is not alone in perceiving that, during the Nazi era, the Jews were still the chosen people. Silvano Ariet concurs: "The Jewish people have been chosen again; in this twentieth century, they have

Two: God's Ark and Hitler's Cattle Car

been chosen to face the greatest possible evil" (p. 164). Unlike Noah, chosen to live because of his righteousness, the Jews of Europe during Hitler's reign were chosen, regardless of their righteousness, not for survival but for death. Unlike Noah, sealed into a container because he was chosen to survive an apocalyptic storm, the Jews of Europe who were transported across a continent were sealed into a container in order that they might die.

Although Jewish reading and Midrashic interpretation celebrate complexity and multiplicity, one central point concerning Noah has consistently preoccupied the rabbis, and that point is raised immediately upon Noah's introduction in Genesis 6:9: "This is the line of Noah.— Noah was a righteous man; he was blameless in his age [*ish tzaddik tamim*]; Noah walked with God." Noah, his family, and the animals in his care had all been guaranteed safe passage through the death that surrounded them for only one reason: Noah was *ish tzaddik tamim,* "a righteous man," "blameless in his age" or in his generation. Wiesel assesses Noah's character as being one of goodness, at least at first ("Noah's Warning" p. 6). His strengths were reflected in his name, which, as Wiesel explains, "means consolation and promise" (p. 6). Frank H. Polak stresses the "notion of stability" which is contained within "positive overtones of the name *Noah*" (p. 71, italics in text). The rest of the world, however, was not blameless: "The earth became corrupt before God; the earth was filled with injustice" (Gen 6:11). Such injustice moves God to repent having ever made the world; consequently, the Lord resolves to destroy the creation. What had Noah done that caused him to be seen as righteous, and thereby allowed his life to be spared?

Rabbinic thinking on this question is polarized. Many follow the assumption that Noah was a righteous man *in* his generation, and that the preposition damns with faint praise, for it implies *only* in his generation. He would not be righteous in another, more benevolent time. Adam and Eve had been expelled from their paradise, and one of their two sons killed the other. God apparently could bear that, but by Noah's time, humanity's sinfulness had become too much for even a loving Creator. The Plaut *Commentary* refers to the Flood story as closing "the first era in man's post–Eden story" and calls it a time of "devolution" and of moral deterioration (p. 61). What had humanity done that so caused the Lord to regret creating them? The "Midrash speculates that it was unbounded affluence that caused men to become depraved.... Hand in hand with material prosperity went an overbearing attitude toward God, whom people judged to be incapable of hearing prayer and of enforcing moral standards" (Plaut p. 61). Walking among the people whose hearts were hard and whose lives were sin-filled, Noah stood out by his righteousness, say many rabbinic thinkers, qualifying their assessment by insisting that Noah himself would not have been exceptional in a better time, a better place. While Noah is praised with a verb implying relationship — he "walked with God" — many rabbis interpret that action as less prestigious than the activity enjoyed by Abraham, the father of Judaism, who talked with God. The verb choice is telling. Talking implies greater intimacy; talking permits two parties to get to know each other on a deeper level. Moreover, Abraham argued with God. Abraham argued and bargained with God to save a city; Noah did not argue with God to spare the world. Noah is not righteous among all people, say many rabbis, because he did not exhibit compassion for those who were to perish in the Flood.

Naturally, there are rabbis who take a different view and insist that Noah's goodness was absolute, in his generation or any other. The Talmud records Rabbi Jochanan's insistence that Noah was blameless only in his age whereas Resh Lakish counters: "He was righteous even in his age; how much more so would he have been righteous in other ages" (qtd. in Plaut p. 61). Neusner seems to side with this supportive position; in his compilation of Midrash, Neusner emphasizes the interpretation that "Noah was found to withstand the trial and so was proved righteous" and that "Noah's obedience, going into the ark when told, coming out when told, explains why he survived the flood, while the rebels, who did not accept God's word, perished" (*Genesis Rabbah* p. 2). Some maintain that because Noah was given time to build the ark, the construction itself was a sign to his neighbors. Certainly the neighboring people would have asked Noah about his boat-building; surely Noah warned them of the flood to come and encouraged them to join his family. Those who drowned did so, according to this view, due to their sinfulness and their inability to interpret the signs about them.

Striking in the Shoah autobiographers' accounts is the determination to endure the Nazis' inexplicable fury, tempered by the grief that the same

Two: God's Ark and Hitler's Cattle Car

violence attacked the writers' loved ones, people who were good, loving, pure, and righteous. The righteous person may have been the lifewriter's parent, a grandparent, a sibling, a rabbi, a child, a friend. Sorrow over the death of a good person is virtually palpable, and no Holocaust memoir is free from such grief. Grief, often unresolved, over the death of an innocent person contributes to the "survivor's guilt" syndrome. Gerda Weissmann Klein writes that her dazed reaction to her "first day of freedom" in 1945 was simply this: "Why am I here? ... I am no better!" (p. 261, ellipsis in text). She has repeated that declaration many times, including in a documentary short film made of her life, *One Survivor Remembers*, and when accepting an Academy Award for that film. When I heard Klein speak in 1996 at a Yom HaShoah service in 1996, 51 years after her liberation, she used the exact same phrase. It is the phrase of the survivor. The arbitrary nature of who lived and who died haunts the survivors; righteousness or its lack was no indicator of who would endure the storm.

Silvano Arieti tries to make sense of the Nazi genocide in his examination of *Abraham and the Contemporary Mind* when he states, "Hitler's implicit intention [was] to destroy the Jews not because they were bad but precisely from a moral point of view because they were good" (p. 116). Arieti's assertion that Jewish *tzaddik*, righteousness, was exactly what Hitler sought to obliterate has, regrettably, an inauthentic ring. While some might imagine that survivors would be comforted by the notion that the Nazis' wrath descended upon them because of their goodness, no Shoah lifewriter whom I have read has posited such a claim. Jews of Hitler's era knew well what Hitler believed and preached about them, and nothing Hitler wrote or said indicated that he reacted out of fear of Jewish goodness. Hitler's position was made abundantly clear from his earliest speeches and *Mein Kampf*. The Nazi refrain about the Jews was repeated throughout its 12-year Reich: "The Jews are our misfortune." The Nazis did not cringe before Jewish righteousness because they could neither see it nor imagine it. Righteous or not, European Jews died by order of the Reich.

After God remembered Noah, the ark was brought safely to dry land. Noah offered a thanksgiving sacrifice to the deity. "Then Noah built an altar to the LORD and, taking of every clean animal and of every clean bird, he offered burnt offerings on the altar. The LORD smelled the pleasing odor, and the LORD said to Himself: 'Never again will I doom the world because of man, since the devisings of man's mind are evil from his youth, nor will I ever again destroy every living being as I have done'" (Gen. 8:20–21). The Lord then creates a covenant, a highly visual one that is celebrated in art and kitsch: "'...never again shall all flesh be cut off by the waters of a flood, and never again shall there be a flood to destroy the earth.' God further said, 'This is the sign that I set for the covenant between Me and you, and every living creature with you, for all ages to come. I have set My bow in the clouds, and it shall serve as a sign of the covenant between Me and the earth...'" (Gen. 9:11–13a). The "bow" has long been interpreted to mean a rainbow, and so the iconography of Noah's successful voyage through perilous waters typically has a rainbow arched above the ark. God speaks, or, more correctly, "the Lord said in His heart" (*Genesis Rabbah* p. 8), that never again will a flood destroy the earth. He promises that seeing the bow will cause Him to "'remember the everlasting covenant between God and all living creatures, all flesh that is on earth'" (Genesis 9:16). Once again the notion arises that God needs a reminder.

Neusner interprets Noah's burnt sacrifice as more than a historical document of ancient cultic practices; rather, he argues that the sacrifice stands, even for our times, as "a substantial and important proposition." "The true sacrifices to God come from those who give their lives for his name," he insists. "So the blood-sacrifice is turned into a symbol for Israel's sacrifice of itself in God's name" (*Genesis Rabbah* p. 9). Such a reading redeems Jewish death, elevating it to martyrdom. A different approach was taken by Professor David G. Roskies when he co-led a literary seminar at the United States Holocaust Memorial Museum, at which I was present. He interpreted the Genesis 9:14–16 passage above with a post–Shoah emphasis. In Roskies's reading, God announces His covenant when the bow appears — but this is no longer the colorful rainbow of popular culture. Rather, in a world that carried on after the six million died, the bow that reminds God of His promise is the bowed archway under which so many Jews passed in Auschwitz and other camps — the bow proclaims the words *Arbeit Macht Frei*. The saying, *Arbeit Macht Frei*, loosely translated as "Work Makes You Free," was displayed on arches, gateways, and posts not only in Auschwitz but in many concentration camps throughout the Third Reich. Millions of prisoners, Jew and non–Jew, walked under or past

Two: God's Ark and Hitler's Cattle Car

such a covenant, a covenant the Nazis had no intention of honoring. Only death would set them free.

Noah departed his ship, setting his feet on dry land for the first time in months or in over half of a year, depending on which *Bereshit* narrative voice the reader wishes to privilege. Perhaps it is good and right that Noah's first action upon stepping foot on dry land was to offer a sacrifice of thanksgiving. Noah's thoughts are not given voice. Its absence begs the question: What words might describe Noah? Thankful? Relieved? Traumatized? Embittered? Overwhelmed? Noah had to start all over again when all that he had known had been destroyed. The silence that hovers over post-deluge Noah might be related to the silence of so many Holocaust survivors, which bifurcates into the silence emanating from the scale of the Shoah and the silence from survivors shushed by a world that did not want to hear.

When the Thousand Year Reich collapsed in 1945, a small percentage of prisoners were able to leave the concentration camps. We will examine the phenomenon of liberation in a later chapter, but at this point, there are a few last words to say about Noah. The Holocaust survivor had to create a new life, just as Noah had to create a post-diluvial life. *Bereshit* tells us that Noah became the first person to plant and nurture a vineyard as part of the process of recreating a destroyed world. Noah drank so much of his own wine that he, inebriated, was discovered "uncovered" by his son Ham. Ham tells his two brothers, Shem and Japheth, about the distressing situation. The author of Genesis paints the picture: "But Shem and Japheth took a cloth, placed it against both their backs and, walking backwards, they covered their father's nakedness; their faces were turned the other way, so that they did not see their father's nakedness" (Gen. 8:23). Noah later awoke from his drunken stupor and was horrified that his son had discovered him in such a state. Violently, albeit verbally, Noah cursed his son Ham, condemning him to the status of a slave (Gen 8:25–26). Noah's drunkenness and the curse he swore upon his own son have caused many readers to puzzle over his behavior.

Noah sought to reestablish his post-trauma life by becoming "the tiller of the soil" as well as being "the first to plant a vineyard" (Genesis 9:20). This is the man who in the next verse is found dead drunk, that same man some rabbis identified as *tzaddik*, a righteous person. "Is this a characteristic of a *Tzaddik*?" marvels Wiesel. "To renew history by getting drunk? Most Talmudic interpreters have judged this incident severely" ("Noah's Warning" p. 15). "To drown one's sorrows" is a common idiom describing inebriation and, when applied to Noah, it is a particularly apt expression. How appropriately yet poignantly Noah acted out his grief: He who survived the flood that drowned all else drowns his own sorrows in his own wine. The flood waters have receded, but those who died are no more; symbolically, Noah floods himself in wine in order to drown out his own agony.

We who did not live through the Event may assume that liberation brought immediate relief and lasting joy, but perhaps it may be more realistic to expect that survivors faced profound difficulties adjusting to life when home, friends, and loved ones had been swept away by the deluge. Ruth Kluger alludes to the strange incident of Ham, who discovers his father intoxicated and naked, as she herself rebuilt her post-war life. Wanting information about relatives who were sent to concentration camps and desiring to know more about activities within various camps, Kluger faces uncooperative people and bureaucracies. "And still I can't get rid of the prickly sense that I am breaking taboos, searching for indecencies, like Noah's children uncovering their father's nakedness, that I am not supposed to know about death and dying" (p. 17). Although the Genesis tale has only one son discovering a drunken, naked Noah, Kluger's allusion does situate her within its emotional context. Noah's son Ham, at the very least, saw his father naked. That in itself does not seem to be a crime worthy of condemnation, especially of receiving a curse, but the Plaut *Commentary* explains Genesis 9:22 thusly: "Uncovering a relative's nakedness was a biblical euphemism for sexual relations.... The story of Ham and Noah should be read, therefore, as one of sexual perversion" (p. 70). Although Kluger does not assume her readers would associate sexual perversity with the Noah allusion, her sense of "breaking taboos" and "searching for indecencies" plunges her into a world of rejection. She found that those who had not endured the concentration camps believed that a young woman should not "know about death and dying." If anyone knew about the death of an entire people, it would have been Noah and his family; it would have to be the Shoah survivor.

Was Noah the first holocaust survivor? If "holocaust" with the low-

Two: *God's Ark and Hitler's Cattle Car*

ercase *h* implies widespread destruction (and not, in Biblical terms, a holy sacrifice consumed by fire), then, yes, he could be considered so. If Noah was the first holocaust survivor, then he established a pattern, a pattern Wiesel observed in his own life and one that he described to Bill Moyers in a videotaped interview. Wiesel states: "When liberation came, our community created immediately ... a community of prayer.... We said Kaddish, the prayer for the dead. And I am not sure really that God was worthy of that Kaddish" ("Facing Hate"). Noah did not seem to question God's worthiness; Wiesel did. Noah, not a Jew, living in the time before God established the Jewish covenant with Abraham, might not have questioned God; Wiesel, a Jew firmly secure in the tradition of arguing with God in lively debate, never shies away from it.

In the Genesis account, God was so dismayed by human evil that He decided to destroy what He had created. The Lord set aside a small remnant of humanity and animals in order that the created life on earth could begin again. In the twentieth century, Hitler blamed the Jews for all the hardships that Germany had undergone and so decided to (re)create a mythical Aryan land; in order to accomplish that, he sought to destroy Jews and others whom he dehumanized. "God remembered Noah" can imply that Noah had been forgotten; Hitler never seemed to forget the Jews, as evidenced by the continued, even escalated, killing of Jews during the war's final years, a time when the Nazi resources might have logically turned from civilian murder to enhanced military efforts. God's rainbow in the sky is a signal of the promise that never again would He destroy the earth by water; the Nazi sign during Hitler's reign as a demigod may well have been the crematoria smoke, a promise to burn all the Jews. God destroyed by water, the Nazis, by fire.

We who have not undergone such a trauma can scarcely imagine what a hard, even bitter, situation it must be to survive when so many others have perished. How difficult to survive, knowing of one's own inevitable human failings and foibles, when those perceived to be more righteous, more *tzaddik*, are dead. Noah and other survivors may have escaped with their lives, but they cannot escape the sounds of the dying. If Noah was a holocaust survivor, then he may concur with Wiesel: "For the camp survivor life is a battle not only for the dead but also against them. Locked in the grip of the dead, he fears that by freeing himself, he is also abandoning them" (*All Rivers* pp. 298–299). To forget the dead is to dishonor them; to remember is to burden one's own life with the weight of incalculable grief. If Noah is an archetype, then his story may be less about God keeping promises and more about the anguish of surviving.

CHAPTER THREE

The Babel of Extermination

> The confusion of languages is a fundamental component of the manner of living here; one is surrounded by a perpetual Babel, in which everyone shouts orders and threats in languages never heard before, and woe betide whoever fails to grasp the meaning.
> — Primo Levi

The Tower of Babel: Genesis 11:1–9

Human cargo, crammed into train compartments originally designed for cattle, shuttled along the railroads of Europe, destined for labor or death camps, as discussed in the previous chapter. The transport was, in itself, such a grueling experience that those who physically lived through it may not have psychologically survived it. Eugene Heimler describes it as a "nightmare three-day journey which bridged the abyss between two worlds.... I had mounted the train of death wearing European clothes, a European man; I alighted at the other end a dazed creature of Auschwitz" (p. 23). Upon descending the train compartment into the abattoir, new arrivals faced an unimaginable reality. Here was a place so demonic that many memoirists refer to it as "the Inferno" or "hell"; other lifewriters seek to convey the place's foreign, bizarre nature of otherness by using such terms as "planet Auschwitz," "the Holocaust Kingdom," and *"l'univers concentrationnaire."* Those who had survived the train journey tumbled into this alternate universe thirsty, starved, weary, demoralized, and confused. They were confronted by Nazi guards who characteristically initiated the new prisoners with a battery of verbal commands and physical blows. Furious orders swirled around the prisoners whose immediate fates were determined instantly by the flick of an SS man's finger or whip. The SS or their myrmidons delivered life-or-death instructions using words foreign to many, if not most, of the arriving prisoners, but the initiation process demanded that the meaning be grasped quickly and accurately.

Arriving at the concentration camps, prisoners were propelled into the camps' pandemonium: Nowhere else does the etymology of Milton's coinage serve the language so well. "Dogs snarl, SS men scream orders, children cry, women weep good-byes to departing men," writes Livia Bitton Jackson of the pandemonium that accompanied her entrance into the death camp (p. 56). Primo Levi alludes not to Milton but to Shakespeare when he observes that, when he arrived at Auschwitz, he had entered a world "filled with a dreadful sound and fury signifying nothing: a hubbub of people without names or faces drowned in a continuous, deafening noise from which, however, the human world did not surface" (*Drowned* pp. 93–94). Some survivors, particularly Elie Wiesel, focus on the phenomenon of silence hovering over the camps' day-by-day existence, a palpable silence he describes as emanating from God and humanity; this topic will be considered in the next chapter. Yet even Wiesel, with his emphasis upon silence, recalls that the "tumult of the convoy disembarking in the night" was augmented by "[h]arsh shouting, stifled crying, soft moans and the barking of dogs" ("Pilgrimage" p. 106). He identifies the noisy confluence that met him upon arrival in Auschwitz to be the actual language of the Third Reich, a tongue he labels throughout his writings as "the language of the night." The parlance "was not human; it was primitive, almost animal — hoarse shouting, screaming, muffled moaning, savage howling, the sounds of beating" ("Why I Write" p. 15). This tumult of sounds — screaming, crying, howling, barking — was omnipresent, as were the sounds of all the languages spoken by a defeated Europe. The nightly routine in her barracks, recalls Liana Millu, included "angry voices, in various languages, ... calling for silence. *Ruhe*! *Cihò*! *Taisez-vous*!" (p. 36, italics in text). With such a cacophony adding to the intensity of an already traumatic situation, it is no wonder that so many Holocaust survivors refer to the noise of the camps as Babel.

Babel is no mere simile. The camps were not *like* Babel; they *were* Babel, insist many survivors in their memoirs. Indeed, the Babel allusion

Three: The Babel of Extermination

is the most consistent and common Scriptural reference made by Shoah autobiographers. If they had been incarcerated within a concentration camp, Holocaust memoirists refer without exception to the strangeness of an imprisoned Europe and its attendant languages — from Norwegian to Greek, from French to Russian — as the macaronic turmoil augmented the omnipresent tension. In Primo Levi's first autobiographical account of life in Auschwitz, he remembers his first night in the barracks, where "from all corners of the now dark hut, sleepy and angry voices shout at me: *Ruhe, Ruhe!*" (*Survival* p. 38, italics in text). He stresses: "The confusion of languages is a fundamental component of the manner of living here; one is surrounded by a perpetual Babel, in which everyone shouts orders and threats in languages never heard before, and woe betide whoever fails to grasp the meaning" (p. 38). Failure to obey a command, even if issued in a language unknown to the hearer, could be fatal. Heimler also uses Babel as a metaphor for the camp's confusion: "It was a strange unreal world to which I awoke. People were talking to one another in every language under the sun. Why was there this noise of Babel in the middle of the night?" (p. 118). Heimler's dizzying juxtaposition of sun/night and hypnogogic/awakened state textualizes the prisoner's disorientation within *l'univers concentrationnaire*.

In many camps, Jews were segregated from other prisoners; however, Jew or not, a prisoner within the Nazi camp system was surrounded by almost every language of Europe. Non-Jewish prisoners of the concentration camp system also defined the camps as Babel. Olga Lengyel recalls in her autobiography, *Five Chimneys*, that the Nazis brought "bruised and starved human beings" into the camps, where "piteous cries rose in every language in Europe: in French, Rumanian, Polish, Czech, Dutch, Greek, Spanish, Italian; who knows how many more?" (p. 83). A particularly aggressive round-up of European deportees "caused changes inside the camp," states Lengyel. "More than ever, Birkenau became a real 'Tower of Babel,' with every kind of language spoken and different kinds of customs practiced" (p. 141). The multiplicity of languages added to the tension inherent within the camps' already stressful situation.

Most autobiographers who employ the Babel allusion identify the camps as Babel when they convey the shock of entering planet Auschwitz; Levi and Heimler are two examples of this. However, the reference may come at any point in a survivor's account. In Henry Orenstein's experience within several camps, he was isolated among his fellow Polish Jews; only near the end of the war was he transferred to a camp massive enough to contain the gamut of the Nazis' European prisoners and where Jews mingle with non–Jews. Orenstein was astonished. "I had never seen such a variety of nationalities, from every part of Europe, by the thousands: Poles, Russians, Jews, Gypsies, Belgians, French, Dutch, Danes, Czechs, Bulgarians, Spaniards, Yugoslavs — each speaking his own language, a true Tower of Babel!" (pp. 227–228). Judith Magyar Isaacson places the allusion near her autobiography's conclusion, when she relates the liberation of her work camp. As a throng of slave-laborers greeted the American liberators, they sang "in a cacophony of tongues. All of Europe seemed represented in the celebration" (p. 117). Her friend exclaimed in amazement, "'It's a veritable tower of Babel!'" (p. 117). A swirl of European languages filled the air above slave labor camps and concentration camps as the war ended in 1945.

The war's end did not end the displacement of European people and their languages. Lena Berg heard a radio broadcast "in all languages the words 'unconditional surrender'" (p. 274), which in turn led to the mass migration of former prisoners seeking home: "The roads of Europe were like swollen mountain torrents in spring, a Babel of people and languages, all former slaves or prisoners of the Third Reich" (p. 275). After the liberation, Helen Lewis was hospitalized, recovering from her physical ordeals; there she met a doctor who "was an elderly, kind German who had volunteered to help in this emergency. He was glad to have found a patient he could talk to in his own language in this enforced Babel from all over Europe" (p. 155). Alicia Appleman-Jurman, originally from Poland and still a child when the war ended, went to an orphanage in Belgium after the Nazis' defeat. European children, originally from various nations, were in the orphanage, having nowhere else to go and no certainty if they had any family left alive. "Sometimes when I thought of the number of languages we spoke, the school seemed to be a small Tower of Babel," Appleman-Jurman recalls (p. 411). Babel reigned everywhere in the Third Reich and held its sway even after the Reich's death-grip on Europe ended.

Just as the Tower of Babel image is the single most common allusion made by Shoah writers, so too is the *Genesis* passage itself one of the most

Three: The Babel of Extermination

familiar stories from the Bible. Such familiarity may lead some to assume that they therefore understand the point of the story, and that the passage explicates one thing: how multiple languages came into the world. However, the short passage is more complicated than a mythic account of ancients trying to make sense of an event; indeed, some autobiographers, notably Levi, find in the Babel tale Jewish history writ small. Babel, to complicate matters, is considered pre–Jewish history, occurring before the appearance of Abraham, the person who ushered in the Jewish covenant with God. Yet Babel and other seminal stories found in the early chapters of the Bible's first book — Adam and Eve, Cain and Abel, Noah and his ark — feature significant motifs important to Jewish history. The short story of Babel needs to be examined in its entirety. To draw attention to particularly important themes, I have italicized key words related to bricks, language, confusion, and dispersal.

> All the earth had the same *language* and the same *words*. And as men migrated from the east, they came upon a valley in the land of Shinar and settled there. They said to one another, "Come, let us make *bricks* and burn them hard."— *Brick* served them as stone, and bitumen served them as mortar.— And they said, "Come, let us build us a city, and a tower with its top in the sky, to make a name for ourselves; else we shall be *scattered* all over the world." The LORD came down to look at the city and tower that man had built, and the LORD said, "If, as one people with one *language* for all, this is how they have begun to act, then nothing that they may propose to do will be out of their reach. Let us, then, go down and *confound* their *speech* there, so that they shall not understand one another's *speech*." Thus the LORD *scattered* them from there over the face of the whole earth; and they stopped building the city. That is why it was called Babel, because there the LORD *confounded* the *speech* of the whole earth; and from there the LORD *scattered* them over the face of the whole earth [Genesis 11:1–9].

Before examining the passage's significance within Holocaust autobiographies, particularly the writings of Primo Levi, a few important features should be considered. As a literary set-piece, Babel is well-wrought. U. Cassuto praises it as "a fine example of Biblical literary art" as he points to the contrasting parallel actions by the builders and by the Lord: The text displays an inverse symmetry between the upward, vertical movement by the people when they build their tower and the outward, horizontal movement by God when He disperses the people across the land (p. 231–232). Alter makes the same point when he observes the "intricate antithetical symmetry that embodies the idea of 'man proposes, God disposes'" (p. 47 note 3). The Genesis passage is well balanced, using approximately the same number of verses in Acts I and III, as it were, with Act II being the climax as God suddenly becomes aware of humanity's hubris. The tale contributes to a Biblical tradition where inanimate objects take on a life of their own — the walls of Jericho, the manna in the wilderness, and, here, the bricks of Babel.

Reading *Bereshit* in English deprives us of word play that is a hallmark of Biblical Hebrew, a language and a style of writing that preoccupies rabbis. Joel Rosenberg is not alone when he insists that the Hebrew Bible defies being effectively translated because of "its saturation with extensive and subtle wordplays" (p. 37). We English readers cannot deduce the text's etymological comment — "That is why it was called Babel" — even though we might speculate that a connection exists to Babylon. We need to know that the text is playing upon two connotations springing from the sound of "babel." Aldo J. Tos supports the Babel/Babylon connection when he states that the ancient Hebrews may have believed that Babylon was the first city in civilization and, consequently, the primal site of corruption: "[T]he Hebrew word *babal*, means 'confuse,' and sounds enough like Babel to be used in folk etymology for the city in which the 'confusion of tongues' first occurred" (p. 68). Thus, Babel establishes a negative tone, with its suggestive inference to Babylon, always mentioned pejoratively in Scripture, and its association with the verb "to confuse" or "to confound."

Similarly missing from the English reader's grasp of the Babel story is the play on words involving two key themes: *bricks* and *let's confuse*. Rosenberg explicates the literary device when he points out that Semitic languages emphasize "consonants — usually three root letters — as bearers of the concept represented by the word" (p. 38). Echoing, reversing, or restating those consonants allows a wide range of word-play possibilities; for instance, Rosenberg points out that the word for *bricks*, *levenah*, metathesizes the letters for the Hebrew *let's confuse*, *navelah* (p. 38). Babel becomes a meaningful allusion for Shoah writers with its threefold stress on a wicked place, bricks, and confusion. Babel suggests Babylon, an evil site; bricks connote toil and slavery; and confusion results when communication fails.

Some who read the Babel passage might dismiss it as an ancient etiological account of how different languages came into the world. The Gen-

Three: The Babel of Extermination

esis passage, or at least where it is placed in *Bereshit*, does confuse the topic; after all, it states clearly that everyone spoke the same language. When the Lord became angry or concerned about human activity, then the Lord "confounded the speech of the whole earth"; yet, oddly enough, this set piece is placed in the middle of the account known as the "Table of Nations." The "Table" records the genealogy of Noah's sons, with each son's heritage recounted with the refrain, "These are the descendants of [Shem, Ham, and Japheth], according to their clans and *languages*, by their lands and nations" (emphasis added). Thus, the chapter before Babel records the existence of multiple languages, and the passage following it continues the linguistic genealogy. Martin Buber suggests that Babel is placed where it is, with its key verbs "to spread abroad" and "to divide," as a way to foreshadow the long-range importance of Babel's message (*On the Bible*, p. 27–28). Why the ancient compiler of *Bereshit* placed the "Table of Nations" accounts as book-ends around the Babel story is a question with ultimately no satisfactory answers.

The Tower of Babel is not a figure of speech for Levi when he was sent to the Buna, a huge facility within the Auschwitz compound where the Reich's workers and slaves were commanded to invent synthetic rubber. Levi captures the twentieth-century equivalent in his description of the Auschwitz Babel, the Buna, itself as despised as the Hebrews despised Babylon. Within the Buna stands the Carbide Tower, a place of infinite labor and relentless sorrow:

> The Buna is as large as a city; besides the managers and German technicians, 40,000 foreigners work there, and 15 to 20 languages are spoken. All the foreigners live in different Lagers [concentration camps] which surround the Buna: the Lager of the English prisoners-of-war, the Lager of the Ukrainian women, the Lager of the French volunteers and others we do not know. Our Lager (*Judenlager, Vernichtungslager, Kazett*) by itself provides 10,000 workers who come from all the nations of Europe. We are the slaves of the slaves, whom all can give orders to, and our name is the number which we carry tattooed on our arm and sewn in our jacket. The Carbide Tower, which rises in the middle of the Buna and whose top is rarely visible in the fog, was built by us. Its bricks were called *Ziegel, briques, tegula, cegli, kamenny, mattoni, téglak*, and they were cemented by hate; hate and discord, like the Tower of Babel, and it is this that we call it:—*Babelturm, Bobelturm*; and in it we hate the insane dream of grandeur of our masters, their contempt for God and men, for us men.
>
> And today just as in the old fable, we all feel, and the Germans themselves feel, that a curse — not transcendent and divine, but inherent and historical — hangs over the insolent building based on the confusion of languages and erected

Imagery from *Genesis* in Holocaust Memoirs

in defiance of heaven like a stone oath [*Survival* pp. 72–73, italics in text, brackets mine].

Why single out the bricks of the Carbide Tower? Levi does so when he catalogues the word in seven different languages. Curiously, one of the premier scholars of Holocaust literature criticizes Levi for using so many languages. Lawrence Langer expresses his impatience: "Readers of [*Survival in Auschwitz*] may wish that they had brought to the encounter an armful of dictionaries. The polyglot vocabulary is exasperating..." (p. 29). However, Langer quotes Levi's list for bread, which we will consider later, as "initiating us into his macrocosm not only in Italian but also in English, German, Yiddish, Polish and Russian, French, Hebrew, and Hungarian" (p. 29). At the minimum, on a surface level, the multiplicity of languages is important precisely because Levi propels readers into the camps' confusion of languages. More importantly, Levi elevates what at first seems to be a simple list into a Midrashic meditation on a word. Precisely with his emphatic attention on a single word—here, *brick*, and later in our consideration, *bread*—Levi's writing becomes Midrashic in its fascination with language, in its attention to detail, and in its prophetic proclamation of Jewish experience. A brick, innocuous as it is, is far from a small detail. Levi's Midrashic emphasis on *brick* manifests the history of Jewish slavery, where bricks are a recurrent theme of oppression.

Long before Germans threw bricks into Jewish stores, homes, and synagogues during Kristallnacht, bricks figured prominently in Hebrew Scriptures as a signifier of hardship. Although modern culture might associate bricks with stability and permanence, Scripture suggests that the very idea of stability is a vain illusion, fueled by human hubris. One Midrash proposes that the Babel story warns us not to devalue human life: "As the tower grew in height it took one year to get bricks from the base to the upper stories. Thus, bricks became more precious than human life. When a brick slipped and fell the people wept, but when a man fell and died no one paid attention" (qtd. in Plaut p. 85). Alter explains that the phrase that he translated as "bake bricks and burn them hard" would be, if literally translated from the Hebrew, "'brick bricks and burn for a burning'" (p. 47 note 3). The emphasis on burning was ominously analyzed by one rabbi when he examined the line, "Come, let us make bricks and burn them thoroughly." The exegete's insight possesses an uncanny prophecy:

Three: The Babel of Extermination

"The word for 'burn them thoroughly' is written as if to be read 'and we will be burned' meaning: 'this people are going to be burned out of the world'" (*Genesis Rabbah* p. 51). Levi's bricks, set amidst the smoke of the crematoria, force readers to consider anew the camps' daily life. His autobiography portrays a place not unlike the Midrashic meditations upon Babel: in both places, powerful men deemed human life valueless.

Although Babel describes a time that is pre-Jewish, the story is fully embraced as a part of Hebrew literary and religious heritage. Jewish history properly starts with the account of Abraham, or Abram as he was known before God initiated the covenant with him. Abraham's story is found in Genesis almost immediately after the Babel tale, and Buber, for one, understands that the world that produced Babel was the world that birthed Abram. Buber reads the Babel story as a symbol which reveals that "no one understands the other. And in the midst of the transformed human world, the world of nations, there stands the unfinished, unfinishable city, Babel, city of 'confusion.' Such is the state of humanity into which Abram is born..." (*On the Bible* p. 28). Abram, the first Jew, began his life in a world that was in chaos. It was a world that God has promised not to destroy (by flood, at least) a second time; the postdiluvian world seemed to be no better than the antediluvian one.

The seminal story involving bricks is the Exodus passage, which is recalled by Jews around the world each spring at Passover. While in Egypt, Jewish slaves labored under a Pharaoh who continually sought to make their burdens heavier. Exodus 5:6–9 recounts the hardship: Pharaoh demanded that "the taskmasters and foremen" compel their Jewish slaves to make bricks without being given the required straw. Pharaoh insisted that the slaves must "'go and gather straw for themselves. But impose upon them the same quota of bricks as they have been making heretofore; do not reduce it, for they are shirkers; that is why they cry, "Let us go and sacrifice to our God!" Let heavier work be laid upon the men; let them keep at it....'" The theme of bricks, then, which may at first appear innocuous in Levi's account, draws connections to Babel, to slavery in Egypt, and to Midrash.

When a Midrash tells of a time "when a man fell and died and no one paid attention," it looks Janus-like, seeing both backward and forward, to pre-Jewish history and to a time when the Nazis actively sought to destroy Jewish history and the Jews. The taskmasters on planet Auschwitz held guns; here was a new Egypt where men and women were forced to labor in back-breaking and spirit-breaking conditions. Should the slaves pause to catch their breath, they would be shot for being "shirkers." The new Babel, the new Egypt, was a place where the Nazis manipulated the slaves to make products for the Reich, but more important to them than useful commodities was the chance to inflict Sisyphean tasks. At some camps, useless work might consist of carrying heavy stones from one quarry to another, only to have to haul the stones back. In the strange world of the concentration camps, the loss of an object might provoke tears, but the loss of life could not, at that time, be grieved.

With their "insane dream of grandeur," as Levi puts it, the Nazi masters became more fantastically powerful than Pharaoh could have imagined. They, like Pharaoh, added burden upon burden upon the Jews. Like Pharaoh, they invented excuses as they blamed the Jews for any perceived faults or slights. Any slowdown or stoppage in labor was punished as an attempt to subvert the Reich. The Dajan, the spiritual leader of the Orthodox who worked with Filip Müller in the crematoria, alluded to Pharaoh when he tried to encourage his fellow Jews. "'In every generation, my brothers,'" Müller recalls him saying, "'there were Pharaohs who wanted to exterminate us, but — praise be the Most Holy — he has always rescued us from their hands'" (p. 67). Müller records that the prisoners "did not believe what he had said"; nevertheless, they departed with a greater sense of peace. Frank Stiffel writes in his autobiography, *The Tale of the Ring: A Kaddish*, of an experience that linked him with Pharaoh's Jews. An SS man took Stiffel, then imprisoned at Treblinka, "to a huge hole in the middle of a forest within the camp. There a detail of Jews was making bricks" (p. 78). Forced to carry heavy racks of bricks to the opposite part of the camp, Stiffel struggled with his burden due to being exhausted and dehydrated. "I kept repeating automatically in my mind, *Avadim Hainu L'Paroh b'Mizraim* — We were Pharaoh's slaves in the Land of Egypt — the sentence with which Father had started each Passover recounting of Jewish suffering and miraculous salvation 3,000 years ago" (p. 79). Religious Jews who worked as slaves under Hitler's regime knew full well that they were joining in the history of Jewish suffering; not all were able to hope for the "miraculous salvation."

Three: The Babel of Extermination

The Tower of Babel does not bear connotations of salvation. Rather, it is better known for the confusion of languages than for the motif of bricks and slavery, and it is in reference to the multiplicity of languages found in the Nazi camps that the Babel allusion serves most frequently. Ruth Kluger describes an image from a favorite book of her childhood: "When the Tower of Babel was built, God threw colored confetti into the crowd, thus damning them to their various languages and misunderstandings: God's wrath as a painted carnival of chance" (p. 32). The colorful image of confetti wars with the dark undertone of the crowd being dispersed; the party-like confetti juxtaposes oddly against the Lord's anger. In the Nazi version of the Tower of Babel, the prisoners were truly damned "to their various languages." The entire language system of Europe was contained within the concentration camp world; naturally, prisoners wanted to be near those who spoke their same language. Many Auschwitz memoirists single out the Greek Jews who ferociously clung to each other, eschewing contact with non–Greeks. Levi mentions a lonely Frenchman greeting each new wave of arriving inmates by asking if anyone spoke French. "Being together with other Norwegians" was the reason given by 23 Norwegian Jews who survived the camps when asked what helped them endure (Eitinger p. 197). Although all European languages were present, there was one dominant language, and that was German.

Prisoners who did not speak German found themselves in a world where masters shouted commands in German. Levi recalls that his initial "collision with the linguistic barrier" was initiated when Italian guards handed him over to the SS; he and his fellow Italians "immediately realized, from our very first contacts with the contemptuous men with the black patches, that knowing or not knowing German was a watershed" (*Drowned* p. 91). His entrance into Auschwitz began with the train doors opening "with a crash, and the dark echoed with outlandish orders in that curt, barbaric barking of Germans in a command which seems to give bent to a millennial anger" (*Survival* p. 19). A prisoner must learn, Levi observes, "to reply '*Jawohl*!,' never to ask questions, always pretend to understand" (p. 33). To pretend might at least buy the prisoners additional time, to live for another few hours or for another day.

The German language dominated the labor camps, concentration camps, and extermination camps. Although German-speaking prisoners had an advantage in understanding the commands, at least when those orders were issued in German, they also suffered by having their language appropriated as "the language of the night." Gerda Weissmann Klein's birthplace was Poland but in an area formerly under control of the Austro-Hungarian empire. Fluent in Polish, Klein identifies German as her first language. The Nazis, muses Klein, "robbed me not only of my youth, of my parents, but also of the comfort of words" (p. 256). The "strident, staccato cadences" were the words that had doomed her parents to a death sentence because they were Jewish (p. 256). Jean Améry, whose birth name was Hans Maier, protests that because the Nazis stole his language from him, he has lost both "home and mother tongue" (p. 54). Born and raised in Vienna, of Jewish heritage but not observance, he saw himself "shut out from German reality and therefore also from the German language" (p. 52). German-speaking victims of the Nazis found that the "meaning of every German word changed for us," ultimately becoming "inimical" (p. 53). Améry, and others like him, mourned the loss of their first language, a previously comforting mother tongue now usurped by the Nazis. Polyglot Jews whose first language was not German also found the language threatening. Appleman-Jurman reflects that "the mere sound of the German language, the way it was used by the Gestapo, made me shiver with fright" (p. 236). The language of Goëthe had been conquered by Himmler, overlord of Hitler's concentration camp system.

Levi sacrificed valuable bread "since there was no other currency" to be tutored in German, so that he would be better able to survive (*Drowned* p. 97). German was the language of the camps' supreme rulers, but orders could be issued in a hybrid version. "'*Schnella, schnella*' (quick, quick), the guard at the door grumbled in the peculiar Slavicized German that was the lager's lingua franca," Millu recounts (p. 35, italics and translation in text). Wiesel identifies Yiddish, Polish, Russian, Ukrainian, and German as the languages which constituted "the concentration camp vocabulary" (*All Rivers* p. 98). Kapos, the SS-appointed prison leaders, expected to be understood even if their fellow prisoners did not know the language spoken. Kapos had the power of life and death over the prisoners in their charge, and the Nazis rewarded cruelty. Newly arrived groups would thrust to the forefront any person who could serve as translator; polyglots were not only indispensable to fellow prisoners but were frequently assigned

Three: The Babel of Extermination

choice jobs which did not require dangerous physical labor. Levi praises those who served informally as interpreters, for they were invaluable for translating such "fundamental commands and warnings of the day" (*Drowned* p. 96). Those orders included such basic instructions and mundane questions as, "'Get up,' 'Assembly,' 'Line up for bread,' 'Who's got broken shoes?'" and so on (pp. 96–97). Without those translators, prisoners would not have been able to respond, and failure to respond correctly could mean death. Noting that most of the Italian Jews who were transported with him did not survive two weeks in Auschwitz, Levi assesses that their inability to communicate with long-time prisoners was the primary factor in their high mortality rate. "The greater part of the prisoners who did not understand German — that is, almost all of the Italians — died during the first 10 to 15 days after their arrival: at first glance, from hunger, cold, fatigue, and disease; but after a more attentive examination, due to insufficient information" (p. 93). The confusion of languages exacerbated tension, despair, and hunger, even to the point of death.

As language took on a life-or-death urgency, some trapped within the camps took pleasure in speaking a foreign language that they learned in school or that had been taught to them by friends or family. Many Europeans were then, and still are, polyglots; if drawing upon a second or third language helped provide a respite and built a friendship within the cruel environment of the camps, then that language was eagerly employed. Orenstein, a Pole, remembers one of his bunk mates, a French prisoner of war, who warmly and patiently listened to Orenstein's attempts to communicate in French (p. 215). In an environment of extreme stress, being able to speak one's native tongue provided some degree of amelioration from the tension. Or, as in the situation that Orenstein mentions, practicing a foreign language learned in happier times might relieve some of the mind-numbing rigors of the day. Levi's interest in foreign languages is evident in his polyglot vocabulary throughout his writings, so it is not surprising that he notes with approval that the Greek prisoners of Auschwitz contributed "to the international slang in circulation" (*Survival* p. 79).

More common than foreign languages drawing people closer together was the situation wherein foreign languages forced people apart. Language segregates, and because of that fact, the parallels with the Genesis story become all the more vivid. Segregation, by definition, draws sameness together and excludes otherness; in the Babel of the camps, same-language groups instinctively banded together. Hostility could and did exist toward other language groups while persons took comfort in surrounding themselves with those who spoke their primary language. Perhaps even more than Western European Jews, who might have been bilingual due to their exposure to other European or classical languages, Eastern European Jews spoke many tongues, juggling languages according to the situation. "We spoke Yiddish among ourselves," Wiesel explains, "responded to others in Romanian or Hungarian or Ruthenian, and we prayed in Hebrew" ("Sighet Again" p. 125). Yiddish helped to unite many a Jew despite the differences of national tongue. Edward Feld identifies Yiddish as the language that "had formed the most intimate connection between God and Israel" and was therefore the "holiest of Jewish secular languages" (p. 101). "As they used to say," Wiesel observes, "God writes in Hebrew and listens in Yiddish" (*All Rivers* p. 292). Yiddish was a language truly loved by many, especially by observant Eastern European Jews.

Yiddish offered to many the ideal expression of Jewish solidarity. Poet Jacob Glatstein, who was born in Poland but escaped the destruction because he immigrated to the United States before the war, found Yiddish to be the perfect vehicle by which to write lament and elegy (Goldsmith p. xxv). After the Shoah, laments and elegies were needed. In one of his poems, Glatstein begs, "O let me come close to the joy of the Yiddish word. / Give me whole days and nights of it" (*Selected* p. 119). Yiddish was then, and is now, sometimes called a Jewish language; then, as is now, it is not common for Gentiles to speak it. Orenstein, though, records a chilling story of a man named Alex, who was a member of the Gestapo (p. 120). Alex "spoke perfect Yiddish" and Orenstein speculates that Alex "must have been raised by a Jewish family, to speak the language so well" (p. 120). The Gestapo agent "would walk around the empty houses calling out in a low voice in Yiddish, to make them think he too was a Jew, and they would answer him"; once the Jews revealed themselves, Alex killed them (p. 120). Beyond that unusual case, Yiddish was, for many, a language proclaiming the oneness of the Jewish people, allowing communication within a religious community when national languages divided.

Three: The Babel of Extermination

For all the comfort that Yiddish generally provided to so many Jews from so many countries within the concentration camps, the language itself also separated and divided. Levi ironically notes that he was imprisoned by the Nazis for the "crime" of being Jewish, yet some of his fellow Jews did not consider him to be Jewish enough since he was not fluent in Yiddish (*Drowned* p. 100). Yiddish-speaking Jews viewed non–Yiddish speakers with suspicion since ignorance of the language could signal assimilation into the Christian culture or disinterest in Judaism. When a group of Yiddish-speaking female prisoners were transferred into Sara Tuval Bernstein's barracks, she recalls them shouting at her with both emotional and physical violence. Bewildered, Bernstein tried to make out what they are saying; she pieced together enough to discern that they were asking, "'What kind of Jews are you that you don't speak Yiddish?'" (p. 241). Similarly, Helen Lewis tells of an influx of 500 prisoners into her camp. "Most of them had had a strict religious upbringing, which gave them a strong sense of identity, but sadly also manifested itself in their hostility to us and their rejection of our group," Lewis writes in *A Time to Speak*. "They all could speak the languages of their home countries, but preferred to talk to each other in Yiddish, a language which I and the rest of my group didn't understand. They bitterly resented our lack of religious ardor..." (p. 75). Knowing or not knowing Yiddish was not the sole sign of a Jew's piety, particularly because Yiddish was more common in Eastern Europe than in Western Europe. Nevertheless, many Yiddish speakers saw the Jews of Western Europe as people who had assimilated and consequently were unfamiliar with practical aspects of a devout Jewish life; a lack of fluency in Yiddish, though, was an unreliable guide to a person's commitment to the faith.

In the linguistic turmoil of the camps, the Nazi language ruled supreme. Levi argues that the German language, as spoken and heard in the camps, was a "hollow language" that "deprives language of its meaning" (Epstein p. 33). The emptiness of the language signified the void sculpted by the Nazis. Devolving from the German, the Nazi "language of the night" was a language whose grammar was rooted in violence, degradation, starvation, and dehydration. The tortures the Nazis concocted defy the imagination. "Torture was no invention of National Socialism," Améry admits. "But it was its apotheosis" (p. 30). Beyond the spectacular displays of sadism, the Nazis made sure that daily life was steeped in their syntax of humiliation.

The rigors of the days and nights in the camps' anti-world guaranteed constant degradations as well as physical and psychological pain. Even the daily distribution of food — an event that eventually broke down as the Allies approached the camps — was engineered to guarantee confusion and heartbreak. The Nazis typically mocked the newly arrived prisoners by not issuing them the basic supplies that they needed to live, including a bowl, the utensil needed to consume the soup that made up the prisoners' diet. Many autobiographers recount missing their first prison meal due to the lack of a bowl. When summing up his first hours in the Janowska labor camp, Dr. Samuel Drix remembers: "I was terribly hungry.... I had not had anything in my mouth for a day and a half. And here was a new tragedy.... [W]e, the newcomers, had nothing to eat from" (p. 64). Drix's experience was multiplied many times over throughout *l'univers concentrationnaire*. Such a situation quickly introduced the prisoners to the Holocaust Kingdom principle known as "organizing," which, in camp parlance, meant to obtain a valuable commodity by any means possible.

Having "organized" a bowl, the prisoner then had to learn how to consume the food that was served. The food was revolting. In order to live another day, the inmates had to force themselves to eat the stale black bread, sip the ersatz coffee, and swallow the moldy vegetables floating in the watery soup. Standing in line to receive the soup required savvy — people at the front were given smaller or more watery portions and those people at the rear of the line might learn that the food was all gone. No matter where one stood in line on a given day, there was never enough nourishment. Frequently there was not enough time to consume what little there was, as Drix discovered when his first meal as a prisoner was interrupted by a German voice shouting, "*Antreten! Antreten!* [Form ranks! Form ranks!]" (p. 64, brackets and translation in text). Ka-tzetnik 135633, the writer who publishes under his concentration camp number, depicts daily life in this manner: "A thousand hearts breathe prayer, a prayer from the deepest depths. A prayer in all the languages of Europe, each summoning it in his own language, each after his custom. No, it is not summoned — it erupts on its own: 'Please God, a big bowl...'" (*Star Eternal* p. 76, ellipsis in text). The prayer is not just for nourishment. "For this is

Three: The Babel of Extermination

not soup in your bowl — it is your life" (p. 76). Each petitioner in his or her own language asking for what he or she would not receive — such was life within the Nazi creation of Babel.

As Ka-tzetnik 135633 dramatizes, each prisoner petitions the deity for a simple, essential item by which survival might be obtained, "in all the languages of Europe," a reference that is hardly hyperbolic. Levi is keenly aware of the Babel of languages that swirled about him in Auschwitz. He describes the panic after early morning roll call: "Some, bestially, urinate while they run to save time, because within five minutes begins the distribution of bread, of bread-Brot-Broid-chleb-pain-lechem-kenyér, of the holy grey slab which seems gigantic in your neighbor's hand, and in your own hand so small as to make you cry" (*Survival* p. 39). Levi's lexicon for "bread" illustrates the reality of a defeated, starving Europe trapped within the camps' electrified wires. One need not be Jewish to be plunged into the linguistic pandemonium which so often expressed itself in the desire for the most basic of requirements: bread and water. Olga Lengyel, a Gentile medical doctor, heard the moans emanating from women in a sealed train. "'Woda ... khleb.' Two words identified them as Russian. We had heard that so often, we knew 'bread and water' in all the languages of Europe" (p. 143, ellipsis in text). Bread and water — these elementary needs were utterly lacking in the universe constructed by the Nazis.

Each day was a struggle to hold onto one's life. In the labor camps, prisoners were worked to death. In the death camps, prisoners could either be worked to death or allowed to deteriorate unto death or be chosen for extermination. The call to Nazi judgment was "the selection," a process by which a Nazi official would determine with a flick of his finger who would live and who would die. That decision was based typically on a cursory judgment of how well or how potentially useful the person looked. Ka-tzetnik 135633 describes the tension before a selection: "In all the languages of Europe — Italian and Yiddish, Polish and Dutch, French and Greek — eyes now ask eyes one and the same question: 'How do I look?' But all with one and the same meaning in the question: 'How do I look?' ... 'Smoke of burnt bodies is one color, no matter what language'" (*Star* p. 96, ellipsis in text). The concept of the smoke over Auschwitz resonates with the smoke arising from the bricks made by the Jews in Egypt, but with a difference. The smoke that in ancient days signaled the Jews slaving to meet the demands of their Egyptian taskmasters is now transformed into the smoke that testifies to Jewish death. The bricks of Babel that scattered the workers and the bricks that the Jews in Egypt died making become in Auschwitz symbols of the Jews themselves.

The smoke, not of bricks baking but rather of bodies burning, is the haunting legacy of the death camps bequeathed to survivors and subsequent generations. If a survivor spent any time at all in a camp where crematoria had been established, in contrast to a slave-labor camp, then the horror of seeing that visible sign of the Nazi intent to destroy will invariably be mentioned in the survivor's testimony. Certainly Wiesel's agonized observations during his first night in Auschwitz are among the best-known lines in Holocaust literature:

> Never shall I forget that night, the first night in camp which has turned my life into one long night seven times cursed and seven times sealed. Never shall I forget that smoke. Never shall I forget the little faces of the children, whose bodies I saw transformed into wreaths of smoke under a silent blue sky.
> Never shall I forget those flames that consumed my faith forever. ... Never shall I forget those moments that murdered my God and my soul and turned my dreams into ashes [*Night* p. 34].

In some cases, such as Millu's autobiography, *Smoke over Birkenau*, smoke assumes titular prominence. Smoke at Auschwitz and other extermination camps signaled that here was a place where Nazis ruled supreme, a place where, as Levi writes in a poem, a person "dies at a yes or no" ("Shemá" Schiff p. 205). One of the best-known poems about the Holocaust is Nelly Sachs's, "O the Chimneys." Sachs draws upon the image of the crematoria and its resulting smoke: "O the chimneys, / On the ingeniously devised habitations of death / When Israel's body drifted as smoke / Through the air!" (Schiff p. 41). The pillar of fire, formerly a sign of God's presence, became in the death camps a sign of God's apparent abandonment.

However, in the Babel story, God is actively making decisions about humanity, and therefore, when survivors invoke Babel, the allusion begs the question of God's activity and of human responsibility in the macabre Holocaust Kingdom. Babel teaches that God's omnipotence will prevail. What does Auschwitz teach? Wiesel sees within the image of the smoke the Nazi assumption of divinity and the Deity's resignation from omnipo-

Three: The Babel of Extermination

tence. In "Facing Hate," a videotaped interview discussing the fatal consequences of prejudice, Wiesel asserts that the Nazis revealed through their orgy of death that they wanted to be gods. They wished to rule as gods, gods of their own universe, and as gods they possessed the power of life and death. The Babel allusion hints at such egotism. One Biblical scholar argues that the Babel tower imagery was patterned after the Mesopotamian temple known as the ziggurat, which "was an artificial mountain, built of clay, bitumen, and unburnt bricks, and ... was considered a high place for a god, whose shrine was located at the top of the structure" (Tos p. 67). Thus, when the story is recounted of Babel's architects desiring to "make a name for themselves," the lust for height suggests their wish for a majestic, godlike place. One Midrash on this subject suggests that the word *name* is equal to *idol* (*Genesis Rabbah* p. 51). Here the Midrash accurately foresees the destructive energy wrapped up in idolatry. The Nazis were aggressively proud in making sure that, wherever they went, their name was known and feared.

In their idolatry in making themselves as gods, the Nazis inverted the deity's action in Genesis 11. Whereas God dispersed the people, the Nazis gathered people. Any person or group whom the Nazis detested — including Jews, Communists, Roma, Sinta, homosexuals, Jehovah's Witnesses, and many more — were gathered, counted, and contained. Shortly before the Torah concludes, God offers the Israelites a choice: "See, I set before you this day life and prosperity, death and adversity.... I call heaven and earth to witness against you this day: I have put before you life and death, blessing and curse. Choose life — if you and your offspring would live — by loving the LORD your God, heeding His commands, and holding fast to Him" (Deut 30:15, 19–20). God offered the Jews life. In their inversion of God's role, the Nazis ordered death. God scattered the people in Genesis 11 in order that they might live; the Nazis gathered so that death would reign. Ettin contends that Babel was a "de-creative act" (p. 118). Certainly the Nazi version of Babel, saturated as it was in torture and death, was the antithesis of creativity.

The Genesis 11 account of Babel potentially speaks of God's benevolence: in God's concern for humanity and the self-destructiveness inherently contained within hubris, God disperses the people for their own good. Yet the Babel story may be interpreted in more than one way, as in the case with any good story.

Imagery from *Genesis* in Holocaust Memoirs

Some read the story as an illustration of God's anxiety. The Tower of Babel story, Genesis 11:1–9, is known in rabbinic literature as "the Generation of Division" (Cassuto p. 226) or "the Generation of the Dispersion" (*Genesis Rabbah* p. 51). Although the divine action of dividing and dispersing the people sounds harsh, even petty, the Nazi activity of summoning and collecting demonstrates the opposite extreme. Nonetheless, reading Babel causes many readers to ask: What was it about the builders' activity that seemed to have so upset God? Some readers, as we have seen, believe that the height of the building suggested that humans wished to climb into the heavenly realms and be like gods, thus threatening the Lord. On the other hand, Otto Procksch argues that the deity treats the builders sarcastically. "God must draw near, not because He is nearsighted," Procksch says, "but because He dwells at such tremendous heights and man's work is so small. God's movement must, therefore, be understood as a remarkable satirical contrast to man's behavior" (qtd. in Plaut p. 85).

The Babel story reflects more precisely on human nature than on the divine, say some rabbis and theologians. Timothy A. Lenchak suggests that Babel is a symbol of humanity's wish to be in opposition to the Lord's plans (p. 44). But one analysis will never suffice for the Midrashic mind. Rabbi Isaac focuses on the word *settled*: "In every passage in which you find a reference to 'settling,' Satan leaps at the opportunity [because Satan is interested in people who live securely]" (*Genesis Rabbah* p. 50, bracketed explanation in text). Jacob Neusner asserts that "the generation of the Dispersion rejected God's rule, and ... they became complacent in their prosperity" (*Genesis Rabbah* p. 51). When humans seek to act as god, Scripture teaches, their actions result in folly. The Midrash goes even further: Being self-satisfied is the beginning of disaster.

Nevertheless, some readers question God's response to the Babel builders. The Supreme Being's response seems more like that of a bully fearful about controlling his territory than an omnipotent sovereign. "If, as one people with one language for all, this is how they have begun to act, then nothing that they may propose to do will be out of their reach. Let Me, then, go down and confound their speech there, so that they shall not understand one another's speech," says the Creator of the universe in Genesis 11:6. The Lord's worried musings do, in fact, sound like the anxious fears of an insecure deity. Lenchak acknowledges the mood set by those

Three: The Babel of Extermination

words when he asks, "Doesn't God sound rather vindictive in this passage?" (p. 44). However, he proposes that the motif of resisting God found in Genesis 11 echoes an earlier one, the Genesis 3 passage in which Adam and Eve disobey God. Both Babel and the expulsion from the garden maintain a common theme, Lenchak argues. The common Biblical theme explores the ramifications of separation and broken relationships; when humans are alienated from each other and from their Creator, the result is trauma (p. 44). Yet one can think of little else that would so alienate humanity from deity as the Holocaust.

God's deeds as recorded in Scripture are often baffling. One of God's most disconcerting acts was the demand in Genesis 22 ordering Abraham to sacrifice his beloved son, Isaac; the next chapter will explore that theological conundrum and its Shoah reverberations.

CHAPTER FOUR

Akeda
The Perversity of Silence

> We have known Jews who, like Abraham, witnessed the death of their children; who, like Isaac, lived the *Akeda* in their flesh; and some who went mad when they saw their father disappear on the altar, with the altar, in a blazing fire whose flames reached into the highest of heavens.
> — Elie Wiesel

The Akeda: Genesis 22:1–19

When Saul Friedländer recalls the Biblical stories he heard as a child in the days before the Shoah, he confesses that those tales meant little to him. However, there was one story in *Bereshit* that had an impact upon him: "We took up the story of Abraham and the sacrifice of Isaac: 'Take now thy son, thine only son Isaac, whom thou lovest, and get thee into the land of Moriah; and offer him there for a burnt offering upon one of the mountains which I will tell thee of...'" (*When* p. 28). The rabbi who shared the story with his charges failed to explain the tale's meaning; Friedländer's nanny and parents also were unable to contextualize it. The parents, after all, had more pressing concerns: "as for my parents, Biblical quotations seemed to occupy them very little at this moment, when the need to flee the country was becoming increasingly obvious" (p. 28). Not surprisingly for the future author, young Friedländer used his imagination as he considered the story; he could picture the patriarch traveling into the desert, accompanied by his son and a donkey and a sword (p. 28). For a time, he put aside his contemplations; later in his life, he returned to the story of Abraham responding to God's request to sacrifice a beloved

Four: Akeda

son. "Then for a long time I forgot the question raised by the awesome text, only to see it arise again later, and with what forcefulness!" (p. 28)

The "question raised by the awesome text" permeates many Shoah survivors' memoirs; in particular, both the question and the text haunt Elie Wiesel. The "question" to which Friedländer refers should surely be in the plural because the "awesome text" generates so many. If we were to imagine the basic plot outline of Genesis 22, the story to which Friedländer refers, then we must ponder its core elements: A father brings his son to the place where the latter will die because the All-powerful has demanded a sacrifice. The father has received a command and he obeys. As he seeks to do his duty, perhaps he experiences terror, resignation, resentment, fear, and maybe even courage. The son knows there is a sacrifice to be made, but he has not yet been told that he himself will be the offering.

Such a scene is not an act only of the imagination. Countless Jewish mothers and fathers during the Nazi era experienced such an ordeal. As the Nazis sent families and villages to the camps, they gathered up European Jewry for slaughter. Families usually tried desperately to stay together; however, upon their arrival at the camps, the families were ruptured as they were segregated by age and by gender. If they were sent to one of the six camps designed to process death, the very old and the very young usually did not live out their first night. Those who survived the first "selection," the Nazi decision as to who would live and who would die, were so horrified by the process that some never recovered. An eerie silence seemed to fill the air as that initial selection was made. Ka-Tzetnik 135633 agonizes in his first autobiography: "They left you without so much as a farewell glance, without a sound. But they know where they're being taken. Why don't they scream? Why don't they weep?! Why is it so quiet here?!" (*Star* p. 100). The quiet filled the void with questions. Anguish resonated in the silence.

Among the many contradictions that comprise *l'univers concentrationnaire* is the fact that the camps were characterized by both noise and silence. Discussed in Chapter Two was Primo Levi's portrayal of the Auschwitz that greeted arriving prisoners: There was the "crash" of the doors opening and the "barbaric barking of the Germans in command" (*Survival* p. 19). However, moments later, Levi sums up the unreality of the scene as the prisoners assessed the situation: "Everything was as silent as an aquarium, or as in certain dream sequences" (p. 19). The silence, often disconcerting, sometimes comforting, seems a paradoxical situation when contrasted with the omnipresent noise, and yet such contradictions seem to be a consistent quality of Nazism. Silence, in and of itself, bears paradoxical qualities: It can comfort or isolate; it can imply protest or consent. Something or someone must be present in order for noise to be made. Noise is a physical reality. Silence, on the other hand, may be noise's spiritual opposite. Noise is finite, material, arising from presence; silence is infinite, metaphysical, arising from either presence or absence.

The silence was palpable. Those singled out for slave labor and extermination felt the weight of silence. Voices which longed to cry out in protest had to restrain themselves, lest the sound bring additional attention and punishment to themselves, their family members, and those in their barracks. Most victims of Nazism learned well before they reached the camps that to speak out, to protest verbally, was to risk not only their own lives but the lives of five, ten, twenty others, or even the lives of an entire community. The victims' suppressed rage was often their sole survival mechanism, but more disturbing than their own silence was that of others. The silence of others was harder to comprehend. The silence of the free world rang in their ears and, chillingly, there was the silence of God, the same God who was constantly being beseeched and implored. The divine silence was, for many, the hardest to bear. Andrew Vogel Ettin admits that "discussing silence in relation to Jewish religion and thought may at first seem paradoxical" because the Jews are known as the people of the word, both the written word of the Bible and the spoken word of God to the prophets (p. 35). However, the silence of the Holocaust Kingdom demands that religious thinkers contemplate the impact of divine silence. André Neher believes that the weight of silence emerging from, or emanating towards, the death camps has had a long-ranging consequence. Neher believes that Jewish thought is beset with a pervasive "sense of anxiety," precisely because of the overarching silence from God and from the world (p. 136). Neher says that thinking about the Event forces us to respond to a "tragic invitation to an encounter with silence" (p. 137). Thoughtful contemplation about the *hurban* and debates about what should have been done will usher the participants into hearing that silence.

Four: Akeda

Silence preoccupies Elie Wiesel, the most prolific and best known of the Shoah writers. Wiesel constantly wrestles with a paradox: The immensity of the Holocaust demands silence (who can speak in the face of so much death?) yet the crimes of the Nazis and the memories of those who suffered require testimony. He is torn between the power of words and the authority of silence. Steeped in Biblical and rabbinical knowledge, Wiesel writes tersely, elliptically, rooted in the Jewish tradition of demanding justice from God. He frequently cites *Bereshit* 22, wherein God asks Abraham to sacrifice his beloved son, Isaac. Inherent within that narrative are questions concerning the nature of God and the phenomenology of silence, as well as its perversity.

The story of Abraham and Isaac found in Genesis 22 is known in the Jewish tradition as the *Akeda*, also transliterated as *Akedah*; in the plural, it is *Akedot. Akedat Yitzchak,* the binding of Isaac, is a more accurate descriptor than the Christian reference, the sacrifice of Isaac. The *Akeda* is a puzzling tale. It is often taught as a triumph of Abraham's faith, a stance which ignores the aspects of the story that Nahum Sarna calls a "soul-shattering event" (p. 156). It is a tale where God asks a father to offer up his son as a holy sacrifice. And not just any son, any beloved son, but the child Isaac, the child of a miraculous intervention, the son in whose light Abraham's other son, Ishmael, is eclipsed. The *Akeda* may be an extant story borrowed from a neighboring tribe which practiced human sacrifice, possibly rewritten to demonstrate the mercy of the Hebrew God. Nevertheless, the Lord's mercy is called into question when one imagines a father and son journeying three agonizing days toward the place of sacrifice.

This is the *Akedat Yitzchak:*

> Some time afterward, God put Abraham to the test. He said to him "Abraham," and he answered, "Here I am." And He said, "Take your son, your favored one, Isaac, whom you love, and go to the land of Moriah, and offer him there as a burnt offering on one of the heights which I will point out to you." So early next morning, Abraham saddled his ass and took with him two of his servants and his son Isaac. He split the wood for the burnt offering, and he set out for the place which God had told him. On the third day Abraham looked up and saw the place from afar. Then Abraham said to his servant, "You stay here with the ass. The boy and I will go up there; we will worship and we will return to you."
>
> Abraham took the wood for the burnt offering and put it on his son Isaac. He himself took the firestone and the knife; and the two walked off together. Then Isaac said to his father Abraham, "Father!" And he answered, "Yes, my

son." And he said, "Here is the firestone and the wood; but where is the sheep for the burnt offering?" And Abraham said, "God will see to the sheep for His burnt offering, my son." And the two of them walked on together.

They arrived at the place of which God had told him. Abraham built an altar there; he laid out the wood; he bound his son Isaac; he laid him on the altar, on top of the wood. And Abraham picked up the knife to slay his son. Then an angel of the Lord called to him from heaven: "Abraham, Abraham!" And he answered, "Here I am." And he said, "Do not raise your hand against the boy, or do anything to him. For now I know that you fear God, since you have not withheld your son, your favored one, from Me." When Abraham looked up, his eye fell upon a ram, caught in the thicket by its horns. So Abraham went and took the ram and offered it up as a burnt offering in place of his son. And Abraham named that site Adonai-yireh, whence the present saying, "On the mount of the LORD there is vision."

The angel of the LORD called to Abraham a second time from heaven, and said, "By Myself I swear, the LORD declares: because you have done this and have not withheld your son, your favored one, I will bestow My blessing upon you and make your descendants as numerous as the stars of heaven and the sands on the seashore; and your descendants shall capture the gates of their enemies. All the nations of the earth shall bless themselves by your descendants, because you have obeyed My command." Abraham then returned to his servants, and they departed together for Beer-sheba; and Abraham stayed in Beer-sheba [Genesis 22:1–19].

The importance of the story in both the Jewish and Christian traditions can scarcely be overstated. Christians read it as a precursor of Jesus' sacrifice, while Jews contextualize it as the supreme last trial of faith to which God subjected Abraham. Just as Abraham bound Isaac to place him on the altar, some rabbis see its long-range implications as the symbolic binding of the Jews to God (Plaut p. 213). The *Akeda*'s central position in Judaism may be heard in auditory reminders during the High Holy days, as the ram's horn, the *shofar*, sounds on Rosh Hashana and at the conclusion of Yom Kippur. The blast of the *shofar* reminds some of Jericho's walls falling at the trumpet's blast, but others hear in it the ram offered in lieu of Isaac. Shalom Spiegel argues that the *Akeda* might contain "the original meaning of Passover" because the Midrash maintains that a drop of Isaac's blood was spilt; therefore, Isaac's blood foreshadows the blood placed on the Egyptian doorposts immediately prior to the exodus out of Egypt (pp. 51–52). Isaac, son of a patriarch and father of a patriarch, clearly is a major figure in Judaism, and yet his life seemed somewhat unremarkable.

Or, it might be more accurate to say that Isaac lived an extraordinary

Four: Akeda

life, although he was not the one who initiated the events for which he is remembered. What is notable about Isaac's life is the way in which events acted upon him. He labored under no illusion that he was the one in control of those events. Because he was a patriarch, Isaac is honored in the triune formula which describes the God of Israel in terms of relationship: the God of Abraham, the God of Isaac, and the God of Jacob. Isaac is placed in the middle of the patriarchal schema since he is Abraham's son and Jacob's father, yet despite his privileged position as patriarch, Scriptural accounts of Isaac's life are surprisingly few.

Isaac was a miracle child, promised by God Himself to Abraham and Sarah, an infertile couple in their old age. According to Scripture, Abraham was 100 years old and Sarah was in her nineties when God gave them the gift for which they had longed, a child. The Lord instructed Abraham to name the child Isaac, a word formed from the verb "to laugh," but that laughter seems to reflect more the parents' immediate skepticism and potential joy than any characteristic belonging to the child. After brief nods to Isaac's birth, circumcision, and weaning, he does not appear again until the deity requests the sacrifice. God's statement in Hebrew is actually a polite request, "please take" (Plaut p. 152). Isaac survived being placed upon the sacrificial altar because an angel stopped his father's hand, but Isaac's life was never the same. Significantly, the Bible records no further interaction between Abraham and Isaac. While death was stopped upon the mountain, it awaited at home. Genesis 23 reports the death of Isaac's mother, Sarah; some rabbis speculate that she died of a broken heart after watching her husband take her only child to be sacrificed.

Isaac's marriage to Rebekah seems to have been a happy one, but a strange note is sounded in their engagement story, a tale in which an emissary meets Isaac's future bride by a well. Betrothals by a well are a common set piece in Scripture, as Alter points out in *The Art of Biblical Narrative*, but with the second patriarch, a passive variation occurs. A ram had already been substituted for Isaac; now, Alter observes, a substitute for Isaac chooses his bride. "Isaac is conspicuous by his absence from the scene," Alter notes; "this is in fact the only instance where a surrogate rather than the man himself meets the girl at the well. That substitution nicely accords with the entire career of Isaac..." (p. 53). Later, Isaac will repeat family history by pretending that his wife is his sister (Genesis 26, a parallel story to a similar incident involving Abraham and Sarah). Finally, an aged Isaac is tricked by Rebekah and Jacob, the younger of his twin sons. Even here, another substitution occurs, a sort of mockery concocted by his wife who conspires to play upon Isaac's infirmity by having the younger son act as if he were the elder. Isaac is less an actor in his own drama and more a person to whom things happen.

The *Akeda* was an event that happened to Isaac. It was a defining moment of his life; less predictably, it became a defining moment in Jewish history. Ernest Namenyi insists in *The Essence of Jewish Art* that the *Akeda* is a dominant and inspiring event in Judaism (p. 34). Artistic representations typically portray Isaac as a young boy or as a teenager because he was old enough to carry his own wood, yet still young enough to be passively obedient to his father. The iconographic portrayal of a young Isaac, submissive to his father, inspires a sympathetic response. However, Biblical scholars disagree over Isaac's age when he made this fateful journey. Louis Berman explains that certain Midrash "raise his age to 25 or 37.... Since it is known that Sarah was 90 when Isaac was born, and said to have died at one hundred twenty-seven, this makes Isaac thirty-seven at the time of the *Akedah*" (p. 62). Portrayals of Isaac at such an age would be unlikely to have the same impact upon viewers. Sympathy inspired by thoughts and images of a vulnerable child might lessen if the victim is a grown man.

Regardless of Isaac's age in Genesis 22, the *Akeda* has also been understood to be a seminal story of what it means to be a Jew. Rabbi Chaim of Tsans reasons: "Two mountains were chosen by God: Mount Sinai upon which the Torah was given to Israel and Mount Moriah upon which Abraham bound his son Isaac and upon which the Temple was built. Now the matter makes one wonder: Why, indeed, was the Temple not built upon Mount Sinai which had been sanctified by the giving of the law?" The rabbi has an answer: "The place on which a Jew bares his neck is sanctified by God more than any other place" (qtd. in Plaut p. 152). Rabbi Chaim of Tsans could not have foreseen the reality of millions of Jews being forced to present their bodies to be destroyed.

"Here," Wiesel declares of the *Akeda*, "is a story that contains Jewish destiny in its totality" (*Messengers* p. 69). Wiesel admits that the story "haunts" him, and its power is such that it has had a "dominant role" in

Four: Akeda

his life (*Evil* p. 172). An admittedly strange story, it is, according to Wiesel, a timeless tale, a never-ending story. "Stretched out on the altar, his wrists and ankles bound, Isaac saw ... that what was happening to him would happen to others, that this was to be a tale without end, an experience to be endured by his children and theirs" (*Messengers* p. 72). "If Isaac's averted sacrifice had involved only Abraham and his son," he says, "their ordeal would have been limited to their own suffering. But it involves us" (p. xiii). Part of the *Akeda*'s timelessness is that it tells the story of a father and son responding to a supreme power's demand for death.

Throughout Wiesel's voluminous *oeuvre*, he wrestles with the implications of God's action in Genesis 22. "In my own way, I speak of Isaac constantly, in all my writings," Wiesel admits. "In fact, I speak of almost nothing else" (*Evil* p. 172). Because Isaac is "the first survivor," his life has something "to teach us, the future survivors of Jewish history" (*Messengers* p. 97). Those who lived through the *hurban* know about the journey of silence, the anticipation of their death, and their lonely walk away from the death site. They may have entered the camp together with their family; those who survived usually left the site alone. Survivors know too the impossibility of returning home and resuming their lives, and they also know how unlikely it is that they will find their loved ones alive. Wiesel finds in the *Akeda* a paradigm for his own experience and those of untold others:

> That is why the theme and term of the *Akeda* have been used, throughout the centuries, to describe the destruction and disappearance of countless Jewish communities everywhere. All the pogroms, the crusades, the persecutions, the slaughters, the catastrophes, the massacres by sword and the liquidations by fire — each time it was Abraham leading his son to the altar, to the holocaust all over again.
>
> Of all the Biblical tales, the one about Isaac is perhaps the most timeless and relevant to our generation. We have known Jews who, like Abraham, witnessed the death of their children; who, like Isaac, lived the *Akeda* in their flesh; and some who went mad when they saw their father disappear on the altar, with the altar, in a blazing fire whose flames reached into the highest of heavens [*Messengers* p. 95].

The *Akeda*, according to Wiesel, occurred not only at Mount Moriah but also at Auschwitz. Wiesel's allusion to Abraham and Isaac's journey contains several themes present within the autobiographies written by Shoah survivors: a family travels together toward death after receiving a summons from a supreme power; a silence pervades the ordeal; and the survivor, shattered, departs the death site alone.

Genesis 22 describes Abraham and Isaac traveling together, accompanied by a few servants, making their way to a destination unknown. Sören Kierkegaard considers the tension, the drama, contained within the essence of the story as a "teleological suspension of the ethical" (p. 54). Kierkegaard's analysis of Genesis 22 remains a pivotal, seminal work that both Jewish and Christian thinkers must interact with when reflecting upon the *Akeda*'s implications. Published in 1854, *Fear and Trembling* continues to demand consideration; contemporary authors who write for a popular audience, such as Rabbi Joseph Telushkin, Rabbi Harold Kushner, and Elie Wiesel, have recourse to it. In an essay entitled "Kierkegaard and Judaism," Milton Steinberg assesses the unlikely dialogue that has sprung up between the Danish Christian theologian's writings and rabbinical thinking. The differences between Jewish interpretations and Kierkegaard's beliefs are vast and significant; nevertheless, when it comes to Kierkegaard's analysis of Genesis 22, Steinberg praises it thusly: "This, be it observed, is such a *midrash* on the *Akedah* as no rabbi in 2,000 years ventured to put forth" (136, italics in text). Thinking about Abraham's three-day walk, Kierkegaard reflects that the patriarch's heart must have been heavy with dread. "If I were to speak about [Abraham], I would first of all describe the pain of the ordeal," Kierkegaard declares (p. 53). Wiesel also contemplates the agony Abraham must have endured. Calling the *Akeda* "an unfathomable mystery given to every generation" (*Messengers* p. 75), Wiesel is sure that Abraham experienced "crushing" and "devastating anguish" (p. 73).

The agony inherent within the journey to the sacrifice forces Kierkegaard and Wiesel, among others, to reflect not only upon silence but also time. "After a three-day journey — which according to Kierkegaard lasted longer than the 4,000 years separating us from the event — father and son ... began their ascent of the mountain," writes Wiesel (p. 72). In *Mimesis*, Erich Auerbach emphasizes the story's timelessness and stillness: "the decisive points of the narrative alone are emphasized, what lies between is nonexistent; time and place are undefined and call for interpretation; thoughts and feelings remain unexpressed" (p. 11). *Bereshit*'s succinct quality contributes to the ominous tone inherent in God's call and Abraham's

Four: Akeda

response. No one's thoughts or feelings, hopes or fears, are conveyed — not God's, not Abraham's, not Isaac's. The unspoken weighs heavily, its precarious balance threatening to tumble into a cry of anguish. The entire passage is "the most poignant and eloquent silence in all literature," asserts E.A. Speiser (p. 165).

The major themes of Genesis 22 are found throughout Elie Wiesel's writings. The *Akeda*'s modern parallel is found in the journeys taken by Jewish fathers and sons, mothers and daughters, during the Third Reich's reign. Wiesel's preoccupation with this Biblical theme extends beyond his autobiographical writings and essays; his concerns are also found in his novels, plays, and his cantata, *Ani Maamin*. With the music composed by Darius Milhaud and the words written by Wiesel, the cantata's title is taken from Maimonides' "Thirteen Articles of Faith." One of those 13 articles of faith is "*Ani Maamin bevait ha-Messiah*: I believe in the coming of the Messiah" (p. 11). In the cantata, the three patriarchs of the Jewish faith transcend time and space; they now see, and live within, the Nazi war upon the Jews. They beseech God to speak out against or to stop the Nazi slaughter. Abraham, Isaac, and Jacob beg God to show mercy, but they are met with what appears to be unresponsive silence. At one point in the cantata, Isaac sings the following words: "An old man / And his son / They speak / In a low voice" (p. 43). What do they speak of? In Isaac's melody, it is of hope. "The father believes in miracles: / Anything can happen, / Even at the last moment, / If only God wills it" (p. 43). But the hope is not enough to allow the old man to look reassuringly into his son's eyes. "Avoiding his son's gaze, / He tells him / That now, / More than ever, / One may not despair" (p. 43). The son mirrors his father's glance turning away from what he loves. "And the son, / Avoiding his father's gaze, / Asks: / 'Does it hurt, Father, say, / Does it hurt to die?'" (p. 43). It is not speculative to assume that millions of children asked their parents that question: Does it hurt to die?

Families suffered together. Wiesel underscores that fact in his first autobiographical account, *Night*, which pulsates with the conundrum of a family member being the source of both comfort and anguish in such a circumstance. Having a family member by one's side often provided much-needed comfort and solace. Isaacson records her mother's reaction once they were reunited after having survived Dr. Mengele's initial selection upon their arrival in Auschwitz-Birkenau. Isaacson remembers that her mother exclaimed ecstatically, "'You're here!... I'm so happy! So happy! I've never been so happy in my whole life!'" (p. 86). Wiesel experienced a similar emotion in his first moments in the death camp. As he explains in *Night*, he and his father were ordered to stand in a specific line. Not knowing whether the line led to life or death, Wiesel recalls that "for the moment I was happy," and the reason for his happiness was simple: "I was near my father" (p. 30). While the joyful emotion expressed by Isaacson's mother and by young Wiesel are at once believable (they are alive and with loved ones) and bewildering (who could be happy in those circumstances?), the altogether different reaction of Wiesel's father is also understandable. "His voice was terribly sad," Wiesel says; "I realized that he did not want to see what they were going to do to me. He did not want to see the burning of his only son" (p. 30). Surely the despair parents felt, knowing that their children could be killed at any moment, is beyond our ability to grasp.

Wiesel identifies Abraham's feeling as he obeyed God as that of "anguish" (*Messengers* p. 72), anguish that Wiesel's own father must have felt. Anguish might have been the only emotion Abraham would have experienced as he walked, day by day. Immediately after placing the "wood for the burnt offering" upon his son, Abraham "himself took the firestone and the knife; and the two walked off together" (Gen. 22:6). This same knife will later be poised over Isaac's bound body. Wiesel uses the knife imagery to draw a subtle comparison between his father and Abraham. At one point during their time in Auschwitz, Wiesel's father is ordered to stay behind as the other prisoners go to work. A selection — the term for the Nazi decision about which prisoners would live and die — was scheduled to occur while Wiesel's father was in camp. The father "felt that his time was short. He spoke quickly. He would have liked to say so many things" (*Night* p. 71). He holds out his few possessions to his son. "'Look, take this knife,' he said to me. 'I don't need it any longer. It might be useful to you'" (p. 71). Wiesel sums up the gift of the knife in two words: "The Inheritance" (p. 71, capitalization in text). The knife with which Abraham is so often portrayed in artistic images is not, for Wiesel's father, an instrument for sacrifice. But by handing over his knife, Wiesel's father has also handed over the iconographic image of Abraham, passing the *Akeda*'s burden to the son.

Four: Akeda

The importance of father and son being together remained paramount for young Elie, who is called by his full name Eliezer in *Night*, throughout his entire concentration camp experience, from their entry into Auschwitz and during the death march as the war drew to an end. In the winter of 1945, with the Red Army fast approaching Auschwitz, Wiesel and his father, both of whom were ill and injured, had to make a decision, a life-or-death decision upon which no accurate information was available to assist them. They had to decide if they should remain in the camp, hoping that their liberators would come before death did, or if they should evacuate the camp, joining the march of victims and their Nazi oppressors, trusting that they were walking towards life. They made their crucial decision based upon the gruesome evidence that literally surrounded them: The piles of skeletons strewn about the camp proclaimed that the Nazis did not intend to leave a single Jew alive. The Nazis would lose the war and sink into defeat with their commitment to keep their promise of annihilating Jewish life and Jewish memory. Even as it became clear in late 1944 and early 1945 that the Allies would be victorious, the Nazis increased the rate at which they murdered. Young Eliezer and his father were forced to make a decision in an ambiguous arena that Levi calls "the Gray Zone." Levi's term hints at the ambiguity surrounding events and decisions when absolutely nothing is known. Nothing was black or white; no choice could be made with confidence, given the absence of information. Left in the camps, the Wiesels reasoned, death would overtake them, either because of their illnesses or because the Nazis would kill them. If they marched, perhaps they would meet the Red Army, or perhaps they could escape, or at least they would not die within the confines of the hated camp. They took their chances on the march.

"I learned after the war the fate of those who had stayed behind," Wiesel says in a characteristically understated manner. "They were quite simply liberated by the Russians two days after the evacuation" (p. 78). Eliezer and his father had made a decision that seemed right, but no amount of reasoning or intuition could guarantee that a right choice would be made in the universe that the Nazis created. And so father and son walked.

The important thing for them, and for so many others like them, was that they were together. "The march continued. The two of them alone in the world, encircled by God's unfathomable design. But they were *together*," states Wiesel, not about his own death march but rather about Abraham and Isaac's (*Messengers* p. 81, italics in text). Knowing that his mother and youngest sister had been killed on their initial night in the death camps, young Wiesel valued staying with his father above all else: "I did not want to be separated from my father. We had already suffered so much, borne so much together; this was not the time to be separated" (*Night* p. 78). But as they walked, it became apparent to them that death was a virtual certainty — the only question was whether it would be from starvation, hypothermia, exhaustion, or murder. Prisoners who stopped to rest were shot; prisoners who tried to escape into forests were shot. Freezing, Eliezer longs for his agony to end. "My father's presence was the only thing that stopped me [from dying].... He was running at my side, out of breath, at the end of his strength, at his wit's end. I had no right to let myself die. What would he do without me?" (p. 82, ellipsis in text). He constantly urged his father to keep moving, to keep living. They needed to stay alive — together.

The emphasis on being together binds the twentieth-century father and son with the patriarchal father and son. Neher argues: "If the *Akedah* had been real (and we know now, through Auschwitz, that real *Akedot* do occur), then everything would have happened to Abraham and Isaac as is related in *Night*" (p. 217). Abraham quietly led his son to a place where he trusted that God would provide; the twentieth-century parallel finds the son leading his father, trying desperately to keep moving, for in movement there may be life. The thought of the father and son, together, causes Wiesel to reflect:

> And so the father and the son walked away together —*ze laakod veze léaked*, the one to bind and the other to be bound, *ze lishkhot veze lishakhet*, the one to slaughter and the other to be slaughtered — sharing the same allegiance to the same God, responding to the same call. The sacrifice was to be their joint offering; father and son had never before been so close. The Midrashic text emphasized this, as if to show another tragic aspect of the *Akeda*, namely, the equation between Abraham and Isaac. Abraham and Isaac were equals, in spite of their opposing roles as victim and executioner. But Abraham himself, whose victim was he? God's? Once more the key word is *yakhdav*, together: victims together [*Messengers* pp. 88–89].

In the cantata, *Ani Maamin*, Wiesel portrays Abraham, Isaac, and Jacob imploring a mute and seemingly indifferent God to stop the geno-

Four: Akeda

cide — or at least to communicate that God cares, if only for pity's sake. Having lived through his own ordeal, Abraham cries out against the modern-day *Akeda*, that replication of the parent bringing the child to death, a murder demanded by a supreme power. He describes what he sees as a protest to the Lord: "A field / Jewish mothers, / Naked, / Lead their naked children / To their sacrifice" (p. 89). In this field Abraham observes "...the priests, / Dressed in black, / Behind the machine guns, / And at the peepholes / Of special installations / In Birkenau and Treblinka" (p. 89). Priests garbed in black attire work on two levels in Abraham's complaint: clergymen wear black and so did the SS. The SS are the priests of death in the Holocaust Kingdom, and throughout much of that Kingdom, the clergymen did not protest. In twentieth-century Europe, mothers and fathers lead their children to the sacrifice. Together: journeying together, suffering together, being victims together.

Livia Jackson describes her own *Akeda* in her autobiography, *Elli: Coming of Age in the Holocaust*. Arriving at Auschwitz and immediately subjected to Dr. Josef Mengele's life-or-death gaze, 13-year-old Livia stood in line with her aunt and her mother. Jackson's golden hair saved her from the initial death selection. Mengele separated Jackson's mother and aunt with his riding stick, forcing them to queue up in separate lines. The mother pleaded for her sister's life but Mengele refused: "'You go with your daughter. She needs you more'" (p. 57). The mother, however, was soon injured when her bunk collapsed onto the level below. Disabled, the mother was ultimately the one more in need of her daughter. Often the mother begged to be left alone so that she might die, but Jackson refused to leave her. The daughter forced the mother to be present at *Appel*, roll call, and to meet the Nazis' demands. As Abraham insisted that Isaac walk up the mountain with him, so too did Jackson command her mother, now lame, to live until the final moment. Determined, Jackson literally dragged and carried her mother throughout the remainder of the war in her desperate — and successful — effort to keep her mother alive.

Wiesel and his father survived the march through the snow in one of the twentieth century's most bitterly cold winters. They arrived at Buchenwald, more dead than alive. The father was terribly ill but the son encouraged him to hold on to life. Addressing his father, Wiesel encourages him: "'Only another moment more. Soon we can lie down — in a bed. You can rest...'" (*Night* p. 99, ellipsis in text). During the war's final days, young Eliezer, still a child in years if not in brutal experience, was so ill, so exhausted, that he could neither compel his father to live nor protect him from all the malevolent forces that assaulted him. Alvin H. Rosenfeld comments upon the inversion of the father/son roles in *Night*. "Wiesel, a storyteller very much within the line of the classical [M]idrashic writers ... [concludes] his memoir with an Isaac surviving the bloody altar but all the father figures dead" (p. 245). Observing the parallels between the Biblical *Akeda* and Wiesel's *Night*, Neher points out that Wiesel's experience is "an *Akedah* in reverse: not a father leading his son to the sacrifice, but a son conducting, dragging, carrying to the sacrifice an old, exhausted father" (p. 217). Wiesel is Isaac; he has lived the *Akeda* in his own flesh. Livia Jackson, too, lived an *Akeda* in reverse as she forced her mother to stand, to walk, to work. Like Abraham and Isaac, Jackson and her mother were able to leave the place of sacrifice alive. Not so for young Wiesel. Eliezer, in an imperfect parallel to Isaac, departed the place of sacrifice alive but without his father.

Shattered survivors found that, for most, there was no use speaking of the pain or the suffering. Pain and suffering in post-war Europe was pandemic: for the victors, the conquered, and the victims, for the military and the civilians. To speak of one's agonizing past would require effort that could be emotionally overwhelming; one would scarcely know how to begin, what to share, and when to stop. Silence hovered over the twentieth-century *Akeda* as well as the Genesis 22 account. The *Bereshit* passage begins with God uncharacteristically breaking the divine silence by asking Abraham to sacrifice Isaac. In their obedience to God, father and son travel, accompanied by their servants, and the air seems heavy with unspoken thoughts. The Plaut *Commentary* points out that once the mountain is reached, the Hebrew text uses "staccato phrases that heighten the tension" as Abraham responds like a somnambulist (p. 146). Isaac breaks the silence by asking where the sacrificial animal is. Abraham responds with the only words that he speaks to his son when he promises that the Lord will provide what is needed. Auerbach states that "the journey is like a silent progress through the indeterminate and the contingent, a holding of the breath, a process which has no present, which is inserted, like a blank duration, between what has passed and what lies ahead, and which yet is

Four: Akeda

measured: three days!" (p. 10). Kierkegaard argues that Abraham's agony was so profound that time itself was shattered: "the journey lasted three days and a good part of the fourth; indeed, these three and a half days could be infinitely longer than the few thousand years that separate me from Abraham" (p. 53). Wiesel calls the journey a "silent march toward that precise point where despair and faith were to meet in a fiery and senseless quest" (*Messengers* p. 86). Wiesel's adjectives, "fiery and senseless," describe the ancient *Akeda* well but are even more appropriate to the modern one.

We may speculate along with Kierkegaard that Abraham might have been too overwhelmed with his pain to speak. Isaac also seemed quiet, and no indication was given that he knew his fate. However, "Isaac was no fool," Jeffrey M. Cohen insists. "His father's evasive answer, '*God will provide the lamb for the sacrifice, my son,*' must have left him very troubled and confused…. Lambs do not roam wild. They are bred in flocks…. After Isaac's question, the dialogue suddenly goes silent. A brooding and telling silence" (p. 241, italics in text). The silence might be one of paralyzed fear, or it might have emerged as Isaac sunk deep within himself to trust in his father's goodness.

The silence of God and the silence of Abraham and the silence of Isaac exist in a void that, as mentioned earlier, Kierkegaard calls the "teleological suspension of the ethical" (p. 54). That is, the Lord, who has defined Himself as benevolent and creative, asks for something evil and destructive. If the Supreme Being undermines the moral and ethical landscape of the universe, how is it possible for humans to trust that Being? God asks, after all, for human sacrifice; as Kierkegaard puts it, Genesis 22 details a "prodigious paradox of faith, a paradox that makes a murder into a holy and God-pleasing act, a paradox that gives Isaac back to Abraham again, which no thought can grasp…" (p. 53). The ethical requirements we demand of God and that God demands of humanity appear to be abandoned in the *Akeda*. How could a loving and compassionate God ask a father to kill his son? And how could Abraham have agreed to such a request? With God's speech and Abraham's acquiescence to it, the ethical dimension of the world, says Kierkegaard, has been suspended. All that we know hangs over the abyss as silence reigns: the silence of others, of the participants, and of God.

Imagery from *Genesis* in Holocaust Memoirs

According to Genesis 22, no words were spoken by Abraham's servants. They were mute travelers, quiet observers. They accompanied Abraham and his son without comment, and they were silent when Abraham returned to them from Mount Moriah, alone. Their silence might represent the silence of others: those who felt powerless, those who agreed with the action, and those who were stunned into muteness. Patterson argues that when "collision with silence" occurs, "it is the silence of the other with which one collides" (*Shriek* p. 33). Shoah survivors frequently mention the distressing effect silence had upon them. Jackson observed that her entire village seemed steeped in silence as the Jews were marched through the streets into the ghetto. Walking past ordinary homes in an ordinary neighborhood, she sensed that even the houses are mute. "Where are our Gentile neighbors? Their doors and windows are shut, shades are drawn on every window" (p. 22). Leitner admitted feeling abandoned when, being marched through the streets on the way to the trains, she looked up at her neighbors' windows and saw no one there. "You could have thrown a morsel of sadness our way while we were dragging ourselves down Main Street. But you didn't. Why?" (p. 16). She did not receive an answer. Bakhtin describes silence as a space where there is a voice which refrains from speech (qtd. in Patterson, *Shriek* p. 34). The physical and emotional space of refrained speech — the stilled voice — was the silence which emanated from the drawn shades; its restraint indicated either a lack of concern, the fear of Nazi reprisal, or implicit consent. Perceiving the silence surrounded them as they left their homes, Jews could accurately predict that a similar silence would await them upon their return.

More haunting than the silence of their impassive, consenting, or fear-struck neighbors was the silence of the dead. No longer would the voices of so many family members and friends be heard. Any person sent to a death camp was surrounded by death; however, Filip Müller's experience at Auschwitz was magnified because his job was to put the gassed bodies into the ovens. At one point, Müller decided that he would join the fate of brave Czechoslovakian Jews who were being prepared for the gas chamber. "...I asked myself what sort of life it would be for me in the unlikely event of my getting out of the camp alive.... In the Jewish school where I knew every nook and cranny there would be silence" (p. 111). One of the doomed Czechoslovakians begged Müller not to join them,

Four: Akeda

urging him to stay alive so that one day he could give voice to their story. Müller acquiesced to the Czechoslovakians' request, discovering in his acceptance of life a new desire to help others survive. When he learned that two Jews planned to escape the camp, he donated physical evidence to serve as proof of the gas chambers' existence. He was confident that once the world learned of "the whole dreadful truth ... surely something would be done to put an end to the mass murder. The rest of the world, so I believed, could not remain silent in the face of what was happening here" (p. 122). Much of the world did know; political powers were informed, evidence had been gathered, millions of people were disappearing from their homes. There were pockets of protests; there were discussions about bombing the train tracks to the concentration camps to disrupt the business of genocide. But, overall, the world remained silent.

In Glatstein's poem, "The German Thinks," he proposes that the Nazis counted on the world's silence: "It was all calculated on the basis of total victory / On silent world-allies" (*I Keep Recalling* p. 188). Although the Nazis did not reach total victory, they seemed to understand that the world's silence was a phenomenon which, in its turn, silenced their victims. The world's mute rejection of Jewish suffering so astonished Wiesel that he titled the first version of his autobiography, an 800-page work written in Yiddish, *And the World Stayed Silent.* Paring down the 800-pages to approximately one-eighth of that for its initial publication in French, *La Nuit,* which became *Night* in English, Wiesel consistently focuses on the theme of silence. He describes his initial encounter with the bizarre world of the death camp: "I pinched my face. Was I still alive? Was I awake? I could not believe it. How could it be possible for them to burn people, children, and for the world to keep silent? No, none of this could be true. It was a nightmare..." (*Night p.* 30, ellipsis in text). Drix heard the silence of the victims and of the world when he watched a new group of prisoners enter the Janowska camp. "Soon a death parade moved on in the direction of the camp. How well we knew this view, which opened our wounds anew—this march of pale, depressed people, broken down physically and mentally, looking about vaguely, with mute expressions of despair on their faces," he recalls (p. 141). Their muteness conveyed a wealth of emotional and ontological information. "The silence was a hundred times louder than shouting, than human yelling. This mute cry should have shaken the earth and heaven" (p. 141). Neither heaven nor earth revealed any sign of being shaken by the horror.

Those who suffered unimaginable hardships bore their ordeal with a "shriek of silence," as Patterson puts it. The silent scream was comprised of survival mechanism, horror, and despair. In one of the most famous passages of *Night,* Wiesel describes a young boy's death by hanging. The "child was silent" as the noose was placed around his neck while the prisoners, also silent, were forced to look at him (p. 61). The chair was knocked away from the boy's feet. "Total silence throughout the camp," writes Wiesel, a silence of sorrow, fear, and disbelief (p. 61). Starved and tortured, living in a world that scarcely seemed possible, the inhabitants could not speak. Eugene Heimler recounts his falling into the camp's silence almost as if it were a pit: "The noises of the camp sounded fainter and fainter. All at once everything became utterly silent. The suddenness with which this occurred threw me into a panic.... I longed to cry out, to scream, to break the silence with my voice..." (p. 39). Ka-tzetnik 135633 chooses one key word to describe the prisoners standing at attention during the selection process: "Silence. Skeletons arranged row on row, standing silent" (*Star* p. 93). Chosen for death, each *mussulman* (a number of spelling variations exist, including *musselman*), a human skeleton, the walking-dead upon whom nothing seems to register, came to realize that death was near. "Soon they will take him to a terrifying Unknown," states Ka-tzetnik (p. 99). "He now drowns in fear. His mouth is full. He cannot scream. But from somewhere within, someone screams a scream beginning wide, flat, grooved, ending rounded, thin, sharpened" (p. 99). The scream itself, coming from "within," may itself have been silent.

The silence enveloped the victims like a shroud. The chorus in Wiesel's *Ani Maamin* dictates: "Jews, you must die, / For the sake of words, / Sacred words / Cursèd words, / Stifled words. / You must die without a sound, / Leave without a prayer, / Saying amen" (p. 85). Wiesel incorporates that silence when describing the decision about whether to stay in the camps or join the march. Three times young Eliezer asks his father about their course of action. "'What shall we do?' My father did not answer. 'What shall we do, father?' He was lost in thought. 'Well, what shall we do, father?' ... He was silent.... He did not answer" (*Night* p. 78). If Kierkegaard is correct in his assessment of the *Akeda* when he argues

118

Four: Akeda

that the story itself proves that there has been a divine abeyance of the ethical, then there is no clear course of action for a person to take. If a deity undermines the supposed structure of the moral universe, ethics collapse. "But if the ethical is teleologically suspended in this manner," muses Kierkegaard, "how does the single individual in whom it is suspended exist?" (p. 61). If a person's very essence is assaulted, at a certain point words of protest and despair seem meaningless. Words cannot sustain themselves with either sound or meaning. Words appear impotent in the face of Nazi power.

God is also silent in the *Akeda,* save for the initial request which launches the action. While Neher ultimately concludes that the Lord was present throughout the Event, he admits that the deity's silence is "serious and alarming" (p. 142). Patterson critiques Neher's assessment linking Auschwitz and silence by stating that it "may be ontologically accurate, but it is Jewishly problematic" (*Wrestling* p. 158). For many inhabitants of planet Auschwitz, the Lord's silence was the most difficult silence to understand because the lack of response, especially before so much fervent prayer, suggested that God was either indifferent or dead. Not all assumed God's silence was indicative of God's impotence. George Steiner states that whole "communities stayed close-knit to the end. There were children who did not cry out but said *Shema Yisroel* and kept their eyes wide open because His kingdom lay just a step over the charnel pit" ("A Kind of Survivor" p. 141). Avner Cohen asserts that the "obligation to sanctify the Divine name" was frequently realized during the Holocaust, when "many Jews ... went to their deaths with joy, following the example of Abraham and the Binding of Isaac" (p. 61). The trust exhibited in such action inspires wonder.

But for others, God's silence was the most difficult silence of all to understand, even for those who had been fervent in their faith. While still in his childhood home in Sighet, a passionately religious Eliezer Wiesel had been groomed in his faith by his parents, his teachers, his rabbis, and Moshe the Beadle. Wiesel's religious and academic education was nurtured on the art of inquiry. "My mother," he recalls, "never asked me whether I had given the melamed [a teacher of religion to the young] good answers, but whether I had asked a good question" (*All Rivers* p. 379). A teacher who appeared much later in Wiesel's life taught him that it "is because a Jew remains attached to his God that he is permitted to question Him" (p. 380). In Sighet, Moshe the Beadle taught young Eliezer that asking questions is at the heart of Judaism. "'Man questions God and God answers,'" Moshe says (*Night* p. 2, spelled Moishe in 2006 edition). But when the questions receive no answers, what then? For many believers, God's silence appears to be the ultimate abandonment.

The deity's silence forced Wiesel's violent rupture with his God as the boy experienced his first night at Auschwitz. The heavens rested impassively overhead even as the crematoria's smoke filled the sky, and he discovered that he could no longer worship God. Wiesel heard men praying around him, but he asked himself: "Why should I bless His name? The Eternal, Lord of the Universe, the All-Powerful and Terrible, was silent. What had I to thank Him for?" (p. 31). The silence proved to be the breaking point at which his childhood faith dissolved. "I did not deny God's existence," Wiesel says of the rupture, "but I doubted His absolute justice" (p. 42). Later, on the eve of Rosh Hashana, a service held spontaneously and illegally by the Jewish prisoners caused Wiesel to observe his own emotional distance: "How could I say to Him: 'Blessed art Thou, Eternal, Master of the Universe, Who chose us from among the races to be tortured day and night, to see our fathers, our mothers, our brothers, end in the crematory? Praised be Thy Holy Name, Thou Who hast chosen us to be butchered on Thine altar?'" (p. 64). Isaac had not been butchered on the altar. God provided a ram for Isaac; why, implies Wiesel, was none given for the millions of Isaacs who lived during the *hurban*?

Arguably, the altar to which Wiesel refers is not the altar upon which Isaac is placed but rather it could be the altar of ritual sacrifice in the days of the Temple. Even so, Wiesel asks the King of the Universe for justice. Abraham, Isaac, and Jacob appeal to God in *Ani Maamin* for mercy because they, the patriarchs, have seen the children of Israel tortured and killed, and they beg God to break the divine silence by responding to their cries. Consistent with his appeals for the people of Sodom and Gomorrah, Abraham tries to reason with God: "The Torah forbids / The slaughter of an animal / And its young / On the same day" (p. 55). Based upon the Torah's prohibition, how is it, Abraham wonders, that the Lord allows the perverse reality of parents and children murdered together daily in the Shoah. "Yet — fathers and sons / Are massacred / In each other's presence / Every

Four: Akeda

day. / Is then a Jew / Less precious / Than a beast? (p. 55). Still the response from the heavens is silence. The Torah speaks; the Lord does not.

Reflecting on Wiesel's first night in the camps, Neher observes that Wiesel's account is "from end to end a rewriting of the *Akedah* in the obscure light of the Night of Auschwitz.... A father and son go to the sacrifice, imprisoned in the silence of God.... But with Wiesel the story of the *Akedah* is suddenly singed, so to speak, with the fires of reality" (p. 216). Neher argues that Wiesel's personal *Akedah*, which was mirrored millions of times during the *hurban*, is "no longer a story invented in the imagination of a poet or a philosopher, and neither is it the story related in the Bible. It is the reality of Auschwitz" (p. 216). Consequently, Wiesel's story combines with the Biblical *Akeda* to compel us to face a most cruel theological question. It is, says Neher, as if the two patriarchs "were suddenly to rise up before us, dripping sweat and blood, exuding life and death, to catch us by the throat and ask us, not 'where is the ram?' (Gen. 22:7), but 'Where is God?'" (p. 216). That final question — "Where is God?" — rebounds in the silence, causing many to break their relationship with God.

Silence, however, is paradoxical. Among its many contradictory conundrums is the fact that sometimes silence implies not indifference but consolation. Jewish mourning rituals acknowledge this fact as those who visit a mourner who is grieving are expected not to speak until the mourner initiates conversation. In a guide to Jewish grief rituals, Rabbi Aaron Levine explains that the Bible compels the visitor's silence and the Talmud promises rewards for the visitor who refrains from speech (p. 76–77). Rabbi Berel Berkovits implores: "Just as God was silent, so we, too, should be silent. For is not speech trite in the face of the silent scream of six million? Is it not a blasphemy to talk in the face of the unutterable?" (qtd. in Harries p. 34). When the Talmud urges silence in the presence of a mourner grieving one death, the implication exists that we must be silent before the millions.

Rabbi Berkovits believes that there is a type of silence that is "a true silence, an evocative silence, a meaningful silence" (qtd. in Harries p. 35). There is a sacred silence, a silence pregnant with divinity. "Just as silence is the most eloquent form of revelation," Neher says, "so the most eloquent means of adoration is silence" (p. 11). Similarly, the sacred books of various religious traditions carry with them a magisterial, spiritual silence. "The Torah," Wiesel remembers of his devout childhood studies, "demanded silence and a kind of sacred respect" (*All Rivers* p. 10). The ineffable inspires a withdrawal from words.

When describing the eve of Rosh Hashana in 1944, Wiesel observed that "thousands of silent Jews gathered" in Auschwitz, fearful with anticipation concerning what God and what the Nazis might have in store for them (*Night* p. 63). Noticing the importance of silence in Wiesel's work, Neher decided to reread the Bible in order to learn more about the Scriptural base of Wiesel's motif. As Neher explains in *The Exile of the Word: From the Silence of the Bible to the Silence of Auschwitz*, the Bible is overwhelmingly a "landscape of silence" (p. 9). God "may ultimately be identified only by Silence," he argues (p. 10). Because the Bible is a book about God, God's creativity and God's interaction with the people of Israel, God's silence can be understood to be one with God; consequently, silence can be creative and nurturing. Neher alludes to an insight uttered by Eleazar ben Judah of Worms: humanity should not be too proud of our human words, for "God is Silence" (p. 11). Therefore, to dwell in silence is to be present to God's own language. Arthur A. Cohen also argues against interpreting silence as an expression of God's apathy. In *The Tremendum*, wherein he attempts a theological interpretation of the Holocaust, Cohen criticizes those who would equate silence with indifference. The "silent God is treated by some of his critics as though speech were the only mark of affect or miracle the only modality of caring; hence silence is ineffectuality and the equivalent of the 'not-God'" (p. 80). A silent God, Cohen asserts, does not necessarily equal an absent one, a *Deus absconditus*. Neher insists that silence is God's own language and, moreover, that God *is* silence. Consequently, God's silence can be a mark of God's presence, according to Neher's reading of Scripture (pp. 10–11). Thus, God's silence could be interpreted as a sign of God's presence made manifest in the death camps.

If God is good and if God's language is silence, then there must have been moments of silence within the camps that seemed to ring with God's presence. Isabella Leitner tells of one such time when her sister, Chicha, was punished by the notorious SS officer Irma Grese. Chicha was forced to kneel for hours on gravel, holding a heavy rock in each outstretched

Four: Akeda

hand. "Thousands of eyes stared at the bonelike creature in the *Lagerstrasse* seemingly holding two mountains, so frail did she look in comparison to the rocks," Leitner says (p. 43). The onlooking prisoners can do nothing but pray, pray in silence. Poetically, Leitner renders the time that her sister held those rocks in her weak hands as the physical embodiment of the war between good and evil (p. 44). Chicha was able to endure precisely because of the silence; the silence of all the dead prisoners "deafens Chicha's ear. Their silence strengthens Chichas's arms" (p. 44). Leitner insists that out of the silence emanating from the live prisoners and from the dead victims, her sister was supported in her ordeal.

While Neher and Cohen's arguments and Leitner's account asserting a benevolent interpretation of God's silence are defensible, the issue of God's silence nevertheless strikes at the heart of many Shoah victims' fears. Moreover, God's silence seems at odds with the Jewish emphasis on hearing. "Hear, O Israel," begins the *Shema*, in the imperative. Ettin observes that Judaism is a faith that stresses hearing; in "the familiar antithesis between the Hellenic and Hebraic views of experience," the Greeks emphasized seeing whereas the Hebrews stressed hearing (p. 35). Nevertheless, a conundrum exists: silence can be destructive and debilitating. Neher states succinctly, "Now Auschwitz is, above all, silence" (p. 141). Yet another Holocaust conundrum arises: How can it be that silence is at once God's language and Auschwitz's reality? While admitting that God's silence catches humanity in an almost paralyzing negative dialectic, Neher ultimately understands the divine silence during the Event to be the same as God's silence throughout the Bible. Neher observes that the Bible is overwhelmingly concerned with silence, yet *Bereshit* begins with God's speech. Out of the void and darkness comes God's voice in Genesis 1:3, and the voice launches a creative calling forth of things that previously did not exist by speaking them into existence. When the Lord proclaimed "Let there be...," whatever was said came into being. The Plaut *Commentary* assesses God's speech "[a]s though He were addressing the universe" (p. 18). Eleven times God speaks forth creation and blessings in the first chapter of Genesis. God spoke, and it was. Neher, however, argues that "God spoke, certainly, but not words," as the Hebrew *davar*, whose primary meanings include *event, word, revelation, fact,* and *commandment*—does not appear until Genesis 11:1 (p. 92). Nonetheless, the Hebrew Scriptures record instances of God speaking to Adam, Eve, Abraham, Moses, Job, and the prophets, to name a handful.

God speaks — sometimes. "God is silent, while all await His Voice," says Neher (p. 15). The waiting for God's voice fills many lines of the Psalms, as people wait expectantly, anxiously, and longingly. But if God speaks in silence, then silence may well be the vehicle by which people are expected to hear. God asks things of people — sometimes. "From Abraham down to the final prophets, there is this succession of men who constantly exist in two dimensions — on the one hand being called, and on the other having the power of responding. And in the dialectic tension of this word extended between a call and a response, silence arises," Neher states (p. 15). The "dialectic tension" is such that silence can be fruitful and productive; but for Abraham and Isaac and their twentieth-century descendants, God's silence comes at a cost.

Jerome I. Gellman considers whether or not humanity can hear God, and specifically, if Abraham did hear God, did the patriarch hear the deity correctly? God's call to Abraham, asking him to take his son to the sacrifice, is, fundamentally, the story of what Neher calls the dialectic between "a call and a response." Gellman argues that the emphasis on divine speaking and human hearing testifies to two problems. God's call as translated into English may be rendered as, "Take your son, your favored one, Isaac, whom you love, and go to the land of Moriah, and offer him there as a burnt offering..." (Gen. 22:2). In Hebrew, the text is much more ambiguous. As Gellman explains, "the Bible does not record an explicit command to kill Isaac, but only a command to 'offer him up' or 'raise him up,' which can mean either a mere 'raising up' or a 'burnt offering'" (p. 25). That implies Abraham could have raised up Isaac, either physically or metaphorically. Wiesel explicates that the "term is *ola*, which means an offering that has been totally consumed, a holocaust" (*Messengers* p. 71). Such a reading suggests that Abraham was correct in his interpretation that his son was to have been a "burnt offering." Gellman argues that God's verbal command to Abraham "constitutes the *problem of hearing*" (p. 2, emphasis in text). But what about Abraham's response? "These questions constitute the *problem of choice*" (p. 3, emphasis in text). The problem of choice is what is so compelling about Abraham's dilemma. "Therefore, though Abraham aroused my admiration," Kierkegaard declares, "he also appalls me"

Four: Akeda

(p. 60). Abraham could have chosen to disobey God, and by doing so, he would not have made the journey in agonizing silence, preoccupied with worry over the impending death of his beloved son.

Abraham's response to God's request may have been a heroic stepping-out in faith, or it may have been, some suggest, something more sinister. A Midrash asserts that "[a] God who asks man what the text [Genesis 22:2] appears to ask is not the true God but one whom man fashions in his own image.... The history of humanity is replete with misdeeds committed in the name of religion" (qtd. in Plaut p. 152). Lippman Bodoff frames the dilemma in his article's title, "The Real Test of the *Akedah*: Blind Obedience Versus Moral Choice"; he explores the implications that "God was testing Abraham's willingness to refuse to commit murder even when commanded by God to do so" (p. 72). Norman J. Cohen argues that Abraham's "zealous behavior" and "self-involvement" mean that he is so "oblivious" to what he loves that he is willing to sacrifice that love (p. 83–84). Michael Brown turns the argument on its head in an article published in *Conservative Judaism* when he asserts that it was Abraham putting God to the test: Would God prove to be a savage deity who demands infanticide, or will God demonstrate mercy?

The more traditional view is that Abraham was an exemplar of faith. Maimonides maintains that God tested Abraham knowing that Abraham would pass the test, and that his faith would be an inspiring light to the nations (Plaut p. 149–150). Buber believes that Abraham's "personal mission foreshadows the national mission of Israel, so his biography is the pattern for the history of the people and must be presented as a living prophecy, as it were" (*On the Bible* p. 31). Despite the seemingly unjust request that God makes and despite the sorrow in his own heart, Abraham trusted that his God was a good God. Kierkegaard, who finds the *Akeda* almost unbearable, nevertheless deems Abraham a "knight of faith," the term he uses throughout *Fear and Trembling*. The Plaut *Commentary* suggests that Abraham's action demonstrates "*emunah*, adherence without faltering, obedience with complete trust" (p. 149). Abraham may be understood to be a man of great faith, a man who trusted his God, a man who knew that God's ways were both beyond his comprehension and his need to understand. Still, "Rabbi Alter draws attention to the use of '*Elohim*' for the Divine name, in the Biblical text," Gellman observes, "rather than the name '*YHVH.*' It is the latter name that is associated with the love of God, whereas the former, '*Elohim*,' is associated with the fear of God. One loves *YHVH*. One fears *Elohim*" (p. 88, italics in text). Was it love or fear, was it obedience or hope, that caused Abraham to take his beloved son to the place of sacrifice? What were the emotions that rendered Abraham and Isaac almost completely mute throughout their ordeal?

Abraham had a choice in responding to God's call. "Call" should be in the plural because God first called Abraham to take his son to the sacrifice, and, secondly, God called out through an angel to stop the patriarch's hand. "And Abraham picked up the knife to slay his son. Then an angel of the LORD called to him from heaven: 'Abraham! Abraham!'" (Genesis 22:10–11). The Midrash speculates why Abraham's name is spoken twice. "The repeated name," explains Rabbi Hiyya, "represents an expression of affection and eagerness'" (*Genesis Rabbah* p. 283). The affection may have been for either the father or the son, or both; the eagerness might have been to stop an unjust execution or to play the part of a rescuer. Rabbi Eliezer ben Jacob counters that the "repetition of 'Abraham' signifies that he was calling not only to Abraham, but to all subsequent generations. For there is no generation without its Abraham" (*Gates* p. 11). However, the generation of Abrahams and Isaacs who lived in Europe between 1933–1945 learned that their *Akeda* was one without a choice. God's call to Abraham and Isaac appeared to promise death; the Nazis' gathering of the patriarchs' children guaranteed death.

We have already considered inversions of Scriptural stories throughout this book; yet as systematic as the Nazis were in their oppression and murder of the Jews, no evidence appears that the Nazis were consciously inverting or perversely mimicking Scriptural stories. Genesis is a text sacred to both Christians and Jews; since most Nazis and their followers were raised as Christians, such famous stories as Babel and the sacrifice of Isaac would presumably have been well known to Germans through church readings, Sunday school, and catechism. The Nazis intended to change that situation. The Nazis regarded all religions with complete disdain; however, knowing that the German people whom they intended to control were predominantly Christians, the Nazis employed Christian motifs, symbols, and imagery to advance their own cause. At one level, the Nazis manipulated Scriptural and Christian themes in order to present a legiti-

Four: Akeda

mate front while undermining traditional meanings. Christian and Biblical concepts could be used for the Nazis' own ends, particularly as the religious ideas could invoke an emotional response from the people. The National Socialist Party, born in the Catholic region of southern Germany, endeavored to be Catholicism without Christianity, according to one historian (Grunberger p. 72). The Nazis exploited pomp, ritual, and ceremony in order to evoke a quasi-religious mood. Ritual enhanced myth; myth and ritual together appealed to devout feelings as Hitler assumed a position of divinity in his own universe.

Early in the Nazis' consolidation of power, they pressured the Christian churches to ban the Old Testament, that is, the Hebrew Scriptures. At the very beginning of Hitler's assumption of the Reich Chancellorship in 1933, prominent German Protestants began to remove "Jewish overrepresentation in the Holy Scriptures and the liturgy" (Grunberger p. 439). Cardinal Faulhaber pleaded a spirited defense of the "Old Testament" in his 1933 Advent sermon series; nevertheless, he was careful to distance Christianity from Judaism: "Let us venerate the Scriptures of the Old Testament!... [T]he church has stretched forth her protecting hand over the Scriptures of the Old Testament.... By accepting these books Christianity does not become a Jewish religion. These books were not composed by Jews; they are inspired by the Holy Ghost!" (qtd. in Mosse p. 258). The Hebrew terms "Amen" and "Hallelujah" were forbidden in one region of Germany, and, in another, Genesis 22 was expressly forbidden: "Abraham's sacrifice of Isaac was excised from the syllabus in Schleswig-Holstein" (Grunberger p. 439). By attacking and deleting portions of the Hebrew Scriptures, the Nazis' actions caused many Jews to perceive accurately that the Nazis were determined to eliminate Jewish history and memory.

God led Abraham to Mount Moriah; the most optimistic reading of the text insists that, although the patriarchs could not know what would transpire, God knew all along that Isaac would not be killed. The Nazi inverted parallel finds the Germans ordering the patriarchs' children to the concentration camps; no optimistic reading about the outcome is possible. Death, and the silence which accompanies it, ruled over that time and place.

Abraham and Isaac walked to the sacrifice together. Isaac carried on

Imagery from *Genesis* in Holocaust Memoirs

his person the necessities for the sacrifice as well as being, ontologically, the sacrifice itself. For European Jews of Hitler's era, they themselves were ontological victims. The word *Auschwitz* has become a synecdoche not only for the entire concentration camp system but also for human-engineered evil. Wiesel perceives within the camps the containment of Biblical stories, themes, and ideals. As he puts it in *Ani Maamin*, the concentration camps ironically were "a biblical kingdom" (p. 33). The Nazi sites of death became "[a] biblical kingdom, where death as sovereign appropriated God's face as well as his attributes in heaven and on earth and in the very heart of man. A biblical kingdom, for every name of every character in every Jewish history book ends up there, extinguished, a forest turned to ashes" (p. 33). Wiesel then names those characters from Scripture and Jewish history: "Moses and Aaron, David and Saul, Ephraim and Menashe, Sarah and Rebecca, Eliezer and Tzipora, Rachel and Jacob: it is the Jewish past, the Jewish memory, that is being resurrected, the better to be destroyed" (p. 35). Eliezer and Tzipora: common names belonging to many Eastern European Jews; the same names borne by Eli — Eliezer — Wiesel and his younger sister, Tzipora, murdered on her first night in the camp, and of whom even now Wiesel cannot bear to speak. "[I]t is the Bible that is being killed, the prophets that are being massacred," Wiesel insists (p. 35). For the vast majority of European Jews, no ram in the thicket emerged to be sacrificed in their place. The twentieth century Isaacs did not have their lives spared.

Genesis 22:18 implies Abraham left the mountain without Isaac. Isaac and his modern counterparts departed from the death site alone and silenced. Emerging from the death site alone came at a terrible cost to the survivor. Liberation brought with it pain as a new life must be created, out of the ashes. Wiesel imagines Isaac's anguish as the man argues with his God: "You made me climb, then descend / Mount Moriah —/ Crushed and silent" (p. 33). The patriarch of ancient times and the contemporary fathers and grandfathers of Isaac and Israel witnessed in their hushed despair: "...my children / Old and Young / Arrive at Majdanek" (p. 33). If Isaac is, as Wiesel suggests, the first holocaust survivor, then the silence that hovered about him as he departed Mount Moriah alone may be seen as an isolating aspect of the survivor syndrome.

Wiesel seems to imply that to be a survivor is to be alone and to be

Four: Akeda

mute, particularly in his characterization of Moshe the Beadle. He becomes a significant embodiment of silence as he appears in *Night* and many subsequent works by Wiesel, albeit variously incarnated as madman or drunkard. "Perhaps he plays such a central role in the world of my novels because he represents the first survivor," Wiesel admits (*All Rivers* p. 60). Moshe, as presented in *Night*, had been left for dead by the Nazis; however, he returned to Sighet so as to warn his fellow townspeople of the Germans' barbarous actions. His tales seem preposterous. The Jews of Sighet refused to believe his stories; the Germans, after all, were veritable paragons of culture. Moshe was certainly mad. No one believed him — surely not even Nazis would toss babies into the air as targets for machine gunners. Who could imagine that men and women would be required to dig their own graves and then present themselves to be murdered? The people hushed Moshe into silence, and their silence enveloped him. Neither believed nor understood, Moshe can only sit and weep. In just a few pages of print, Wiesel creates a paradigm of the survivor: "Messenger of the dead, he shouted his testimony from the rooftops and delivered it in silence, but either way no one would listen" (*All Rivers* p. 60). The survivor is a messenger of the dead, for the dead; he or she is a person who longs to speak out, to testify, to warn, but the audience did not want to hear.

Glatstein describes in his poem, "The Survivors," those who emerged from the Shoah's ruins: "Ridden with pain, / Enslaved, trampled, / Tortured, beaten, / Shamed, silenced" (p. 236). Liberation proves for many to be exceedingly bitter as a veil of silence enshrouds and segregates the survivors. During the war, as in Moshe's situation, people did not want to listen to a firsthand account of Nazi cruelty; the tales seemed too bizarre, too far-fetched. After the war, people did not want to hear the stories of Nazi horrors; everyone was too busy, creating a new life out of the rubble. And now, more than a half-century after the war, some still refuse to hear. Patterson evaluates the Moshe parable as demonstrating that "many ... survivors were locked into their own silence by the silence they encountered in others" ("Annihilation" p. 214). Wiesel's status as a survivor means he is both Isaac and Moshe.

Silence's conundrum — it can signify support or indifference — accompanies survivors into their post-war lives. Wiesel is not alone in repeating the muteness which the townspeople of Sighet forced upon

Moshe, although Wiesel's writings may constitute the most eloquent expression of this paradox. In the documentary film *The Long Way Home*, one survivor explains that others compelled her into silence; the people who had not experienced the Shoah did not wish to hear about it. Consequently, the survivor learned not to speak of the Event. Lucille Eichengreen had a similar experience; she describes the uncomfortable atmosphere when she, a recent immigrant, lived briefly with an American couple while attempting to rebuild her life. "They didn't quite know what to say to this 'creature' from the concentration camps. Most of our time was spent in uneasy silence" (p. 176). So the survivors learned, as Moshe did, that there are at least two reasons why they must be silent: Their tales are so horrific that they can scarcely be believed, and their stories implicate all who hear them — including their listeners and their God.

CHAPTER FIVE

Israel in Auschwitz
A Malediction Forbidding Mourning

> Who will wrestle with the angel? I beg you, Rabbi, let me into the secret of the angel who wouldn't reveal his name to Jacob! Was Jacob himself the angel? Did Jacob wrestle with himself? And like me, didn't he know his own name?
> — Ka-tzetnik 135633

Jacob Wrestles with the Angel: Genesis 32:23–33

Photographs and newsreel footage from the liberating British, American, and Russian armies captured images from the death camps, existing as an eerie parody of the Western ghost town, now that the rulers of the Night had fled. Too ravaged by starvation, disease, torture, and despair to exult, the faces of the concentration camp prisoners stared blankly into the camera. There were some prisoners who smiled and cheered, but, for the most part, the prisoners looked like the living dead; camp slang called them *musselmen* (the word itself spelled in numerous ways). *Musselmen* were those persons who had submitted to their fate, those who no longer had the physical or emotional energy to care whether they lived or died. The camera captured the physical reality of the *musselmen*, well known and ubiquitous within the camps, but unimagined beyond the electrified perimeter: Here they stared blankly by the camp's fence; there they shuffled aimlessly in the dust. Even the prisoners who appeared to be stronger than the *musselman* displayed relatively little emotion. Their withdrawn attitude revealed the emotional and physical deprivation they had endured as they observed the liberators passively.

Euphoria was rare. Opening her memoir with the flat assessment, "We have been liberated," Bertha Ferderber-Salz wonders: "Birds sing in the trees; the smell of spring is in the air; we have been liberated! But what has freedom to do with me? Do I really deserve to enjoy it?" (p. 15). Occasionally the cameraman of the liberating army would photograph a group cheering or a person weeping. As this was the prisoners' first opportunity to feel anything openly, the dominant repressed emotion was grief. The tears photographed by the liberators' cameras captured some joy, but most were tears of sorrow. Wiesel describes the lack of joy: "Strangely, we did not 'feel' the victory. There were no joyous embraces, no shouts or songs to mark our happiness, for that word was meaningless to us. We were not happy. We wondered whether we ever would be" (*All Rivers* p. 96). A few prisoners might touch or kiss the hand of a passing liberator, but many were too ill, too close to death, for such an expenditure of energy. Many thousands of prisoners would die in the days and months following their liberation. Some who survived would be condemned to continue living in the same despised camps, or ones not dissimilar to them, in the hours, months and years ahead as Displaced Persons.

The Allied soldiers who liberated the camps were stunned by what they saw. Alexander Donat's description of his specific experience speaks generally for the concentration camp survivor. "The soldiers of Patton's Third Army were shaken as the filthy skeletons in striped uniforms embraced them, weeping, kneeling to kiss their hands, mumbling incomprehensible thanks. In that hour of liberation we wept as we had not wept during all the years of martyrdom; we wept tears of sorrow, not tears of joy. Our liberation came too late; we had paid too high a price" (p. 290). Drawing upon his own experience and his formal interviews with other survivors, psychologist Emanuel Tanay explains that the "moment of liberation was rarely remembered as a joyful experience. It was the end of one form of suffering and the beginning of another" ("On Being" p. 26). Adding to the prisoners' grief was the knowledge that their liberation had not been the goal of the armies that had come their way. They recognized that they "had not been rescued. Our freedom was merely a by-product of the defeat of our oppressors" (p. 25). Wiesel affirms Tanay's perspective: "Yes, Hitler lost the war, but we [the Jews] didn't win it. We mourned too many dead to speak of victory" (*All Rivers* p. 96). Liberated from the Nazis, most concentration camp survivors did not experience instantaneous freedom. As the conquering armies and governments decided what to do with the emaciated prisoners, the survivors lived on in the very camps that the Nazis had run. Although free of the SS, selections, and gas chambers, still the former prisoners lived behind barbed wire and locked gates. Living in the camps was far from ideal; nevertheless, it was a sort of limbo that — at its best — gave the former prisoners time to build up their strength, strength they needed to begin the next phase of their lives.

Concentration camp prisoners who lived until liberation were surrounded by the bodies of fellow victims as well as the memories of their dead. Soon they discovered that the very fact that they were alive would subject them to criticism. Tanay and his camp compatriots would soon learn that they would be challenged; their existence continually "had to be justified and explained" (p. 25). Shoah survivors, as demonstrated in the previous chapter, became, in some measure, Moshe the Beadle from Wiesel's *Night*: they warned, they described, they testified, but few listeners wished to hear or believe their stories, their tales of wrestling with the Third Reich. Once the war was over, those Moshes were challenged by others who had no concept of what the liberated had endured. The survivors were asked how it was that they lived when others did not, and often survivors were suspected of committing immoral or indecent acts that enabled them to live. Victimized again, the survivors of 1945 either had to remain in the camps as they tried to decide how to rebuild their lives, or they had to make their way back home — a place that for many no longer existed, either psychologically or physically.

The long war had destroyed much physically: Many homes, neighborhoods, and towns had been eviscerated by bombs and other ravages of war. Survivors who left the camps found in the shattered physical world of post-war Europe a mirror of their own emotional and psychological world. Europe lay in ruins. Many Jews returned to their hometown knowing that their neighbors had betrayed them and that their homecoming was unwanted. Livia Bitton Jackson describes her experience tersely: "Open gate. Dark, empty courtyard. Bare rooms covered with dust. And something else. In the middle of every room there is a heap of human excrement" (p. 194). Moreover, throughout Eastern Europe, particularly Poland, many Jewish survivors were killed upon their return home. Anti-Semitism did not end with Hitler's defeat. There were Poles, among other nationalities, who were so incensed that there were still Jews alive that they murdered the Jews, now on an individual basis and not on an industrial scale. "Incredibly," notes historian Martin Gilbert, "the killing of Jews continued in Poland for more than two years after Germany's surrender" (p. 240), with approximately 1,000 Polish Jews murdered during that time (p. 241). Many *hurban* autobiographers record the stunned look of disapproval on their neighbors' faces when they returned from the camps. The Gentiles were frequently not restrained in wondering out loud how it was that Hitler had failed in his mission to kill all the Jews. Rebuilding a life was difficult; some would even say, impossible. "It becomes more and more clear to me," writes David Wdowinski in his autobiography, "that it is far easier for people to live with the six million dead than with the few thousand survivors" (p. 16). The documentary film *The Long Way Home* shows viewers the multiple obstacles survivors faced. One survivor is quoted in the film as saying flatly: "It is better to be a defeated German than a liberated Jew." Out of the ashes — literally, for many — survivors had to create a new life.

Survivors began to repair their lives, some more successfully than others, as implied by the suicides among some of the Shoah's best-known authors, who include Bruno Bettelheim, Jean Améry, Tadeusz Borowski, and Primo Levi. In attempting to recreate a "normal" life, many survivors changed their names for a variety of reasons, some of which will be examined later in this chapter. At this point, I wish to assert the significance of a name change for the Holocaust autobiographer, and later in this chapter, I will present several memoirists whose first-person accounts are published under a name different from their birth-names. The subject of naming preoccupies author Ka-tzetnik 135633, who returns, again and again, to the Biblical story of Jacob wrestling with the angel. Jacob received his new name, Israel, during the course of his struggle.

The pseudonyms under which Shoah autobiographers publish transcend the merely literary *noms de plume* as they point to a profound change, an interior transformation brought about by external events. Ka-tzetnik

Five: Israel in Auschwitz

135633 demands special attention, although we will examine many other names shortly. Born Yechiel Feiner in Poland, he changed his name to Yehiel De-Nur after the war; once he began writing of his experiences in *l'univers concentrationnaire*, he chose not to publish as Feiner nor as De-Nur, but rather as Ka-tzetnik 135633. The designation "Ka-tzetnik 135633" is wholly strange to most readers, so his publishers inevitably place an explanatory note in each book, quoted here in full: "K.Z. (German pronunciation Ka-tzet) are the initials of *Konzentration Zenter* (Concentration Camp). Every K.Z. inmate was known as 'Ka-tzetnik Number...'—the number itself being branded into the flesh of the left arm. The author of this book is Ka-tzetnik 135633." I will refer to him by his authorial name of his Shoah literature, Ka-tzetnik 135633, or as Ka-tzetnik. Vividly describing his stay in the Holocaust Kingdom in his two autobiographical works, *Star Eternal* and *Shivitti*, Ka-tzetnik 135633 finds the story of Jacob's wrestling match with the angel an apt allusion for survivors, for it contains such themes as struggling against a mighty power, receiving a new name, and being blessed while enduring an injury.

In order to appreciate who this Jacob is as he wrestles with a supernatural power, a brief review of his story is in order. Jacob, the patriarch whose name would be changed to Israel, is an important figure in Jewish history, and his name even today concludes the three-part formula by which the God of the Jews is invoked in one of the central prayers of the liturgy: The God of Abraham, the God of Isaac, and the God of Jacob. However, when readers turn to his story in Genesis, they are often surprised at what a shifty character he was. His mother Rebekah had longed for children throughout her marriage to Isaac, the same Isaac who was bound, placed upon an altar, and awaited death by the knife in his father Abraham's hand. Rebekah's anguish over her infertility ended when she conceived at long last, and twins at that. However, she feared that she would not survive her pregnancy because of the violent struggle of the twins within her womb. Esau was born first; Jacob followed, grasping his brother's heel. English readers bring their own associations to the word "heel." A positive association suggests that Jacob was grounded; a pejorative connotation is that Jacob was himself a heel, a scoundrel. The Plaut *Commentary* explains that Jacob (*ya-aqob*) holds on to his brother's heel (*akev*), with the original Hebrew insinuation that "Jacob tried to overreach his brother" (p. 173). Jacob's grasp on Esau's heel revealed his fetal struggle and foreshadowed a lifelong sibling competition.

From the start, the fraternal twins were completely different from one another. Parental preferences underscore those differences: Esau was the father's favorite son while Jacob was the mother's. By cunning, Jacob twice received something precious that rightfully belonged to his elder brother: Esau's birthright and Esau's blessing, both key elements of primogeniture. Fearing for his life due to Esau's anger over the stolen blessing, Jacob ran away to safety in his uncle's community. Some 20 years later, Jacob desired reconciliation with his twin, and he traveled homeward to see if Esau might welcome him. He had reason to fear that Esau might still resent him passionately; although many years had passed, old angers do not necessarily dissipate. The night before the brothers' meeting, Jacob selected hundreds of goats, rams, and cattle to give to Esau as a present. Jacob sent his traveling companions — wives, children, servants, and animals — across the river Jabbok (note the homophonic Jabbok to *ya-aqob*, Jacob), while he stayed on the shore by himself.

Here is the story of Jacob and his wrestling match with the stranger:

> Jacob was left alone. And a man wrestled with him until the break of dawn. When he saw that he had not prevailed against him, he wrenched Jacob's hip at its socket, so that the socket of his hip was strained as he wrestled with him. Then he said, "Let me go, for dawn is breaking." But he answered, "I will not let you go, unless you bless me." Said the other, "What is your name?" He replied, "Jacob." Said he, "Your name shall no longer be Jacob, but Israel, for you have striven with beings divine and human, and have prevailed."
>
> Jacob asked, "Pray tell me your name." But he said, "You must not ask my name!" And he took leave of him there. So Jacob named the place Peniel, meaning, "I have seen a divine being face to face, yet my life has been preserved." The sun rose upon him as he passed Penuel, limping on his hip. That is why the children of Israel to this day do not eat the thigh muscle that is on the socket of the hip, since Jacob's hip was wrenched at the thigh muscle [Genesis 32:25–33].

Biblical scholar Nahum Sarna declares: "This story, unparalleled in biblical literature, is thoroughly bewildering" (p. 203). It is indeed mystifying, as the Genesis author does not explain many crucial aspects of the narrative. Readers do not know why Jacob wanted to be left alone by the river the night before he was to meet his brother. Readers are not told who the person (if person is the correct word) was who wrestled with Jacob. The wrestling match appears at once to be violent yet benevolent. Although

Five: Israel in Auschwitz

readers of Hebrew Scripture know the importance of the name — a name signifies the being's essence — it is not clear if being injured is worth the blessing (if that is what it was) of being given a new name.

The Genesis passage demands study with an eye on three of its key ingredients: names, places, and actions. Names are of utmost importance in the Hebrew Scriptures, as evidenced in the Genesis 2:19–20 story of Adamic naming, that is, when the animals were brought to Adam in the Garden of Eden. More than a mere label, Adam's naming of the creatures meant that he perceived its ontological reality, its essence, and the name reflected that understanding. Many, if not most, proper names in the Bible bear etiological or etymological significance, as in the *Bereshit* portion above, wherein four proper nouns are specified: Jabbok, Jacob, Peniel, and Israel. English-speaking readers might catch the homonym of Jacob/Jabbok, but those who read Hebrew learn even more: "The Hebrew of Jacob's name is *ya-aqob*, the river's name is *yabboq*, and the verb for 'wrestle' is *abaq*, so Jacob's name is echoed and emphasized throughout [the] text" (Weis p. 103). Sarna points out that "he wrestled" in Hebrew may be transliterated as *va-ya'abek* (p. 204). Subsequently, the repetition of *yah* sounds in the Hebrew rendering of *Jacob*, *Jabbok*, and *wrestle* combine to create an emphatic statement about the importance of person, place, and action, all of which culminate in a name changed, elevated, to Israel.

The *-el* suffix in Hebrew proper nouns designates God; *Israel* and *Peniel*, two of the proper names in the wrestling story, are consequently two nouns with etymological ties to God. *Peniel* is credited in Genesis as signifying having seen divinity "face to face," a word which merges *paneh* or *panîm*, "face" and *elohîm*, "God" (Kodell p. 65). Jacob's old name stresses his grasping, fraternal struggle with its word play on the noun *heel*, the lowest part of the human body. His new name keeps the struggle intact but replaces it with a higher, heavenly adversary since *Israel*, Jacob's new name and the Jewish homeland's future name, means "to contend with God." Geoffrey H. Hartman argues that because of "this unmediated encounter, everything shady in Jacob is removed: the blessing he stole he now receives by right; and his name, tainted by his birth and subsequent behavior, is cleared. No longer will he be called Jacob, that is, Heel or Usurper, but Israel, God-fighter — quite a title" ("Struggle" p. 8). Anson Laytner sees within the blessing of the name *Israel* the spiritual foundation for what he calls the uniquely Jewish way of prayer: arguing with God. Therefore, the name *Israel*—"to contend or to strive with God"— suggests that the divine/human relationship is factious, contentious, and tumultuous. Such a vision differs greatly from Islamic or Christian perspectives that emphasize complete submission to, or quiet cooperation with, the Divine.

The setting of Jacob/Israel's struggle with God is important. Jacob wrestles by the river that echoes his own name, Jabbok. The desert tribes of the Middle East often used rivers and seas in their literature as symbols of danger. Sarna observes that rivers have been, throughout human history around the world, the site of literary tales wherein humans must contend with the spirits of the water (p. 204). Because waters, such as rivers, lakes, and oceans, could be unpredictably dangerous, ancient people suspected that they contained evil spirits or powers that sought to destroy humans (p. 204). Sarna's explanation, while helpful, limits the story's power by emphasizing ancient anxieties, particularly among desert tribes, who would logically fear the unknown, such as large bodies of water. Jungians would see the river's importance in a different light. Rather than water being an environment that hosts hostile, exterior forces, the Jungian reads water as an emblem of interior transformation. "Water is the commonest symbol of the unconscious," declares Carl Jung. "Psychologically, therefore, water means spirit that has become unconscious.... The descent into the depths always seems to precede the ascent" (p. 302). A Jungian reading allows a wider range of psychological and spiritual interpretations than does Sarna's more anthropologically-based assessment. A Jungian interpretation would permit readers to understand Jacob's struggle as a battle from the self-obsessed depths to the God-aware heights, a spiritual transformation worthy of the name "Israel."

Yet the battle that Jacob fought was a mysterious one, and his battle was set amidst a story which in itself is ambiguous. Translators of this passage usually assign either a proper noun or a common noun to the masculine pronoun, but, for much of the Hebrew account, Jacob and the stranger are simply referred to as "he." Thus, the tale stresses its enigmatic action precisely because, as is so often the case in Biblical Hebrew, ambiguous antecedents make identifying the pronouns difficult. Weis notes that "Jacob wrestles with his opponent; the audience wrestles with the text.

Five: Israel in Auschwitz

Jacob wrestles in the dead of night ... and the text keeps the audience equally in the dark" (p. 101). We cannot clearly tell who is being injured, blessed, renamed. Hartman wonders, though, at the "twisted" nature of the story "because while it is Jacob who is wounded, it is his antagonist who immediately pleads for release" ("Struggle" p. 11). Logic commands us to assign a proper name or at least a common noun to the ambiguous pronoun; even though Hartman observes that it is the antagonist who begs to be let go, the pronouns themselves simply are not clear. Translators assign to the angel (if that is who or what he is) the lines wherein he nervously observes that daybreak is near, dodges the question of his name, and gives both blessing and injury.

Even as the pronouns are elusive, so too are the nouns. The passage is frequently referred to as "Jacob wrestles with the angel"; the text itself, however, calls the stranger by a common noun, "man," and a proper noun, "God." As Kodell observes, "Jacob's adversary is identified as a man (*ish*) in verse 25, but in verse 31 Jacob says, 'I have seen God (*elohîm*) face to face'" (p. 65). Hartman states, "Even if he is an angel and not God, no other patriarch, no other Biblical character except for Moses has so direct and dangerous an encounter with a divine agent" (p. 7). A Biblical pattern exists in which a being who first appears to be a man turns out to be an angel of God, who, in turn, may become synonymous with God. A precedent for Jacob's encounter with man/angel/God may be found in a story involving Jacob's grandfather, Abraham.

Genesis 18 portrays the patriarch relaxing in his tent to escape the heat of the day when "[t]he LORD appeared" to Abraham (Gen. 18:1). When Abraham looked up, "he saw three men standing near him" (Gen. 18:2) and consequently rushed to offer hospitality to the three visitors. The story could be read as simply highlighting Middle Eastern hospitality customs; Abraham wished to refresh the traveling strangers with a meal, a normal occurrence within his culture. However, the text suggests that these three men are somehow physical manifestations of the one God. Significantly, during his offering of hospitality, Abraham heard his Creator make a promise. The Lord foretold Isaac's birth to Abraham and Sarah, a blessing that would take place in nine months (Genesis 18:10, 14). God was willing, according to this passage of Genesis, to speak to humans face-to-face, albeit disguised.

Imagery from *Genesis* in Holocaust Memoirs

Abraham's grandson, Jacob, also apparently had an encounter with the Deity. If God is willing to appear to people, to talk with an individual, then it is within the realm of Midrashic tradition to speculate that Jacob wrestled with the Lord. Yet the text will not allow one interpretation to be advanced with complete confidence; the critical interpretations span the spectrum. Psychoanalytic views abound: Fass provides a psychosexual reading wherein Jacob wrestles with himself and his desires; Kodell suggests that Jacob wrestled with the unrecognized Esau; Weiss maintains that Jacob wrestles with the blessings he has received. One Jungian, Esther Spitzer, argues that "Jacob's struggle with the Adversary was a numinous confrontation with the Shadow, or the dark, selfish side of him" (qtd. in Plaut p. 223). A Freudian, Dorothy F. Zelig, sees in the "mysterious figure" aspects of the "dangerous forces of the id and the strength of the super-ego" (qtd. in Plaut p. 224). One Midrash says Jacob wrestles with Esau's guardian angel. David Patterson acknowledges in *Wrestling with the Angel* that numerous interpretations exist, but the idea he finds most compelling is that the mysterious figure is the Angel of Death.

If the text is ambiguous, the result is less so. By receiving a new name, Jacob has been found worthy of that name. He has contended with God and prevailed, a verb that Weis explains may be interpreted as "you have endured" or "you have shown the ability to endure" (p. 104–105). In this respect, Jacob, the one who became Israel, is the spiritual progenitor of Shoah survivors. His children experienced a dark wrestling match in a place and time that Wiesel calls The Kingdom of the Night. Like Jacob, many contended with a mighty power; some prevailed, leaving the site injured. Some departed with a new name.

Ka-tzetnik 135633 reveals in both his fiction and nonfiction work his obsession with Jacob's battle. In his first autobiographical account, *Star Eternal*, an elliptical and thematic examination of concentration camp life, he grapples with questions of self-knowledge, self-understanding, and self-identification, all contained within an allusion to Jacob's wrestling match with the stranger. The following passage is a concentration camp discussion between a beatific rabbi, the Rabbi of Shilev, and a bitter 22-year-old man named Ferber, whom readers may interpret to be the author because of his questions, and possibly because of the similar sound to Ka-tzetnik's birth name, Feiner. The Rabbi asks: "'Can't you see, Ferber, God's

Five: Israel in Auschwitz

spirit hovering here now above this Destruction and Creation? Can't you feel that Jacob — in our bones — now wrestles with the Angel? We are the sinew of his thigh-vein in this struggle! Be strong, my son, at this moment you must be strong...'" (p. 106, ellipsis in text). Ferber responds with a question: "'Rabbi of Shilev, for whose sake does Jacob wrestle with the Angel, if his children did not cross the river, but stayed here in the blackness of the night?'" (p. 108). The rabbi's response is mystical and potentially beatific: "'From the very blackness of this night Jacob will bring forth the name "Israel." Before that, the morning star will not arise'" (p. 108). If the name *Israel* means "God-contender," then the Rabbi seems to imply that the modern-day Jacobs will prevail and that eventually the sun, with its promise of hope, will appear.

The Rabbi of Shilev understood Jacob's wrestling match as indicative of the struggle against the Night, a battle that was fought in Biblical times as well as the rabbi's contemporary time. Just as Jacob emerged from the battle blessed with a new awareness of his ability to endure, so too did the Rabbi imply that something good could emerge from the darkness. God will acknowledge those who contend with God. The Rabbi asserted that "we," the children of Jacob now imprisoned within the camps, "are the sinew of his thigh-vein" (p. 106). The descendents are one with the patriarch; they are one with his struggle. More than the children of Jacob, the concentration camp children of Jacob/Israel compose his body. Yet to be the sinew of Jacob's thigh is not only to participate in his fight against an unearthly power, it is to be the site of injury as well. It was there, at the joining of the hip and thigh, that the angel debilitated Jacob.

Despite the battle, despite the injury, despite the curious timelessness in which the battle takes place, the Rabbi of Shilev implied that Genesis teaches that there will be blessing. Just as *Israel*, Jacob's new name, is understood to be a blessing, so too, the Rabbi hinted, will a blessing come, but it will happen in darkness. Jacob's fight, continuing with the children of Israel against the power of the Nazis, is fought in a timeless state. An odd cessation of time occurs: "the morning star will not arise" until an action — Jacob's name change — is accomplished.

Ka-tzetnik 135633's second autobiographical account, *Shivitti*, unfolds the author's own wrestling match with the demons of nightmares and distress resulting from repressed memories of Auschwitz. He learned of a psychiatrist in Holland who administered the drug LSD to help patients relive trauma in order that they might be reconciled to it, thereby allowing them to put the ordeal behind them. Poetic and grueling, *Shivitti* details Ka-tzetnik's memories and hallucinations as he coped with what is now called post-traumatic stress; he faced his fears, both in his normal state and while being given LSD clinically. In one hallucination, the author was back in Auschwitz; he cried out to the man he identifies as his "rabbi and mentor": "'See for yourself, Rabbi! The barracks is [sic] packed with skeletons. Any moment now they'll take us by the truckload to the crematorium. Did Jacob wrestle with the angel for our sake? Let me into the secret, what was the angel after?'" (p. 61). Images whirled before De-Nur/Ka-tzetnik's eyes as he stayed within his hallucination. He continued his theological exploration with the Rabbi: "'Who will wrestle with the angel? I beg you, Rabbi, let me into the secret of the angel who wouldn't reveal his name to Jacob! Was Jacob himself the angel? Did Jacob wrestle with himself? And like me, didn't he know his own name?'" (p. 61) The words of the text indicate the struggling and the questioning that are part of Jacob's story, of Israel's story, the story of Israel in Auschwitz.

The Kingdom of the Night was both a physical and a spiritual reality. If Israel, that is, the Jewish people, wrestled with an angel, "what was the angel after?" The battle was waged during the Holocaust, a time period that Wiesel calls "Biblical times" ("We are" p. 33). As Wiesel insists: "It is the Bible that is being killed, the prophets that are being massacred" (*Ani* p. 35). The patriarch wrestled against an adversary, but that incident alone seems unlikely to produce a name change. Perhaps the battle was so pitched that Jacob never felt the same and therefore could not return to his given name. Perhaps the intensity of the struggle was such that Jacob forgot or repressed an essential part of who he was; perhaps losing his name was the source of Jacob's injury.

One question posed in *Shivitti* is particularly poignant for those who experienced the Holocaust and who had their names stripped from them: "And like me, didn't he know his own name?" Most of us take for granted that we know our own names, and most of us assume that we will keep the same name all of our lives. At least that is true for men. In contemporary American culture, women who marry must decide whether or not they will keep their given last name, itself a patriarchal inheritance, or

Five: Israel in Auschwitz

assume their husband's name, or hyphenate the two. The book of Genesis posits that to know a person's name is to know something of that person's essence. To change one's name, or to have it changed, is an unusual situation and could reflect how a person sees himself or herself. Ka-tzetnik suggests that Jacob needed a new name precisely because he "didn't know" the old one.

After the liberation, most Shoah survivors were eager to return to their old names; others were reluctant. Having been transformed, some needed to maintain that break with the past. Ka-tzetnik 135633 describes his personal life as afflicted with unresolved grief and repressed memories which spilled forth into vivid nightmares; the rupture between the person he was before the war and the number he became was so violent that even hearing his name inspired fear. Ka-tzetnik describes in the foreword to *Shivitti* his first LSD session, an experience he entered into with great anxiety: "I don't know why my knees were trembling. It was as if a long-sealed passageway, deep within me, had burst open and a tidal wave of horror was breaking over me.... Perhaps it was a succession of events that unleashed this wave: being called by my own name" (p. 1). Disconnected from his "own name," he underwent intense physical reactions upon hearing it. Estranged from his name because the Nazis had taken it from him, he might have reacted so strongly to his name because it reminded him of the extent to which the Nazis had ruptured his life. The "Ka-tzetnik" designation renders him a faceless prisoner in the crowd, and he is emphatic that he speaks *of* the others but not *for* them. Nevertheless, his specific number belongs to him alone. It is he who writes, and no other. Even as he recognizes the other prisoners in the camp, his concentration camp designation also carries with it an effect of timelessness. His very name suggests that Ka-tzetnik 135633 is still there in the camps.

In the penultimate chapter of *Star Eternal*, he, a liberated Ka-tzetnik, stands on a street corner and observes himself in the third person. "The sleeve of his Ka-tzetnik uniform is ripped to the shoulder. He gazes at the six digits of the Ka-tzetnik number on his forearm. The blue outlines of the digits streak before his eyes: a blue river" (p. 118). No longer does Jacob wrestle by the river Jabbok; his descendents have the site of their battle inscribed upon their flesh. This "blue river" does not hold the psychological or spiritual promise Jung saw in water imagery; rather, the contemporary Jabbok seeks to pull its bearer back into the anti-world. No Jungian ascent into awareness beckons for the Ka-tzetnik. How can the modern-day Jacobs depart from the scene of their wrestling match when they carry its stain? In the LSD therapy sessions Ka-tzetnik experienced, he returns again and again to the site of his trauma. There is no escape, and he knows it: "I stare at the Germans climbing into the cobalt of the Auschwitz skies, climbing up the ladder to the watchtowers, whose turrets pierce the dome of dawn. Shadow-figures ascending the ladders heavenward like angels, climbing Jacob's ladder.... It's crystal clear to me that this is Their world, Their planet, Their natural law, and this is Their sky" (p. 57). The Nazi overlords reign supreme. They alone decide who is worthy to bear a name.

The subject of naming engages literary theorist Philippe Lejeune to such an extent in his study *On Autobiography* that much of his theory is based on the reality of the author's name. Identifying what he calls *le pacte autobiographique*, Lejeune insists that the author's name and the promise of the author's life story invite the reader into an agreement, the autobiographical pact. He proposes, even as he acknowledges autobiography's amorphous qualities, that most readers assume an autobiography to be a "narrative recounting [of] the life of the author" that "supposes that there is *identity of name* between the author (such as he figures, by his name, on the cover), the narrator of the story, and the character who is being talked about" (p. 12, italics in text). The name on the cover is synonymous with the narrator, typically expressed in the first-person singular pronoun, which equals the character's life story that is being related. "In order for there to be autobiography (and personal literature in general)," he says, "the *author*, the *narrator*, and the *protagonist* must be identical" (p. 5, italics in text). The name on the cover should match the name inside the text.

Therefore, a published autobiography initiates a relationship with its readers because "the autobiographical genre is a *contractual* genre" (p. 29, emphasis in text). The fact of the autobiography's publication implies an "implicit or explicit contract proposed by the *author* to the *reader*, a contract which determines the mode of reading of the text and engenders the effects which, attributed to the text, seem to us to define it as autobiography" (p. 29, emphasis in text). According to Lejeune, the reader's response to the text is launched, in part, by the author's name on the book's cover and the absence of any invitation into a fictional pact. For all its myriad ambiguities, autobiography is an extreme proposition, Lejeune believes, for it "does not include degrees: it is all or nothing" (p. 13). Thus the autobiographical pact — that the author's name establishes a synonymous relationship between the author's life and the protagonist's story — is a promise.

Such a stance explains readers' sense of outrage when sham memoirs are perpetrated upon them. Upon discovering that a text they read as nonfiction was, in fact fiction, readers may feel betrayed. The moral imperative of truth-telling — at least grounded in what the lifewriter understands to be true — is all the more heightened when discussing Holocaust texts. Because the phenomenon of Holocaust deniers still inexplicably exists, when a purported Holocaust autobiography turns out to be a fictional account, the ever dwindling group of survivors is at risk of being accused of perpetuating a fiction. Such was the situation when *Fragments* by Binjamin Wilkomirski was exposed as a hoax. This is especially relevant in the case of Shoah survivors' memoirs and lifewritings, important as they are as nonfictional testimonies and eyewitness accounts.

Lejeune roots his argument in the importance of names. Arguing that "the problems of autobiography" are directly situated "in relation to the proper name" (p. 11, emphasis in text), he insists that the text must "honor" the author's name or "signature" (p. 14). Lejeune's analysis of the proper name leads him to create a nine-fold schema wherein he places the relationship of the author to the protagonist:

> [W]e can classify all the possible cases by bringing into play two criteria: the relationship of the name of the protagonist and the name of the author, the nature of the pact concluded by the author. For each of these criteria, three situations are possible. The protagonist (1) has a name that is different from the author; (2) has no name; (3) has the same name as the author; the pact is (1) fictional; (2) absent; (3) autobiographical. In articulating these two criteria, we obtain theoretically nine combinations; actually only seven are possible, the coexistence of the identity of the name and the fictional pact, and that of *the difference of name and the autobiographical pact being excluded by definition* [p. 15, emphasis mine].

Yet Shoah texts bring up textual circumstances that Lejeune dismisses as impossible. The author's name does not match the name given of the protagonist, even though a non-fiction pact has been established. Shoah

Imagery from *Genesis* in Holocaust Memoirs

autobiographers are modern-day Jacobs. As Jacob left the Jabbok injured and with a new name, so too did many Holocaust survivors leave the death camps injured and renamed. However, the wrestling match for their names started long before their arrival at the camps.

When the Nazis began their systematic assault upon the Jews, they targeted names, among many other personal aspects of human lives. The issue of names as it involved German Jews arose even before Nazism; Bismarck, for instance, insisted that "national pride is deeply wounded by those cases in which Jews with Eastern Jewish names have adopted particularly nice German surnames" (qtd. in Friedländer *Nazi Germany* p. 35). As soon as the Nazis assumed national power in January 1933, they began legal maneuvers to corner the Jews and "Jewish" names. By late April 1933, "the use of Jewish names for spelling purposes in telephone communications was forbidden," reports Saul Friedländer (p. 37). By 1935, as the Nazis sought to de-Judaize the arts, Jews were forbidden to change their names to more Aryan-sounding appellations (p. 134-135). Still another "decree announced that from January 1, 1939, Jews who did not bear the first names indicated on an appended list were to add the first name Israel or Sara to their names" (p. 254). The names Israel and Sara became, in the Nazi lexicon, a mockingly parodic summation of Jewish names, according to Friedländer (p. 255). Dictating which names Jews were allowed to use was yet another strategic attack on Jewish identity.

The ultimate strategy was the Final Solution. For many Jews who arrived at the death camps, their names were duly recorded in the camp's register and would thereafter be used only for official record-keeping — of which many records are preserved, locked in vaults, awaiting scholarly scrutiny. Prisoners had a number on their prison garb and/or a number burned into their forearm. Not every camp tattooed its prisoners, but the blue-ink prison number textualized the nightmare world of the Nazi concentration camp and has, to a large extent, come to symbolize the entire system. Yaffa Eliach considers how devastating the tattooing must have been for the newly arrived Jews; they had been "stripped of everything, even their names" (*Hasidic* p. xix). Shirley Russak Wachtel remembers the exact moment when she had her humanity taken away from her: it was when she was tattooed with a number (p. 58). She no longer had a name; instead, she was reduced to a series of numerals (p. 58). Moreover, soon

Five: Israel in Auschwitz

after her entry to the camp, she overheard the commandant call a German shepherd by its name, Otto: "A dog is given a name," she observes, "...but we ourselves are but numbers" (p. 64). The Nazis were not unique in assigning prison numbers to their victims; the prison number has long been, and continues to be, an emblem of shame, punishment, and loss of individuality. Most prisoners resume their lives by reclaiming their name and abandoning their number. One enduring consequence of the Shoah, however, is the physical scar many survivors bear on their arms: their concentration camp number.

"On my left forearm," Améry reflects, "I bear the Auschwitz number; it reads more briefly than the Pentateuch or the Talmud and yet provides more thorough information. It is also more binding as a basic formula of Jewish existence" (p. 94). Améry's choice of the word "binding" is significant. There are basic formulas, to be sure, of Jewish existence—reciting the *Shema* ("Hear, O Israel...") would be one. Another form of binding is indeed physical. Devout Orthodox men bind the *tefillin* around their arm and their head. Rabbi Joseph Telushkin explains that each weekday morning, men will place the small black box on their head and arm and secure the box with straps, thereby actively participating in "a Jew's relationship with God" (p. 661). Améry's concentration camp number became a tangible sign of his relationship with the Nazi powers.

The strangeness of Ka-tzetnik 135633's "name" causes it to stand out in a bibliography, and while, to my knowledge, he is the only survivor who publishes under his concentration camp number, most lifewriters mention their assigned numbers. David Patterson puts it this way: "Thus, seeking the recovery of their humanity, the authors of numerous memoirs set out to recover a name by remembering a number" (*Wrestling* p. xii). Patterson then provides eight examples of autobiographers who specify what their number was (p. xii–xiii); those eight are representative, as the list could be far longer. "I became A-7713. After that I had no other name," recounts Wiesel in *Night* (p. 39). Levi describes receiving his number, 174517, as having "been baptized" (*Survival* p. 27). His terminology is appropriate. While baptism has, on one level of Christian theological interpretation, associations with being washed clean from impurities, a physical act that links it to the Jewish *mikveh*, there are deeper associations upon which Levi draws. Baptism means, for Christians, being initiated into Christ's death; Levi's "baptism" signals his immersion into what Katzetnik calls "Auschwitz death" (*Star* p. 96)—an entire universe devoted to death.

The prisoners' numbers contained information, both for the camps' interned cognoscenti and their German overlords. The numbers were processing data for the Nazis. The prisoners learned how to read the subtext of the numbers, a system that Levi calls "the funereal science of the number of Auschwitz, which epitomize the stage of destruction of European Judaism" (*Survival* p. 28). Levi explains: "To the old hands of the camp, the numbers told everything: the period of entry into the camp, the convoy of which one formed a part, and consequently the nationality. Everyone will treat with respect the numbers from 30,000 to 80,000: there are only a few hundred left and they represented the few survivals from the Polish ghettos" (p. 28). The low numbers indicated that the prisoners had survived the system thus far; the opposite was true for high numbers. "As for the high numbers they carry an essentially comic air about them, like the words 'freshman' or 'conscript' in ordinary life. The typical high number is a corpulent, docile, and stupid fellow..." (p. 28). Such a fellow, Levi continues, can be conned out of his soup or manipulated into some sort of service, so naïve is he to the ways of the alternative universe in which he finds himself. Moreover, being called by a slang-form of one's number could reveal how others assessed that prisoner's mental state. Levi recalls a certain individual who was known only as "Null Achtzehn": "He is not called anything but that, Zero Eighteen, the last three figures of his entry number, as if everyone was aware that only a man is worthy of a name, and that Null Achtzehn is no longer a man" (p. 42). He was not even his full number. Everyone knows instinctively, as Levi states, that a person is "worthy of a name"; the Nazis capitalized upon that fact by taking away the name, demoralizing their victims.

The prison numbers contained information, as we have seen. Sometimes the numbers in themselves were a reason to bond with another person. Filip Müller, whose autobiography explicates what it was like to be a *Sonderkommando*, that is, a slave-laborer in the gas chambers and the crematoria, recalls a friendship that developed between a French prisoner and himself. "Although I was only an ordinary prisoner, while he was one who wielded a good deal of influence, he was very kind to me simply

Five: Israel in Auschwitz

because the numbers with which we were both tattooed were very similar" (p. 53). In such a manner, prisoners could find ways to subvert the humiliations imposed upon them. There was no one singular response to the prison number; prisoners had different reactions to their numbers. Erna F. Rubinstein, for instance, felt a certain relief when she looked at the digits burned into her skin: "I was to be a number from now on, Number A-19348 forever after. Curiously, as a number it was easier to cope. Stripped of clothes, feelings, moral obligations, and human qualities, one was better off being a number" (p. 130). Rubinstein bore her number as an automaton, using it as a shield against any feelings concerning the present and any associations from the past. With so much of their former life stripped from them, some prisoners felt it best to leave their names behind as well. Isaacson describes an unusual encounter with a kindred spirit: "I reciprocated by giving my name — a rare exchange in Birkenau" (p. 80). Viktor E. Frankl remembers his first moments at the death camp when he was surrounded by others who were unable to "grasp the fact that everything would be taken away" (p. 12). Absolutely everything — and that included one's name. Frankl evaluates that "the first phase of my psychological reaction" to the death camps was the moment when "I struck out my whole former life" (p. 12). To be reminded of the past was to be made aware of all that had been stolen; acknowledging that there was no past seemed to help some cope.

As soon as liberation came, the prisoners shed their numbers — at least, those who wore them only on their clothes. For those whose numbers were inked into their skin, the prison number was harder to abandon. Some survivors chose to have their numbers removed by a doctor or a tattooist. In *Return to Auschwitz*, Kitty Hart details her unsuccessful campaign of persuasion to have her mother, who endured the camps with her, see a doctor in order to remove the skin and its numbers. Hart eventually achieved her success after her mother's death, "and now it is in pickle along with my own. A gruesome relic; but such relics must be preserved" (p. 23). Hart includes photographs of both skins with their numbers with this annotation: "My mother's Auschwitz tattoo, 39933, and my own, 39934, removed from our forearms after the war and preserved as evidence of the days when we were just nameless numbers in the death camp" (pages of photographs not numbered). In abandoning their numbers, survivors rejected their prisoner status and reclaimed their personhood. Author Ka-tzetnik 135633 may appear to be the exception to that rule; however, he published literature other than Shoah texts under his Israeli name Yehiel De-Nur. When De-Nur wrote about the *hurban*, however, he wished to honor those who were never able to reclaim their rightful names, and so he kept the Ka-tzetnik designation.

The individual's name is an essential part of who each individual is. "Writing their memoirs, all survivors assert their name," Patterson argues, "the name that came under assault during the Shoah" ("Twilight" p. 22). While I concur with Patterson's statement, I think that a further step must be taken in analyzing the name phenomenon. I am intrigued by the number of Shoah lifewritings where incongruity exists between the name on the cover and the name of the lifewriter. The reality of the situation undermines Lejeune's confident assertion that the names can and must be identical. "We know all too well how much each of us values his/her name," Lejeune states (p. 14). Despite his examination of multiple nomenclature possibilities, Lejeune does not bring up the subject of Shoah survivors' name changes.

Survivors' name changes occurred for a variety of reasons, reasons that resonate with Ka-tzetnik's preoccupation with Jacob wrestling with the angel. The Jews who were liberated had wrestled with the mighty power of *Night and Fog*; many lifewriters regard their old selves as dead and what exists now as something quite different. Holocaust autobiographies signal the cataclysm undergone by the authors with the disruption of name and narrator. One could, of course, quickly challenge my assertion by pointing out the long and respectable history of the pen name. Lejeune observes: "A pseudonym is a name that is different from the one found in vital statistics.... The pseudonym is the name of an *author*. It is not exactly a false name, but a pen name, a second name, exactly like the one a religious assumed upon taking orders" (12, emphasis in text). I disagree with Lejeune on this point. An author chooses his or her own pseudonym. As for those entering a religious order, depending on the order's tradition, the individual would either submit a choice for a religious name or would have a name assigned. Thus, while the monk or nun may or may not have self-selected the name, the decision to enter an order was voluntary, presumably. There are many reasons a person — and an author —

Five: Israel in Auschwitz

might choose a new name, but with the Holocaust lifewriter, the name may reveal the persistence of the Nazi ontological attack. *Hurban* memoirists' lives have been fragmented, and the rupture is textualized in the conflict of names. Among such autobiographers whose lives and names were forever changed by the Final Solution are Michal Berg/Alexander Donat, Celia Landau/Lucille Eichengreen, Lucjan Salzman/George Lucius Salton, Hans Maier/Jean Améry, and Pavel Friedländer/Saul Friedländer.

The author of *The Holocaust Kingdom* is Alexander Donat, yet a short declarative sentence opens the second paragraph with the words, "My name was Michal Berg" (p. 3). Readers' expectations are thus quickly undermined on the book's first page: Why does Michal Berg have the name Alexander Donat on the book's spine and cover? Why does Berg refer to himself and his birth name in the past tense? Added to that mystery is a footnote in the current edition of Donat's memoir, wherein the editor states that the author's "actual name was Aleksander Grynberg" (p. 3, footnote 1). To complicate the matter even further, the author's son states in his "Afterword" that his father's birth name was Mojzesz (Moses) Grynberg, and was called Saszek and later, Alexander (p. 316). A reader may suspect that the clash of names mirrors the disruption in the lives of those whom the Nazis singled out for death. The dissonance in nomenclature indicates a larger pattern found in Shoah autobiographies, a testimony concerning the absolute break between the life lived before the Nazis' rise to power and the life lived after their defeat.

Berg/(Grynberg)/Donat eventually explains the name change, a change which both blessed him and injured him in a manner that asks us to recall Jacob's name change to Israel. Before the war, Michal Berg was content with his life, enjoying his work and building a satisfying relationship with his wife and son. That life disappeared upon the arrival of the Nazis. He suffered through a series of nine concentration camps, including the most infamous: Auschwitz, Majdanek, Dachau, Treblinka, and Ravensbrück. In 1944, barely able to function, Berg kept receiving contradictory advice from fellow inmates about whether it was better to stay where he was, in Vaihingen, or to try to get transferred out of the camp by being assigned to a different work crew. In the Gray Zone, as Levi calls the concentration camp world, information was spurious, uncertain, and ever-changing. When the situation turned against Berg, he describes how his destiny — his life and his death — changed because of his exclusion from the work crew list.

> The list had been turned over to the Germans and there was no room for me. As I stood there in the corridor, dejected, a young boy approached. He was weeping. His family had been murdered, he told me, and he had only one brother left. Now he was being transferred and his brother was remaining in Vaihingen. I had a brainstorm: "Let's swap places," I said.
> I could barely keep the boy from kissing my hands.... His brother fixed it up with our Lagerälteste [barracks' leader] so that when he called out the numbers of those to be transferred I would step forward and he would simply not notice it: the Germans did not know us by name anyway. And so it was done. When the Lagerälteste called out, "Number 1398, Donat," the name by which I was henceforth to be known, I took my place in the column to be shipped out [p. 221, brackets mine].

Michael Berg became Alexander Donat because he and another switched places, a decision that seemed to be mutually beneficial. Berg/Donat learned what happened to the young boy who became Michal Berg: "Later we learned that two weeks after we left, all work on the Vaihingen construction project ceased and the remaining workers were sent [to a different site]. All of them died in the killing labor of that impassable swamp except for one man..." (p. 221–222). That one person was not the boy, Alexander Donat, who had only wanted to be with his brother. The author reflects: "Officially, I died there, too. Had it not been for that chance, last-minute encounter, I would have shared their fate. *Hic obiit Berg, Donat natus est*; here Berg died and Donat was born" (p. 222, italics in text). One must wonder at the author's choice of Latin for his explanation. Because Berg's death was decreed by non–Jews, Berg suggests that it was most appropriate to announce the death and birth in a language not associated with Jews. Moreover, the Latin conjures up Catholic associations, thereby underscoring Berg/Donat's death and resurrection. Perhaps it is simply the heteroglossia of a learned man. Regardless of the Latin, Michal Berg honors the life of Alexander Donat, a young boy who died as a slave to the Nazis in a swamp, and ransoms him, as it were, from anonymous death.

Lucille Eichengreen identifies her pre-war name at the beginning of her autobiography by portraying her loving father waking her with a kiss on her cheek. She recalls him saying, "'It's time to get up, Celia'" (p. 1). Celia Landau survived the Holocaust, but her family did not. War-rav-

Five: Israel in Auschwitz

aged and alone, she made her way to the United States in 1946. "I was a long way, not only in miles, from the life I had known and the little girl I had been," she mused about her entry into New York City (p. 175). She had to tell herself "over and over again how lucky I was, [yet] I felt forsaken in a strange land" (p. 177). Her exile made her feel adrift, and as many other survivors discovered, the physical presence of a survivor made others feel uncomfortable. Landau tried to cope, and soon her adaptation to American life extended to her very name. Her friend "suggested that I apply for American citizenship and, at the same time, change my first name from Cecilia to Lucille. [She] pointed out that my German and Polish nickname, 'Cilli,' would be pronounced 'silly' in English. 'Lucille sounds more American,' she stated. I decided to follow her advice, but I kept Cecilia as my middle name" (p. 178). Celia experienced a situation common to immigrants to the United States: she must adjust to American lack of language proficiency by changing her name so that Americans could find it easier to say. A European Cecilia Landau is transformed into an Americanized Lucille Landau and, after her marriage, to Lucille Eichengreen. The name transformation testifies not only to the Americanization of a Shoah survivor but also to the name change that most women undergo upon marrying, a cultural-linguistic signifier that proclaims a shift, potentially, in how women might see themselves. If Cecilia felt any regret upon changing her first name—and the tone of her writing implies that she did—readers might wonder if she were reluctant to part with her family name, Landau, her last connection to her beloved father, murdered by the Nazis.

Lucjan Salzman tells his story in *The 23rd Psalm: A Holocaust Memoir*. A Polish Jew, Salzman survived ghettoes, slave labor camps, and concentration camps; after liberation, he eventually made his way to the United States in 1947. He summarizes his condition as an immigrant: "I was nineteen. I spoke little English, had barely any education, no money, and only a few belongings other than the clothes on my back" (p. 228). Such was the case for countless survivors; many did not know the language of the country that accepted them after the war; young Jews had little formal education because it had been banned early in their youth; there was no real opportunity to possess belongings or money. Teenagers, though, had the best chance for survival in the camps; they were neither too young nor too old, sparing them the immediate selection for death. Adolescents might typically have had more physical stamina than those who were younger or older. When Salzman arrived in New York, he was asked by an immigration officer if he wanted to "Americanize" his name (p. 228). "I remembered the danger, under the Germans, of having a Jewish name. In an instant I, Lucjan Salzman, became George Lucius Salton" (p. 228). Americans reading that sentence might be startled, believing that no Jew should fear having a "Jewish name" in the United States. However, it might be well to remember that many Jews, particularly Western European Jews, had viewed pre–Nazi Germany as a pinnacle of education and culture. Millions of European Jews could not have dreamed that an industrial-style slaughter, an anti–Semitic genocide, would have been generated by the Germans, of all people.

Michal Berg willingly kept another's name in order to honor that person's memory, whereas Lucille Eichengreen changed her first name so that she would not appear "silly." George Lucius Salton selected his own new name so as to avoid any potential anti–Semitic attack. Jean Améry rejected his birth name, Hans Maier, because his home country of Germany had rejected him. Neither an autobiography nor a memoir, Améry's *At the Mind's Limits* is, as the subtitle suggests, a series of intellectual "contemplations by a survivor on Auschwitz and its realities." His book is nevertheless insistently autobiographical, as every page records his encounter with the Third Reich and his subsequent scars. Améry himself does not reveal that the name on the book's cover was not the name he had received at birth. Rather, in the book's foreword, Alexander Stille uncovers the hidden nomenclature discrepancy. Stille explains that "Jean Améry was born in Vienna in 1912 with the name Hans Maier. Améry is an anagram of the alternate form, Mayer. The story of how Maier became Améry is the story of his life" (p. vii–viii). Maier's story begins with his father, a Jewish man who "died fighting for his Kaiser before his son could get to know him" (p. viii). Despite his father's military death in the Kaiser's service, his son would learn later that to Hitler, no matter how long a Jewish family had lived in Austria or Germany or how patriotic that family had been, they were still foreigners, usurpers. Countless German and Austrian Jewish men who ended up in ghettos and concentration camps were bewildered that their military service (or their fathers') to the Kaiser in the Great War did not spare them harsh treatment. The dismissal of Améry's father's sacrifice combined with the physical torture the SS meted out to him caused him to break with his homeland.

German and Austrian Jews labored, whether they were segregated or assimilated, says Améry, under the mistaken belief that they were at home in a country in which they had lived for generations. "We, however, had not lost our country," Améry reflects, "but [we] had to realize that it had never been ours. For whatever was linked with this land and its people was an existential misunderstanding" (p. 50). Such a "misunderstanding" would cost their future generations their lives. Surviving the war despite the physical and psychological torture inflicted upon him by the SS, Améry felt compelled to reinvent himself. "Exactly how to define myself I did not know, since my past and my origin had been confiscated from me" (p. 58). No longer willing to accept Germany, the country, its heritage, or its language, the German Hans Maier became French intellectual Jean Améry. Even that was not enough to transcend his haunted past; acknowledging that to be tortured once was to be tortured forever, Améry killed himself.

Unlike the authors mentioned above, Saul Friedländer did not experience planet Auschwitz, but his life was radically altered because of the Nazis. Born Pavel Friedländer to non-observant Jews living in Poland, he survived the war in France because his parents placed him in a Catholic boarding school. As a condition of his acceptance into the school, he was baptized, catechized, and raised thereafter as a Catholic. His parents' acquiescence to the school's insistence upon young Pavel's baptism must have been heart-wrenching, the adult Friedländer admits; however, he qualifies that acknowledgment. Many devout Jewish parents would not have allowed their children to be baptized, but Friedländer's parents were not religious Jews, so he presumes that the parental dilemma might not have been too searing. To survive the war as a Catholic meant many aspects of Pavel's boyhood would have to change. His name had to be changed; certainly, all Jews in hiding from the Nazis had to change their names if they maintained any contacts with the outside world. For Pavel Friedländer to keep his birth name would endanger not only himself and his family, but his protectors as well. Under the potentially fatal circumstances, it was essential that his name become both French and Catholic: "Paul-Henri Ferland, an unequivocally Catholic name to which Marie was added at my baptism, so as to make it even more authentic, or perhaps because it was an invocation of the protection of the Virgin, the heavenly mother safe from torment, less vulnerable than the earthly mother who at this very moment the whirlwind was already sweeping away" (*When Memory* p. 79).

Children adapt and, over time, Pavel Friedländer was forgotten, even by Pavel Friedländer himself. Vulnerable as children are to their environment, Paul-Henri Marie Ferland became a devout Catholic. So devout, as a matter of fact, that he considered whether he had a call to the priesthood. He explored his possible vocation with a priest, a man who asked him a question that changed his world. The priest stunned Paul-Henri with the query, "'Didn't your parents die at Auschwitz?'" (p. 137). The question became a turning point for the boy. In a dark and murky chapel, Pavel Friedländer/Paul-Henri Ferland found his mind reeling; the physical environment symbolized the darkness of the boy's memory. He realized with discomfort that he did not know what the name Auschwitz meant; he did not know that a Jewish genocide had occurred (p. 137). The priest's question launched the young man on a quest to rediscover his identity. "For the first time," Friedländer remembers, "I felt myself to be Jewish" (p. 138). The priest's attitude "profoundly influenced" the boy because the priest spoke of the Jews "with so much emotion and respect" (p. 138). Among the first actions that Paul-Henri Marie took in reclaiming his past was to return to his first name: "…I asked people to stop using my borrowed name and reassumed the name that was mine" (p. 139). But Pavel's name change is not one of mere return, as a reader can judge by seeing the author's name on the book cover as Saul Friedländer. To Friedländer, Pavel represented the child in Prague, a youth whom the Nazis considered Jewish and yet who was completely uninformed about Judaism. At the age of 15, he left France "to fight in Eretz Israel"—the land of Israel (p. 162). His life became a spiritual trek to find an authentic and vital Jewish life.

Part of that experience was learning Hebrew and taking the name Saul, the Hebrew form of his name. He discovered that learning to read Hebrew allowed him to understand the Bible more fully (p. 12). "The Bible soon fascinated me, and the simplest passages we read were perhaps those that bore the most powerful message, that were infused with the most intense poetry" (p. 12). Because of his fascination with the Scriptures, he began to see parallels between Biblical lives and his own; consequently,

Five: Israel in Auschwitz

that led to his name change. "For me, for example, who had changed my name from Paul to Shaul (Saul) upon arriving in the country, the story of this first king of Israel, told in the Book of Samuel with so much controlled force, became the very image of the tragic: called against his will, and then abandoned by all, even by God, who refuses to answer" (p. 12, parentheses in text). Once again in Shoah lifewriting does the theme of God's abandonment arise. As God forsook the first king of Israel, so too, implies Friedländer, did God desert the twentieth century children of Israel.

The difference in names used before and after the war points to the battle waged by the survivor, a battle of holding onto life, just as Jacob held onto his opponent. A physical and psychological battle ensued for Shoah victims. For those with names other than those given to them before the *hurban*, the clash between pre-war and post-war names may itself represent conflict. Steiner asserts that recognition, even self-recognition, is at its core an aggressive act. "It is, surely, notable that the theory of personality, as it develops from Hegel to Nietzsche and Freud ... is essentially a theory of aggression," he states (*Bluebeard's* p. 52). Our self-awareness emerges out of battle: "All recognition is agonistic. We name our own being, as the Angel did Jacob, after the dialectic of mutual aggression" (p. 52). If Jacob wrestled with the Other, that man/angel/God, then he contended with and prevailed against other powers. If, however, as discussed earlier, Jacob wrestled with himself, as some suggest, then his wrestling match was his struggle within himself. Fass argues, based on an interpretation by Maimonides, that the story should not be read "as about what was happening *to* Jacob, but as about what was happening *within* Jacob.... Alone and in the dark, Jacob wrestled with the darker side of his own being..." (p. 147, italics in text). If, as Steiner suggests, Jacob wrestled with himself, then his agonistic conflict was interior; if, as Fass proposed, Jacob wrestled with his own desires and fears, then Jacob named himself.

The Jews of the Shoah knew clearly enough who their adversary was and with whom they struggled, but, like Jacob, they were injured in the fight. For many, the injury was located in the psyche. Psychologists attest to a survival mechanism employed by some during extreme trauma: the individual essentially wills the self into a split personality. As the ordeal progresses, the victim safely tucks away, as it were, the self-perceived true self and creates an exterior self who must physically endure the event. Such a coping mechanism has helped countless victims by enabling them to get through the trauma. While this helps the victim survive an ordeal, a lingering negative effect occurs when the self is unable to unify after the event. The reintegration of the "true self" proved for many to be a difficult or impossible procedure. The traumatized self remained fragmented.

The Shoah autobiographer sometimes bears witness to his or her own fragmentation. Ka-tzetnik 135633 provides one of the more dramatic textual proofs of his own life's disruption and those whom he honors by publishing under a prison number. All Holocaust lifewriters face the challenge of telling their own unique story using the first-person pronoun, because by writing "I," that "I" signifies an "I" taken away from them under horrific circumstances. In some cases, the lifewriter feels his or her own "I" to be too remote to use comfortably. The autobiographer must wrestle with conveying in words events that defy the imagination. In the case of a survivor having had multiple names, he or she must decide which name to put on the book's cover. With the relatively rare exception of autobiography written in the third person (and Lejeune devotes an entire chapter to that unusual situation), most lifewritings are told in the first person, so that the "I" of the text is understood to be identical to the author's name on the book jacket, which contribute to Lejeune's assertion that an autobiographical pact exists. Most Shoah autobiographies are written in the first person, with the "I" serving as an eyewitness, but some, such as Ka-tzetnik, refrain from the "I." Reclaiming the "I" forces survivors to return to the camps where that "I" was stripped from them; consequently, some Shoah lifewriters seem to testify to their life's displacement by their pronoun usage.

Star Eternal is written primarily in the second person although eventually all pronoun forms are employed. Writing an autobiography in the second person is extremely rare, and a reader could argue that Ka-tzetnik chose this unusual narrative strategy because he could not bear to place himself, his "I," back in the camps. It is not Ka-tzetnik's "I" who is sent to Auschwitz; rather, "you" are. You are whisked away from everything you know; you are starved; you are beaten; you long for release. In such pronoun usage, the Holocaust did not happen to someone else's "I" nor to another's "he" or "she"; instead, "you" are the one pulled into planet

Five: Israel in Auschwitz

Auschwitz's gravity. Only near *Star Eternal*'s conclusion does the author switch to the third person; only in the final chapter does the first-person pronoun emerge, as Ka-tzetnik muses over the juxtaposition of *Wiedergutmachung*—German reparations—and his murdered mother.

Elie Wiesel speaks of himself using the first person in *All Rivers Run to the Sea*, at least for 416 pages; however, in the book's final two pages, he shifts to the third person. He concludes his memoir with an account of "the groom" who, as he paces before his wedding, is fearful that his emotions will overpower him. Wiesel, now distanced to a more anonymous "he," recalls important family members who cannot be at the wedding— his mother, father, and sister, all of whom were murdered by the Nazis. The anticipation of his wedding, an intimate yet public moment, to "the woman he loves" (p. 418) causes the author to displace himself. Yet it is the same author who began his book by acknowledging the fact that an autobiography promises "a special pact with the reader," a pact that promises "a willingness to reveal all" (p. 16). Only a naïve reader would expect an autobiographer to reveal all. Wiesel's shift to the third person at the point in his text that is at once the description of a joyful event and the conclusion of his memoir suggests either modesty or the persistence of mourning.

Ka-tzetnik is keenly aware of the rupture in his life as expressed in his Shoah writings. In *Shivitti*, he shares his interior trauma of being called by his name when he serves as a witness in the Eichmann trial. The Israelis, having captured the fugitive Adolf Eichmann, brought him to Jerusalem to stand trial for his active role in genocide. Ka-tzetnik records his reaction to a judge's question when he took the stand to testify about the concentration camps. When the judge asked if his name is De-Nur, to which he replied affirmatively, he is asked, "'Then why do you hide behind another name in your books?'" (p. 70). The inquiry shakes him: "A routine question, ostensibly, but the moment it flashed into my brain all hell broke loose. Not only did they want me to melt the two identities into one, but they wanted a public confession..." (p. 70). De-Nur/Ka-tzetnik reacted violently, albeit interiorly. In a certain sense, he was two people; he was an Israeli writer and he was a Shoah author. Those two were separate, and the judge's question seemed to him to force a melding of those two entities.

The act of writing about the trial and his reaction seemed to bring about an epiphany for Ka-tzetnik. He confesses that it was only as he was writing the words for the book *Shivitti* that he realized that he was writing in the first person (p. 70).

> Until now, all of my books have used the third person, even though I've had to go through contortions doing so. All I've ever written is in essence a personal journal, a testimonial on paper of I, I, I: I who witnessed ... I who experienced ... I who lived through ... I, I, I, till half through a piece, I suddenly had to transform the *I* into *he*. I felt the split, the ordeal, the alienation of it, and worst of all — may God forgive me — I felt like the Writer of Literature. But still I knew unless I hid behind the third person, I wouldn't have been able to write at all [p. 71, ellipsis and italics in text].

Writing in the third person was the only way, until his psychological breakthrough in Holland, that De-Nur could face Ka-tzetnik's past.

Ka-tzetnik's discomfort during the Eichmann trial was not strictly an interior crisis; Hannah Arendt notes with disapproval his testimony in her important and controversial *Eichmann in Jerusalem* (p. 224). Prior to judging his performance, she sets up his need to explain his name. "He started off, as he had done at many of his public appearances, with an explanation of his adopted name. It was not a 'pen name,' he said. 'I must carry this name as long as the world will not awaken after the crucifying of the nation ... as humanity has risen after the crucifixion of one man'" (p. 224, ellipsis in text). Ka-tzetnik seemed to take too long to explain himself, and even then, too poetically, for Arendt's taste. Arendt's frustration with him indicated that she was impatient with, or unaware of, Ka-tzetnik's psychological need to hide "behind the third person."

Some Shoah survivors admit that writing in the first person is a challenge, almost an indomitable one. Eugene Heimler explains that he had to disassociate himself from the turmoil that surrounded him in the concentration camp: "I began to view myself as if I weren't myself at all, but someone quite different, as though I were at home, sitting comfortably in an armchair, watching the scenes of some film of which I myself was the hero being projected before my own eyes" (p. 92). However, Heimler wrestles with how to think of himself—first person or third person: "I seemed to be attempting to justify this trick of thinking in the third person by the conviction that I was watching scenes from the chapters of a book I would one day write, which made it essential to lower this little curtain between myself and the world. That this book might be written in the first person singular I never dared to think" (p. 92). Only the distance of time, with its occasional gift of diminishing pain, allowed Heimler to make use of the "I."

The coping mechanism of splitting oneself into two is recognized by mental health care professionals as a necessary, even inventive, way for a person to survive extreme trauma. Stiffel admits to using that psychological device when he was tortured by the SS. "I made myself separate from me," he states, watching himself and his beaten body as an outsider (p. 146–147). Such a strategy was not restricted to Jews, nor was it limited to only war-time duration. Charlotte Delbo, who was arrested by the Nazis because of her Communist activities and later sent to Auschwitz, explains that she did the same. "I live within a twofold being. The Auschwitz double doesn't bother me, doesn't interfere with my life. As though it weren't I at all. Without this split I would not have been able to revive" (p. 3). Because the camps were an entirely different universe, as the often-used phrase *l'univers concentrationnaire* suggests, then having an "Auschwitz double" may have been the most understandable means to survive that anyone could have used.

The long-term effects of extreme trauma and the incomplete nature of liberation itself have a profound impact upon survivors; nevertheless, it must be stated that most survivors were thankful that they — somehow — lived until liberation. The fact that many, if not most, could eventually reclaim a life that had happiness and normalcy in it is impressive. Lena Berg rejoiced when she discovered that both her husband and her child were also alive: "Life had the promise of new happiness. We were not only liberated, we were saved" (p. 312). Judith Magyar Isaacson credits a question posed to her after a speech as the impetus for writing her autobiography. A college student who had heard her speak of the concentration camp asked her, "'After all you've been through, how can you smile? So freely? So often?'" (p. xi). Survivors' autobiographies are filled with the names of children and grandchildren, many of whom are named for deceased family members, as is traditional in the Jewish community; the names often pay tribute to loved ones who perished in the war.

Yet even as they relate happy occurrences, most survivors reveal the effects of a life lived in the midst of so much death. Everything is tainted.

Imagery from *Genesis* in Holocaust Memoirs

Isabella Leitner exults when she and her husband learn that she is pregnant; she cries out to her murdered mother, "*Mama, you did not die!*" (p. 97, italics in text). Upon her son's birth, she again addresses her mother: "He is the sound of your soul. He is the voice of the six million" (p. 98). Whether or not the son can bear the burden of the six million is not addressed. Significantly, the title of Leitner's lifewriting is *Fragments of Isabella: A Memoir of Auschwitz*. All Shoah autobiographies are fragments: a book can contain only a fragment of the ordeal undergone by the author, and the fragmented author bears the trauma's wounds.

The fragmentation of extreme trauma, suggested by Holocaust writers in their name changes and in their pronoun usage, is profound. Individuals who experience post-traumatic stress show such long-term symptoms as insomnia, nightmares, and an inability to trust. Donat, for instance, reports in a postscript to *The Holocaust Kingdom* that he has enjoyed a happy marriage and a good relationship with his son (p. 363). "Of course," he states, casually yet tellingly, "I have sleeplessness and nightmares..." (p. 363). Only comparatively recently has post-traumatic stress syndrome been described and categorized by mental health care professionals; in the late 1940s and throughout the subsequent decades, survivors were on their own as they coped with various symptoms, including flashbacks to the horrors they experienced. Survivors may rebuild their lives and create new families, but, for most, there are homes, belongings, and loved ones that can be neither forgotten nor replaced. David Wdowinski admits that "those of us who have survived are condemned unto death to an incomprehensible loneliness" (p. 18). Survivors who were unable to build trusting relationships experienced a solitary life.

Solitude is an important element in the wrestling match between Jacob and the stranger, according to Geoffrey Hartman. He grounds this upon a rabbinic insight that saw a connection between Jacob and God. On the evening before reuniting with his brother, Jacob stayed alone by the river; some rabbis link his aloneness with the aloneness of God as found in Deuteronomy 33:26, "There is none like God" ("Struggle" p. 7). Hartman argues: "The word alone acquires two senses: only Jacob, among all men, is noble and straight enough to be compared with God; but also, more radically, the loneliness of the human Jacob in this encounter can remind us of the aloneness of God" (p. 7). If Shoah survivors are like

Jacob, then they, too, bear the trait of the loneliness of Jacob. As Wiesel observes, survivors, who are necessarily in exile from their former lives, are marked by solitude ("We Are" p. 27). Fractured from the battle with self, with others, and with a higher power, the survivor's autobiography testifies to the long-term consequences of the fight. When the self is broken, it may be that it can never be made whole. The individual departs the concentration camps, the war is over, but the rupture is deep.

And We Are Not Saved, the title of Wdowinski's autobiography, emphasizes his sense of liberation as a by-product, not a goal, of the successful Allied armies. In Wiesel's cantata, Jacob cries out to God: "Do you hear, / God of my father and my father's father? / My struggle with the angel / Ended in defeat. / Israel lost—/ And I did not know it" (*Ani* p. 47). Auschwitz represented defeat, a defeat that carried into post-war life. The liberation ended one struggle on one level, but those liberated from Nazi tortures had many battles left to fight. "Where is it, this liberation?" asks Ka-tzetnik (*Star* p. 110). Many Jews did return home; many were met with defiant attitudes expressing surprise that any Jews were still alive. Out of necessity, many survivors created new homes and new lives in countries other than their homelands.

Some, such as Saul Friedländer, found a physical and spiritual home in *Eretz Israel*, the land of Israel; others were displaced throughout the Diaspora. Most survivors found instructions, implicit and explicit, from those around them that they were to keep silent about their ordeal. Kitty Hart entitles her memoir's first chapter, "The Promised Land," which is not Israel, but rather it is England. She conveys her sense of excitement that after being "close to death so many times," she and her mother face a new and hope-filled life in England (p. 11). However, her uncle who greeted them upon arrival "staggered us by saying firmly: 'Before we go [home] there is one thing I must make quite clear. On no account are you to talk about any of the things that have happened to you. Not in my house. I don't want my girls upset. And I don't want to know'" (pp. 11–12). Hart's experience was common. A new life had to be forged, often in a new country that necessarily meant a new language, and in the midst of creating a new beginning, the old could not be discussed.

Wiesel identifies his situation as "exile" and defines that estrangement from his native home as pervasive. "It envelopes all endeavors, all explorations, all illusions, all hopes, all triumphs, and this means that whatever we do is never complete. Our life is not complete, and lo and behold, our death is not complete..." ("We Are" p. 27). Nothing is or feels complete. Incompleteness is a hallmark of autobiography. All autobiography is fragmentary, the Shoah texts only more so. "In the life I live and experience from within myself," Bakhtin observes, "my own birth and death are events which I am in principle incapable of experiencing" ("Author" p. 104). Since a person cannot express his/her perspective on his/her birth or death — those highly significant and dramatic moments of an individual's life — a sense of wholeness is necessarily absent from autobiography.

Jacob wrestled by the river Jabbok, and his children wrestled within Auschwitz. Were they blessed in that struggle? Wiesel would refute such a claim. In *Ani Maamin*, Jacob pours out his anguish to God: "As for me, O God, I yearn to die as Jacob —/ To prevent Israel from being. / You promised me so many things, my Lord. / You promised me to watch over Israel —/ Where are you? What of your promise? / You promised me blessings for Israel —/ Is this your blessing?" (p. 23). The questions are legitimate ones, both for Jacob, now Israel, and for those who underwent the Nazi assault.

David Patterson analyses the Nazi attack on Jewish names and personhood in *Wrestling with the Angel*. Recalling "an ancient Jewish legend" (p. xiv), he tells the story: after a person is buried, the Angel of Death escorts that person into the Holy One's Presence where a test is given. "The question is the same for all, but for each the answer is different" (p. xv). The question? "What is your name?" (p. xv). Based in the Hebraic understanding that a name carries with it ontological significance, to know one's name is essential, in both this life and the next. Patterson uses that legend throughout his analysis on the Nazi rupture of Jewish life and names, and he convincingly argues that a survivor asserts his or her name when writing an autobiography. While Patterson is right, the question lingers for many Shoah Jews: which name? Jacob wrestled with a power and received an injury even as he received his blessing— his new name. The Jews of Hitler's time also struggled against a mighty force. They too were injured. Survivors might say that their liberation was a blessing, but, like Jacob's, the gift is attached to an unforgettable hurt. Some see the trauma as not unique to European Jews of the Third Reich, but they understand the wider implications throughout the entire Jewish community, even to today.

In his memoir *Turbulent Souls*, Stephen Dubner traces the remarkable spiritual journey his devout Catholic parents experienced as they left the Judaism of their childhood to embrace the theology and lifestyle of 1950s American Catholicism. Reclaiming a Jewish identity of which he was unaware, Dubner finds the Jacob story an apt one: "...for to be a Jew was to live forever with the knowledge that the Holocaust had scarred your people as irrevocably as Jacob had been scarred by his encounter with the angel" (p. 283).

Genesis records that Jacob's name change was a blessing, and, as Hartman aptly comments, the name Israel is a more elevated name than that of "heel." Many of Jacob's twentieth-century children had their names changed; however, those names cannot always be seen as an elevation. The scars from their *hurban* battle are deep within the skin and the psyche. Liberated from a world of death into a world of grief in order to begin their mourning, survivors learned to live with their broken lives, if they could. Less a joyful embrace of freedom, liberation became for many a lacuna.

CHAPTER SIX

Fratricide

> The burnt offering exudes a fiery glow in the dark. In heaven a chimney opens to receive the smoke of Abel's offering as it ascends ever upward into the all-consuming void. Cain's upward gaze is riveted on the opening in the heavenly chimney, on the fiery glow of Abel's offering; on the flaming torch of Jews that is in the empty field of the border town. His hand sweeps up into the salute: *Heil Hitler!*
> — Ka-tzetnik 135633

Cain and Abel: Genesis 4:1–26

By concluding this study of Biblical imagery with a focus on Cain and Abel, we must return to an early chapter of *Bereshit*. However, it is appropriate to end the study with this particular Scriptural text. The philosophical implications made by several Shoah lifewriters who allude to humanity's first murder demand contemplation. Significant among the Second World War's legacies of horror, as generated by the Nazis' bloodlust, is the sheer number of people killed. Even beyond the genocide perpetrated by the Nazis, modern technology and military progress ensured greater numbers of combatant deaths as well as civilian deaths. Appalling too is the number of people slaughtered by the Nazis, a number that is greater than the six million Jews. Yet the core meaning of the Holocaust is that six million Jews, some one million of them children, were killed, and they were murdered in genuinely horrifying ways. How the Final Solution was implemented, and how successful it was, and the relative inaction of the world, comingle into anguish when studying the Shoah. The Nazi war against the Jews forces us to consider a theological conundrum: As Wiesel puts it, the Holocaust can be understood neither with God nor without God (*Evil* p. 52). Even if God is completely removed

Six: Fratricide

from the struggle to understand the Shoah, there is still the mystery of why one group of people would wish to murder another group. Several lifewriters see in the genocide the ancient story of Cain and Abel, acted out on the world stage by Hitler.

A word about the masculine terms that I will use in this chapter: Throughout this book I have avoided using sexist language, although at times I needed to use masculine pronouns in reference to the Lord, as that was how the Hebrew Scriptural writers saw the deity, and I used masculine pronouns when speaking about rabbis who, until very recently, were always men. Because of the Genesis story that I will now turn to — Cain and Abel — I will refer to the broader implications of their story by using masculine terms such as brother, mankind, and fratricide. Certainly women killed other women during the Event, particularly female camp officials, kapos, and their collaborators. The number of men who killed other men significantly outweighs the number of female murderers, and so, within the historical and Biblical context, the use of the term "fratricide" seems appropriate. For some Shoah autobiographers, the Biblical brothers' story propels to the forefront the physical and metaphysical injustice of killing. By drawing upon the Cain and Abel story, Jewish writers link their common humanity to the Germans and their collaborators, a commonality the Nazis refused to see. A Jew and a German, mortal enemies at the time (at least in Nazi eyes) were, at the most profound yet basic level, brothers. Thus the Germans and those who co-operated with them were engaged in fratricide as they murdered Jews, Roma, homosexuals, priests, nuns, Communists, Jehovah's Witnesses, and countless others.

Genesis 4 tells the story of Adam and Eve's sons, born in a post–Eden existence. After being banished from Paradise, their old life permanently shattered, Adam and Eve nevertheless showed the human trait of resiliency as they created a new life for themselves. Their new start generated new birth as Eve bore Cain (Genesis 4:1) and then another son, Abel (Genesis 4:2).

> Now the man knew his wife Eve, and she conceived and bore Cain, saying, "I have gained a male child with the help of the LORD." She then bore his brother Abel. Abel became a keeper of sheep, and Cain became a tiller of the soil. In the course of time, Cain brought an offering to the LORD from the fruit of the soil; and Abel, for his part, brought the choicest of the firstlings of his flock. The LORD paid heed to Abel and his offering, but to Cain and his offering He paid no heed. Cain was much distressed and his face fell [Genesis 4:1–5].

Imagery from *Genesis* in Holocaust Memoirs

Deftly and succinctly, the boys enter into Judeo-Christian myth. Robert Alter explains that Cain's name, whose etymology ties it to *smith*, is, in Hebrew, *qayin*, which "puns on the verb *qanah*, 'to get,' 'acquire,' or perhaps, 'to make'" (p. 16, footnote 1). Acknowledging that Genesis does not provide an etymology for Abel's name, Alter suggests that "it has been proposed that the Hebrew *hevel*, 'vapor' or 'puff of air,' may be associated with his fleeting life span" (p. 16, footnote 2). Furthermore, a traditional typological reading of the story concludes that because Cain was a farmer and Abel was a shepherd, an historic tension exists between the occupations. The first children born of the first humans, at least as far as the stories of Genesis 1–4 are concerned (the subject of Cain's wife need not concern us here) reveal that although they are siblings, one resents the other. In a plot device that will echo throughout Scripture, the elder brother feels threatened by the younger.

Abel lives for only a few verses. Sarna speculates that it must have been, at one time, part of a longer work; what *Bereshit* offers "is tantalizingly incomplete. The narrative of events is extraordinarily terse and sketchy" (p. 28). After establishing that Abel's sacrifice was more pleasing to God than was Cain's (rabbinic speculation abounds why that was so), Abel is tempted to kill his brother. In a poetic passage, God warns Abel, and, for the first time, the word *sin* occurs in the Bible:

> And the LORD said to Cain, "Why are you distressed, / And why is your face fallen? / Surely, if you do right, / There is uplift. / But if you do not do right / Sin couches at the door; / Its urge is toward you, / Yet you can be its master." Cain said to his brother Abel ... and when they were in the field, Cain set upon his brother Abel and killed him. The LORD said to Cain, "Where is your brother Abel?" And he said, 'I do not know. Am I my brother's keeper?" Then He said, "What have you done? Hark, your brother's blood cries out to Me from the ground! Therefore, you shall be more cursed than the ground, which opened its mouth to receive your brother's blood from your hand. If you till the soil, it shall no longer yield its strength to you. You shall become a ceaseless wanderer on earth" [Gen. 4:6–12, slashes and ellipsis in text].

These compact six verses contain three important elements: the ellipsis following Cain's statement to his brother, God's question to Cain, and Abel's blood crying out from the earth. Each of these three elements will be considered over the course of this chapter.

The Plaut *Commentary* speaks specifically about the ellipsis that immediately follows "Cain said to his brother": "The text does not quote

Six: Fratricide

what was said. The Septuagint and Targum supply these words: 'Come, let us go out into the field.' However, the omission of what Cain said may be a purposeful ellipsis" (p. 44). Thus, some Biblical translators feel compelled to provide Cain's missing, and perhaps explanatory, words. Knowing the outcome, translators may have felt that their interpretation was logical. Other translators were content to abide with the ellipsis. Because readers are not told by the Biblical writer what Cain said to Abel, the lacuna resonates powerfully out of the void. The inversion of the story, as realized during the Final Solution, is that the Nazis very clearly stated their intention regarding the Jews during the Wannsee Conference, the gathering of the minds that planned the mass murder. Their specific goals and plans were not explicitly relayed to the rest of the world, but many could correctly interpret the Nazis' intentions.

Seven times the author of Genesis points out that Cain and Abel were brothers. Seven is a significant number in the Hebrew Scriptures; clearly, the Biblical author wished to emphasize the familial relationship between the two young men. Ultimately, Abel's murder teaches humanity that "all homicide is at the same time fratricide" and that any "crime against [a human being] is a sin against God" (Sarna p. 31). A Midrash on this first murder, this fratricide, asserts that the lesson is "that one man's life is equal to all of creation" (qtd. in Plaut p. 49). If the Talmud teaches that "to save one person is to save the world entire"—a rabbinical precept contained within, and made widely known by, Steven Spielberg's film *Schindler's List*—then it must also be true that to take one person's life is to assault the entire world. The principle "that one [person's] life is equal to all of creation" is at the heart of Holocaust allusions to Cain and Abel.

At first glance, it may appear that Cain and Abel is a natural story to convey the context of the Nazis and the Jews. Cain committed the violent act. The Genesis author provides no clear motivation. Jealousy is usually understood as a primary cause of the violence; the concept of sin may be external (it was an entity that couched by Cain's door) or it may be internal (a symptom of the soul's perversity). Abel was Cain's innocent victim. If the genocidal Nazis are Cain and the murdered victims are Abel, the division of Nazis/Cain and Jews/Abel is clear and logical.

Abel J. Herzberg equated the Jews with Abel, whose blood cries out from the ground. He saw the theme of Cain and Abel murderously played out when he was incarcerated at Bergen-Belsen for the crime of being Jewish. Designated a "privileged Jew," Herzberg was in the unusual situation of having the physical materials — paper and pencil — by which he could keep a diary. This journal, only recently printed in English, provides a fascinating glimpse into Bergen-Belsen's daily life. Originally written in Dutch, Herzberg captured the effects of systematic starvation, exposure to deadly diseases, and the impact of mind-numbing, constant fear. He wrote with literary skill and theological insights about the events that surrounded him, even as the diary recorded the toll camp life took on him. Life and death swirled in an unending pattern of night and day, despair and hope. In echoes of Biblical language, he notes: "it becomes evening and it becomes morning. One day there will probably be peace again and then war again" (p. 53). Scriptural images weave throughout his writing, but a dominant motif is that of Cain and Abel.

Of particular relevance is his September 4, 1944, entry. In a remarkably theologically dense entry, before hunger's disorientation hampers him, he reflects on two types of religious belief: the monotheists and the polytheists. The fatal collusion of worldviews between the monotheists and polytheists intrigues Herzberg, although he does not designate who he assigned to each particular religious viewpoint. The monotheists, nevertheless, must certainly be the Jews, who worship one God, the God of Abraham, Isaac, and Jacob. The polytheists, given the context of Herzberg's writing, must be either the Nazis specifically, with their pagan-like worship of Hitler, or the polytheists could be all Christians generally, because the concept of the Trinitarian Godhead is seen by non–Christians as polytheistic. Herzberg argues that the polytheist hates the monotheist. In his diary, he invents a scenario wherein the monotheist, the Jew, is a symbol for memory. Herzberg puts it this way: the monotheist confronts the polytheist "with the incomprehensible, agonizing question: Cain, Cain, where is your brother Abel?" (p. 67). The monotheist, the Jew, is a sign of a people who worship one God, but in Herzberg's entry, the Jew becomes a sign of God. God asked Cain where Cain's brother was; in Herzberg's diary, the Jew asked the same question to the non–Jew.

According to *Bereshit*, it was the Lord who confronted Cain concerning Abel's whereabouts; it was the deity who heard the cries of Abel's blood from the earth. Herzberg revisits the theme of Abel's blood in his Septem-

Six: Fratricide

ber 16, 1944, entry. After reflecting upon the Nazi dedication to such idols as strength, victory, and being hard as metal, Herzberg challenges those Nazi ideals. He attacks their validity, if only with a pencil on paper, arguing that those are not true virtues. "Yet the Bible says one has to be righteous. And it not merely says it: but its voice screams, screams in one's blood: 'Cain, Cain, where is your brother Abel!'" (p. 97). With his citation of Genesis 4:9, Herzberg raises two important points: that of the blood itself crying out and that of God asking the murderer where the murder victim is.

Genesis states that Abel's blood cried out from the ground. Perhaps it cried out for recognition, so as not to die forgotten; perhaps it screamed for justice. Rabbi Telushkin observes that in Hebrew, the word translated as *blood* is *d'mei* (p. 27), a noun in plural form — *bloods* (p. 28). The Mishnah concludes that because the word is in the plural, the collective voices of the unborn join in Abel's plea (Plaut p. 49). In Auschwitz, in Bergen-Belsen, and throughout the Reich, the unborn descendents of the murder victims may also have cried out. In a few cases, people such as Primo Levi and Abel Herzberg recorded those cries.

Another significant aspect of Genesis 4:9, mentioned earlier in this chapter and brought up by Herzberg, is that of God asking a question. Judaism is a faith that prizes questions; appropriately, God asks many questions of humanity in that record of origins, *Bereshit*. The Lord's direct question of Cain concerning Abel is the fifth question posed to humanity; both the question and the answer — such as it is — linger throughout the millennia.

According to Genesis, the first question posed by God was, "Where are you?" The Lord asked this of Adam in Genesis 3:9b immediately after Adam and Eve ate the forbidden fruit. The question could be read as a legitimate query by a limited God, or it could be a more ontological invitation for Adam to confess his transgression. Wiesel understands the divine question to be "the primordial question" that compels humanity to constantly assess its role in any given situation (*Evil* p. 157). Adam's inadequate answer causes the Lord to issue two follow-up questions: "Who told you that you were naked? Did you eat of the tree from which I had forbidden you to eat?" (Gen. 3:11). Later in the story of humanity's beginnings, God challenges Cain's emotional reaction to the rejected offering:

"Why are you distressed, / And why is your face fallen?" (Gen. 4:6). Immediately after Cain's slaying of his brother, God asks: "Where is your brother Abel?" (Gen. 4:9). Readers might suspect the question "Where is your brother Abel?" to be in the same mode as the first divine question, "Where are you?" Either the author of *Bereshit* wanted to portray a divine being who was not omniscient and therefore did not know Adam's and Abel's whereabouts, or the portrayal is of an omniscient God who did know but posed the question to invite a response from the guilty. The question itself held the possibility of the respondent entering into a healing dialogue with the Creator.

Cain's reaction was markedly different from his father's answer to God's first question. Adam said, according to Genesis, "I heard the sound of You in the garden, and I was afraid because I was naked, so I hid" (Gen. 3:10). Adam's declaration can be interpreted as a sheepish admission or a confrontational justification, but at least it was some sort of answer. When asked about his brother, Cain did not feel compelled to tell the truth to the Deity. Cain defiantly lied with the retort, "I do not know" and continued with the flippant, "Am I my brother's keeper?" (Gen. 3:8b). That the Lord does not reply to Cain's belligerent question has subsequently preoccupied the rabbis and other theologically-minded readers. The Plaut *Commentary* itself asks questions about Cain's response. "Why is God silent when men kill each other? Where does His power begin and where does it end? God asks man to account for his deeds. Man in turn asks God to account for His" (p. 48). The *Commentary* says that such an interpretation "is appealing" because of its "great urgency today but also because it allows for a direct continuation of the Eden story"; that is, Eden offered a life-and-death scenario while post–Eden poses the choice between good and evil (p. 48). Jews within the Third Reich were in an unprecedented life-and-death situation, but they were not given the choice between good and evil — evil was forced upon them. The Nazis who so single-mindedly sought to exterminate their "inferiors" were confronted by moral choices; they, in the mode of Cain, chose evil.

Isabelle Leitner refers to Cain's comment in her autobiography when describing how solicitous her brother, Philip, was of his sisters and his mother when they all were imprisoned in Auschwitz. However, Leitner's allusion is rooted more in popular culture than in the Scriptural text.

Six: Fratricide

Recalling his many kindnesses and virtues, she says, "Philip, more than any of us, is like my mother, whose heart truly was governed by the words 'I am my brother's keeper'" (p. 29). This not-uncommon misremembering of Genesis 3:8b places human responsibility and compassion within the sentiment that Leitner expressed — an individual does have a duty towards another human being. Cain questioned whether to show care and concern for his sibling (and therefore his fellow human being) was his role. No doubt Philip Leitner's attitude, and not Cain's, is the morally correct one to have, and consequently that may be the reason why the Biblical text is so often misquoted.

That the Jews of the Third Reich could be equated with the murder victim Abel is not surprising. What may be more uncomfortable would be the second way in which the Cain-and-Abel allusion functions, wherein the Jews are identified with Cain. Both Primo Levi and Abel Herzberg explore this connection.

Levi spends considerable time in *The Drowned and the Saved* relating several stories told by Dr. Miklos Nyiszli, a Hungarian doctor forced to experiment on prisoners by order of the infamous Dr. Mengele. Nyiszli published his own memoir, *Auschwitz: A Doctor's Eyewitness Account*, but Levi adds a spiritual dimension. Levi retells Nyiszli's account of the Nazi SS men playing soccer with the Jewish workers of the crematoria, the *Sonderkommando*, known by the initials SK (*Drowned* pp. 54–55). Levi captures the surreal quality of on-looking SS and SK men, cheering on their teams as they play soccer, appearing as if "the game were taking place on the village green" rather than where it was, "at the gates of hell" (p. 55). Levi depicts the bizarre event through the lens of theological interpretation as he imagines the Nazi masters gloating over their Jewish slaves. "Behind this armistice one hears satanic laughter: it is consummated, we have succeeded, you are no longer the other race, the anti-race, the prime enemy of the millennial Reich; you are no longer the people who reject idols" (p. 55). As is common with Levi's prose, his word choices are telling: "satanic" captures the demonic grotesqueness of the situation, the game played in hell, initiated by the inferno's rulers; "consummated" emphasizes both a sense of completion and the connotations of sexual intercourse; "succeeded" establishes the Nazis' triumph over the Jews, a people whom they saw as no longer worshipping only one God, the God of Israel. Levi continues his imaginative Nazi stream of consciousness: "We have embraced you, corrupted you, dragged you to the bottom with us. You are like us, you proud people: dirtied with your own blood, as we are. You too, are like us and like Cain, have killed the brother. Come, we can play together" (p. 55). Spoken, as it were, by the victorious SS to the defeated SK, the SS gloat that they have made their murder victim Abel become one of them, the race of Cain. Brothers have been killed. Families have been burned. The blood cries out from the ground.

Many Shoah survivors, as well as students of the Event, have contemplated the Nazi perversity of pitting Jew against Jew. This divide-and-conquer strategy was considered in an earlier chapter, but the Nazi setting of one Jew against another was seemingly endless. The Nazis devised plans wherein Jews had to police other Jews, which was enforced within both the ghettos and the camps. The Nazis forced Jews to select fellow Jews for deportation, which was part of the responsibility of the ghettos' *Judenräte*. The Nazis created a system wherein Jews were forced to oppress emotionally and physically beat other Jews, as did the *kapos* in the slave-labor and concentration camps. Most grimly of all, within the death camps, the Nazis compelled Jews to assist in the mass murder of other Jews and to dispose of the corpses. Not all of the Nazi concentration camps were extermination camps, although death was everywhere in the Holocaust Kingdom. In the camps that were devoted to systematic murder, the Nazis used Jewish slave labor to cram live bodies into gas chambers and then remove the bodies to the crematoria or to huge pits. According to Levi, the slaughter, initiated by the Nazis who then made the Jews handle the bodies, merged murderer and murdered.

Herzberg recognized the complexity of the Cain and Abel motif playing out in front of his eyes. We have already considered his entry wherein he saw the Jews as Abel. In a different entry, yet written around the same time, he links the Jews with Cain. His lengthy September 1, 1944, entry shows the writer preoccupied with the war's fifth anniversary. He contemplates the mystery of why the Nazis persecute the Jews. The Jews are a people, he says, "who are convicted of crimes they have not committed, who are persecuted yet are innocent, who look at each other and whatever we may think of each other, *know* we are innocent..." (p. 53, emphasis in text). The vitriol poured out upon the Jews throughout the centuries

Six: Fratricide

has created a situation that finds them to be "the eternal scapegoat, the brother of him who was beaten to death, who are branded with the mark of Cain the fratricide..." (p. 53). Although Herzberg does not imply that the Nazis are the hapless Abel, his reference to the Jews being Cain may well surprise many readers.

That Cain was "the eternal scapegoat" suggests to Herzberg that the Jews, eternal scapegoats, are in the line of Cain. Every Jew within the Third Reich had been condemned to be a scapegoat. The ubiquitous phrase, *Die Juden sind unser Unglück*, the Jews are our misfortune, was not unique to Hitler and the Nazis, but they successfully drilled that mantra into the national psyche. Because he is a Jew, Herzberg writes that he was "brother of him who was beaten to death" (p. 53). Such a situation was literally true for Herzberg. His daily life was surrounded by his brother and sister Jews who were beaten to death, to name but one of the almost infinite ways by which the Nazis murdered their victims. As a Jew in a concentration camp, he and millions of other Jews were "branded with the mark": the clothes of the prisoner, the yellow triangle of the Nazi-despised Jew, the shaved head, and, for many, the prison number tattooed on the skin. Genesis states that the Lord "put a mark on Cain, lest anyone who met him should kill him" (Genesis 4:15b). What the "mark of Cain" is, is ambiguous. Genesis does not inform readers what that mark was, and so the text invites a multitude of possibilities. The mark might have been a special garment that Cain could take on or off, or perhaps it was an irremovable symbol on the skin that was prominent for all to see. One school of thought understands the mark to be "a sign of protection against blood revenge"; as such, it was not a punishment or a symbol of rejection (footnote Plaut p. 45). Thus the mark offered protection. Some rabbis understand the mark to be ontological: "Cain himself was the sign that warned men against murder" (p. 45). He embodied the warning, carrying it with him throughout his exile.

Cain's mark and exile might be signs of a relatively benign punishment. Cain's words, as conveyed in Genesis, hardly convey sorrow, but one Midrash considers the primal murderer as capable of regret, and that may be the reason that blood was not demanded for blood. The story is told in *A Rabbinic Anthology*; springing Midrashically off the few words "And Cain went out" (Gen 4:16), one rabbi speculated that Adam, not surprisingly, asked his son about the Lord's judgment (Montefiore p. 316). Cain told his father that he had expressed his sorrow to the Lord and the Lord pardoned him; "When Adam heard that, he smote his face and said, 'Is the power of repentance as great as that? I did not know it was so'" (qtd. in Montefiore 316). The Midrash is intriguing. Was Cain capable of repenting? Cain is not the most reliable of narrators; did he tell his father the truth? Perhaps Cain did repent, off-stage, as it were, where so often the rabbis' imaginations love to roam. If so, Adam's anguish may convey disappointment with himself that he had not repented when the deity challenged him about his transgression. On the other hand, Adam's reaction may reveal anger towards God. Is repenting all that is required for a person to get off, virtually scot-free, from a crime as extreme as murder? And if that is so, and if Midrash comments on modern times, then is that why so many murderers throughout the Holocaust Kingdom received little to no punishment? Left unsaid, as Cain's imagined words were, are expressions of repentance from almost all Nazis and their collaborators.

Whether or not Cain repented before his Creator, Genesis states that he received a mark. More common than interpreting the sign as one of protection is to see the "mark of Cain" as a punishment, a permanent sign pointing to Cain's sin. Wiesel draws upon such an association when he reflects upon the Eichmann trial: "Could there be any punishment for crimes of this magnitude? Cain, after all, exterminated half the human race when he killed his brother, Abel, yet his only punishment was to bear the mark of his crime on his forehead" (*All Rivers* p. 348). Wiesel reads the mark as a sign of Cain's criminality. Such a view is neither unique nor new. The mark of punishment inspired the Christian Church of the thirteenth century to impose such a sign on the Jews: The Fourth Lateran Council, convened by Pope Innocent III in 1215, issued a decree that Jews must wear on their clothes a large, obvious mark, which was typically "a solid yellow circle sewed on to an upper garment" (Telushkin p. 185). Centuries later, the Nazis followed the Lateran Council's lead by requiring Jews to wear a distinctive mark on their clothes; at first, in some locations, it was a blue-and-white arm band, but more commonly, Jews were later required to wear prominently on an outer garment a yellow patch with the word *Jew* on it or a yellow Star of David. Pope Innocent III, prior to the Fourth Lateran Council, wrote in a letter: "'Jews, like the fratricide

Six: Fratricide

Cain, are doomed to wander about the earth as fugitives and vagabonds, and their faces must be covered with shame'" (qtd. in Telushkin pp. 185–186). It appears to be in this spirit that Herzberg writes his reflection on his situation: The Nazis understood each individual Jew to be Cain, a moral leper, someone who needs to be sent out from the body for the common good. Cain and his descendents were a people to be despised and sent into exile. The mark is ignominious, inviting the contempt of the righteous.

When Levi asserts that the Nazis pulled the Jews who they forced to work with them down to their own level, a satanic depth, he conveys a certain desperate energy. Herzberg, however, portrays Cain as a more passive figure than does Levi. For Herzberg, Cain is "the brother of him who was beaten to death"; in this scenario, Cain bears the grief of a survivor, but not the weight of responsibility for committing the fatal violence. While it may not be a common reading of Genesis 4:6–12, it may serve adequately for the twentieth century counterpart.

Still another interpretive level of meaning exists for the Cain and Abel story: It becomes a mystical linking of Jewish Biblical myth with all of Jewish history. As envisioned through the LSD hallucinations of Ka-tzetnik 135633, Cain and Abel stand as an emblem for the eternal human struggle that has played itself out through time. In the previous chapter of this book, we examined Ka-tzetnik 135633's autobiographical writings, including *Shivitti: A Vision*. As a reminder, Ka-tzetnik describes in *Shivitti* his attempts to overcome the Shoah's post-traumatic effects by trying medicinal LSD therapy. The author reveals his preoccupation with Jacob, as we have seen, throughout his nonfiction writings, but in *Shivitti* he sees in the Cain and Abel story Jewish history writ small.

The third medically supervised LSD treatment had Ka-tzetnik seeing himself back in the Auschwitz barracks. The man to whom he spoke kept transforming, moment by moment, into important people of his life, including the Rabbi of Shilev and Vevke the cobbler. Bewildered, Ka-tzetnik said to the man he now sees as Vevke, a man he knew to be dead: "'But Vevke, I saw you lying outside on the heap of corpses behind the barracks'" (p. 59). "'One moment I am Abel, brother to Cain,' Vevke replies, 'one moment I am being bound to the altar; one moment I am crucified in Jerusalem, and one moment I am Reb Nachman the Bretzlaver; one moment I am Vevke with the cobbler's bench, and one moment I am the scab-faced Rabbi of Shilev'" (p. 59). Vevke's pronouncement, funneled through a hallucination, equates the Jewish victim of the Nazis with the totality of Jewish history as conveyed in Biblical myth. Projected onto Vevke is the vast panorama of Jewish history. Vevke was therefore Abel, the first murder victim; Vevke was Isaac, living out the *Akeda*; Vevke was the Jewish Jesus, nailed to a cross; Vevke was the Rabbi of Shilev, whose eyes focused upon God even in the depths of an Auschwitz hell. It is a history, be it of all humanity or of the Hebrew people specifically, that is linked with life, murder, near-murder, and death. It is a story of sin and of obedience, of self-assertion and of spiritual submission.

The co-mingling of ancient Jewish history and myth with modern times shaped Ka-tzetnik's fourth LSD vision. In his penultimate session, he again observed the themes of Genesis played out in Auschwitz. He saw himself digging a grave, and across from the grave stood a Jewish man who had on his head a tefillin, an element of the phylacteries a devout Jew uses for prayer. Mocking Germans crowned the tefillin with thorns, thereby ridiculing the man while equating him with Jesus. Out of the tefillin flowed the letters that make up the *Shema*; those letters floated above the Jew's head. Ka-tzetnik saw a fiery heaven and an earth filled with darkness. "A hand reaches down and grasps this firebrand to kindle Abel's offering" (p. 78); the implication is that the hand must be the Lord's. "The burnt offering exudes a fiery glow in the dark. In heaven a chimney opens to receive the smoke of Abel's offering as it ascends ever upward into the all-consuming void" (p. 78). Cain had a response to the reception of that gift: "Cain's upward gaze is riveted on the opening in the heavenly chimney, on the fiery glow of Abel's offering; on the flaming torch of Jews that is in the empty field of the border town. His hand sweeps up into the salute: *Heil Hitler!*" (p. 78). Was Cain, the first killer, the prototype of the murderous Nazi?

A hand — God's? — reaches out from the heavens and ignites Abel's gift. A hand — Cain's — gestures with the Nazi salute. A hand — Abel's — is not seen, but it had prepared the offering that was acceptable to God. Eternity, myth, and modern history merge in Ka-tzetnik's vision. Ka-tzetnik equates the goodness, the preferment, of Abel's sacrificial gift with the very bodies of Jews being burnt in the crematoria. He presents a com-

Six: Fratricide

plex image: The smoke of Abel's burnt offering lifts up into a "void," yet beyond that emptiness is a heaven with a chimney that captures the smoke. The words "burnt" and "chimney" demand that readers associate Abel with the Jewish victims suffering and dying in the Nazi death machines. Abel's offering becomes Abel himself, dispatched to the heavenly sphere: Cain stands alone as he swings his hand up into the well-known Nazi gesture and the cry, Heil Hitler!

Readers of the Judeo-Christian texts may assert that God did not necessarily have favorites among God's children, but *Bereshit* does state that God judged Abel's gift to be better than Cain's. That is clear, although not explained. A reader might conclude that Scripture suggests that the Lord had a chosen one, a highly favored one, and in the primogeniture culture of the time, it would have been shocking to the elder son that he was not the favored one. Abel could be a foreshadowing figure of the chosen people; Cain could be a warning. Just as God warned Cain that sin, like a vicious beast, was crouching at his door, but Cain allowed sin to master him, so too might the story of Cain himself be a cautionary tale. It states that defiance of God leads to this becoming: a murderer. Ka-tzetnik's evocation of Cain's Nazi salute, the sweeping right hand motioning with vigor into a straight line, declaring allegiance to the Führer, implies that the Germans made a choice, a choice that led them away from a peaceful life with God to a Thousand Year Reich littered with millions dead.

The primal tale of the primal murder testifies both to our common humanity and to our common vulnerability. Dan Pagis captures the timelessness of Adam and Eve, Cain and Abel, in his poem, "Written in Pencil in the Sealed Freightcar." Having endured a Ukrainian concentration camp in his youth, Pagis managed to escape near the war's end; later, he made a commitment to writing poetry in Hebrew. The unutterable that was textualized in Genesis when Cain lures his younger brother to his death is captured in the poem, although the persona is Eve, who herself is being transported to her death in one of Hitler's cattle cars. "Here in this carload / I am Eve / With my son Abel / If you see my older boy / Cain son of Adam / Tell him that I" (Schiff p. 180). In some editions, an ellipsis follows the final "I." Eve has a message, and it has the urgency of life and death. Her circumstances do not allow her to complete the message. Her message and her life have been cut short.

Pagis, like Ka-tzetnik, renders the timeless, transcendent myth of our first parents and their children into a specific time and place within modern memory. Genesis, and the people who fill its pages, have much to say about life and death, joy and sorrow, the beginnings of things and, as in the case of the Shoah, tragic endings.

Epilogue

In the beginning was the Holocaust....

— Elie Wiesel

In my examination of Genesis allusions found in Shoah survivors' autobiographies, I led readers through a journey, safely and vicariously, paralleling the experience of many European Jews during the Third Reich. We have examined the trajectory of the Holocaust experience through Genesis citations as we have pondered the expulsion from paradise/home; the transport through/to death via Noah's ark/cattle cars; the imprisonment of European nationalities and languages with the Tower of Babel motif; the demand for human sacrifice by a higher power with references to Abraham and Isaac and Hitler; the wrestling match with a mysterious power, be it divine, angelic, demonic, or simply human; and the moral and theological implications of Cain's murder of his brother Abel as demonstrated in the Third Reich. My goal was to explore the manifold implications present in the Biblical images employed by the lifewriters and to demonstrate the complex resonance between the Holocaust and the Scriptural story that operate in a Midrashic manner.

Bereshit is a text concerned with beginnings. How appropriate are the survivors' references to it because at every stage of their Nazi-engineered degradation, life began anew. An old life passed away — usually violently — as each new stage made the previous one look paradisiacal. An old life vanished as the Nazis forbade the Jews to work, to go to school, to sit on park benches, to listen to the radio, or, in some places, even to enjoy the company of their pets. An old life disappeared as Nazis set up food restrictions and manipulated Jewish names. An old life died when a prison number was tattooed on the skin. An old life was eclipsed by a new one, over and

Epilogue

over again. For 12 years, the Nazis shrank the world of the European Jew until, for millions, there was no life left at all. Those who survived and had the courage to write their memoirs give to the world a valuable contribution.

Some scholars might argue that the Biblical book of Exodus serves as a more appropriate text for survivors to engage with than Genesis. Michael Goldberg, for instance, asserts in his provocatively titled book, *Why Should the Jews Survive? Looking Past the Holocaust toward a Jewish Future*, the themes of freedom and empowerment found in Exodus should inspire Jews. In our focus upon Genesis allusions, we have occasionally glimpsed references to Exodus. Frank Stiffel alluded to Exodus and Pharaoh's cruelty in his autobiography, *The Tale of the Ring: A Kaddish*, when he reflected on his harsh and meaningless work. Filip Müller quoted the Orthodox leader who reminded the crematoria workers that Pharaohs have existed throughout the millennia, intent upon destroying the Jews. Certainly the motifs of slavery, deliverance, and freedom link those who suffered in the Holocaust with those who suffered in ancient Egypt. Goldberg believes that the Jewish people have been pulled down too long by the gravity of the Holocaust, and so he suggests that Exodus offers hope and encouragement. His argument bears merit, but I agree with Emil Fackenheim and others who see in the *hurban* a rupture that the mere passing of time will not be able to mend. Jews, and any other people who have been systematically oppressed, can be empowered by Exodus; nevertheless, the stories told in *Bereshit* are critical to self-understanding.

Genesis encourages self-reflection at both a personal level and a cultural level. Far from the simple book that some contemporary readers mistake it for, Genesis contains stories that are complex, compelling, and paradoxical. It is, as the title proclaims, a book of beginnings, and Wiesel reflects that the "Jew is haunted by the beginning more than the end" (*Messengers* p. xii). The beginnings of stories often propel the plot to go in a certain direction. In light of the genocide that occurred during the Second World War and that continues in different parts of the world today, it may be too optimistic to say that we should try to overcome being haunted by beginnings. If humanity can transcend that state, then perhaps we can actually learn from history's past traumas.

Imagery from Genesis *in Holocaust Memoirs : A Critical Study* has by

Epilogue

no means exhausted the subject of Holocaust autobiographies and their Biblical allusions. Some autobiographers refer to the Psalms, to Ecclesiastes, and to the major prophets. Allusions to Job exist, but not to the extent that might be predicted, given the nature of Job's losses and sufferings; this is likely due to the perception that Job was not Jewish. The ordinary practice of faith within the camps — an illegal activity — demands further study, as well as extraordinary religious events, such as lifewriters who believe that they saw Elijah or angels. Comments about Moloch and the golem should be considered. The attitude of the nonpracticing Jew towards devout Jews is also a topic ripe for exploration. I plan to examine Christian allusions made by Jewish lifewriters; references to Calvary, crucifixion, and resurrection appear throughout various autobiographies. Moreover, a critical analysis of literary allusions to Shakespeare, Goëthe, Kafka, Dante, among other authors who populate Shoah memoirs, could deepen our appreciation of intertextual resonance.

"In the beginning," Wiesel says — and some would accuse him of being too pessimistic, too dire — "there was the Holocaust. We must therefore start all over again" ("Jewish Values" p. 285). If, from the start of humanity, there was the Shoah, then does that imply that the *hurban* was preordained? Inevitable? I do not think so, and I suspect that neither does Wiesel. Rather, Wiesel suggests that the ramifications of the Holocaust reverberate back into the beginning of time. As I argued in the introduction, literary allusions reflect back to the earlier work; something similar happens in history. The Shoah might not have happened if only certain actions had been taken. Surely the Holocaust was not destined to occur, fated thusly by a divine being, nor was it doomed to happen, although Genesis teaches that a murderous impulse exists in the human heart. But because the Event did happen, the shock waves were not limited to the contemporary time of its occurrence, but it spread to the past and to the future. We citizens of the twenty-first century are who we are partially because of the Holocaust.

If Wiesel is correct when he says that we must start afresh, then we must not ignore everything that came before. To read survivors' texts may be, in some small measure, a way to honor those whom Hitler sought to annihilate. To read is to participate in the act of memory, a critical component for the autobiographer and, as discussed in the introduction, for the Jew. We who read have much to learn.

Bibliography

Primary Texts

Améry, Jean. *At the Mind's Limits: Contemplations by a Survivor on Auschwitz and Its Realities*. 1980. Trans. Sidney Rosenfeld and Stella Rosenfeld. New York: Schocken, 1990.

Appelman-Jurman, Alicia. *Alicia: My Story*. New York: Bantam, 1990.

Bau, Joseph. *Dear God, Have You Ever Gone Hungry?* Trans. Shlomo Yurman. New York: Arcade, 1990.

Berg, Lena. "Lena's Story." *The Holocaust Kingdom: A Memoir* by Alexander Donat. Washington, D.C.: Holocaust Library, 1999; 257–278.

Bernstein, Sara Tuvel. *The Seamstress: A Memoir of Survival*. New York: Berkley, 1999.

Cyprys, Ruth Altbeker. *A Jump for Survival: A Survivor's Journal from Nazi-Occupied Poland*. Ed. Elaine Potter. London: Constable, 1997.

Delbo, Charlotte. *Days and Memories*. Trans. Rosette Lamont. Evanston: Mallboro, 2001

Donat, Alexander. *The Holocaust Kingdom: A Memoir*. Washington, D.C.: Holocaust Library, 1999.

Dribben, Judith. *And Some Shall Live*. Jerusalem: Keter, 1969.

Drix, Samuel. *Witness to Annihilation: Surviving the Holocaust A Memoir*. Washington, D.C.: Brassey's, 1994.

Dube, Alfred. "And Where Was God?" unpublished ms. held in archives of the United States Holocaust Memorial Museum.

Eichengreen, Lucille, with Harriet Hyman Chamberlain. *From Ashes to Life: My Memories of the Holocaust*. San Francisco: Mercury, 1994.

Ferderber-Salz, Bertha. *And the Sun Kept Shining...* New York: Holocaust Library, 1980.

Frankl, Viktor E. *Man's Search for Meaning: An Introduction to Logotherapy*. Trans. Ilse Lasch. New York: Simon & Schuster, 1962.

Friedländer, Saul. *When Memory Comes*. Trans. Helen R. Lane. New York: Farrar, Straus & Giroux, 1979.

Hart, Kitty. *Return to Auschwitz*. New York: Atheneum, 1982.

Heimler, Eugene. *Concentration Camp*. New York: Pyramid, 1959.

Hillman, Laura. *I Will Plant You a Lilac Tree: A Memoir of a Schindler's List Survivor*. New York: Atheneum, 2005.

Isaacson, Judith Magyar. *Seed of Sarah: Memoirs of a Survivor*. 2nd ed. Urbana: University of Illinois Press, 1991.

Jackson, Livia E. Bitton. *Elli: Coming of

Bibliography

Age in the Holocaust. New York: New York Times, 1980.

Ka-tzetnik 135633. *Shivitti: A Vision.* Trans. Eilyah Nike De-Nur and Lisa Herman. San Francisco: Harper, 1987.

———. *Star Eternal.* Trans. Nina De-Nur. New York: Arbor House, 1971.

Klein, Gerda Weissmann. *All But My life.* New York: Hill and Wang, 1995.

———. Yom HaShoah address. Edmond Historical Society Museum. Edmond, Oklahoma. 27 May 1996.

Kluger, Ruth. *Still Alive: A Holocaust Girlhood Remembered.* New York: Feminist Press at the City University of New York, 2001.

Leitner, Isabella. *Fragments of Isabella: A Memoir of Auschwitz.* Ed. Irving A. Leitner. New York: Crowell, 1978.

Lengyel, Olga. *Five Chimneys: A Woman Survivor's True Story of Auschwitz.* Chicago: Academy Chicago, 1995.

Levi, Primo. *The Drowned and the Saved.* Trans. Raymond Rosenthal. New York: Summit, 1986.

———. "Shemá." *Holocaust Poetry.* Ed. Hilda Schiff. New York: St. Martin's Griffin, 1995; 205.

———. *Survival in Auschwitz and The Reawakening: Two Memoirs.* Trans. Stuart Woolf. New York: Collier, 1973.

Lewis, Helen. *A Time to Speak.* Belfast: Blackstaff, 1992

Millu, Liana. *Smoke Over Birkenau.* Trans. Lynne Sharon Shwartz. 1947. Philadelphia: Jewish Publication Society, 1991.

Müller, Filip. *Eyewitness Auschwitz: Three Years in the Gas Chambers.* Ed. & trans. Susanne Flatauer. New York: Collier, 1973.

Nomberg-Przytyk, Sara. *Auschwitz: True Tales from a Grotesque Land.* Trans. Roslyn Hirsch. Eds. Eli Pfefferkorn and David H. Hirsch. Chapel Hill: University of North Carolina Press, 1985.

Nyiszli, Miklos. *Auschwitz: A Doctor's Eyewitness Account.* Trans. Tibere Kremer and Richard Seaver. New York: Fawcett Crest, 1960.

Orenstein, Henry. *I Shall Live: Surviving Against All Odds, 1939–1945.* New York: Touchstone, 1987.

Pagis, Dan. "Written in Pencil in a Sealed Freightcar." *Holocaust Poetry.* Ed. Hilda Schiff. New York: St. Martin's Griffin, 1995; 180.

Rubinstein, Erna F. *The Survivor in Us All: Four Young Sisters in the Holocaust.* Hamden, Connecticut: Archon, 1986.

Salsitz, Norman. *A Jewish Boyhood in Poland: Remembering Kolbuszowa.* As told to Richard Skolnik. Syracuse: Syracuse University Press, 1992.

Salton, George Lucius, with Anna Salton Eisen. *The 23rd Psalm: A Holocaust Memoir.* Madison: University of Wisconsin Press, 2002.

Stiffel, Frank. *The Tale of the Ring: A Kaddish.* New York: Bantam, 1984.

Szalet, Leon. *Experiment "E": A Report from an Extermination Laboratory.* New York: Didier, 1945.

Wachtel, Shirley Russak. *The Story of Blima: A Holocaust Survivor.* West Berlin, New Jersey: Townsend Library, 2005.

Wdowinski, David. *And We Are Not Saved.* New York: Philosophical Library, 1963.

Wiesel, Elie. *After the Darkness: Reflections on the Holocaust.* Trans. Benjamin Moster. New York: Schocken, 2002.

———. *All Rivers Run to the Sea: Memoirs.* New York: Alfred A. Knopf, 1995.

———. *From the Kingdom of Memory: Reminiscences.* New York: Schocken, 1990.

———. *Messengers of God: Biblical Portraits and Legends.* Trans. Marion Wiesel. New York: Summit, 1976.

Bibliography

_____. *Night.* Trans. Stella Rodway. New York: Bantam, 1960.

_____. *One Generation After.* Trans. Lily Edelman and Elie Wiesel. New York: Random, 1970.

_____. "Pilgrimage to the Kingdom of Night." *From the Kingdom of Memory.* New York: Schocken, 1995; 105–21.

_____. "Sighet Again." *From the Kingdom of Memory.* New York: Schocken, 1995; 123–9.

_____. "Why I Write." *From the Kingdom of Memory.* New York: Schocken, 1995; 13–21.

Secondary Texts

Alter, Robert. *The Art of Biblical Narrative.* New York: Basic, 1981.

_____. *Genesis: Translation and Commentary.* New York: Norton, 1996.

Appelfeld, Aharon. "After the Holocaust." Trans. Jeffrey M. Green. *Writing and the Holocaust.* Ed. Berel Lang. New York: Holmes & Meier, 1988; 83–92.

Arendt, Hannah. *Eichmann in Jerusalem: A Report on the Banality of Evil.* Rev. & enl. ed. New York: Penguin, 1992.

Arieti, Silvano. *Abraham and the Contemporary Mind.* New York: Basic, 1981.

Auerbach, Erich. "Odysseus' Scar." *Mimesis: The Representation of Reality in Western Literature.* Trans. Willard R. Trask. Princeton: Princeton University Press, 1953; 3–23.

Bailey, Lloyd R. *Noah: The Person and the Story in History and Tradition.* Columbia: University of South Carolina Press, 1989.

Bakhtin, M.M. "Author and Hero in Anesthetic Activity." *Art and Answerability.* Eds. Michael Holquis and Vadim Liapunov. Trans. Vadim Liapunov. Austin: University of Texas Press, 1990.

_____. "Discourse in the Novel." *The Dialogic Imagination: Four Essays.* Ed. Michael Holquist. Austin: University of Texas Press, 1981; 259–422.

Berenbaum, Michael, and Yitzchak Mais. *Memory and Legacy: The Shoah Narrative of the Illinois Holocaust Museum.* Lincolnwood, Illinois: Publications International, 2009.

Berman, Louis A. *The Akedah: The Binding of Isaac.* Northvale, New Jersey: Jason Aronson, 1997.

Bodoff, Lippman. "The Real Test of the *Akedah*: Blind Obedience Versus Moral Choice." *Judaism* 42(1993): 71–92.

Brown, Michael. "Knight of Faith or Man of Doubt? A Contemporary Reading of the Akedah." *Conservative Judaism* 35(1982): 17–23.

Buber, Martin. *I and Thou.* Trans. Walter Kaufmann. New York: Scribner's, 1970.

_____. *On the Bible.* Ed. Nahum N. Glatzer. New York: Schocken Books, 1968.

Carmy, Shalom. "The Long and Winding Road: By Way of Introduction." *Jewish Perspectives on the Experience of Suffering.* Ed. Shalom Carmy. The Orthodox forum. Northvale, New Jersey: Jason Aronson, 1999; 1–20.

Cassuto, U. *A Commentary on the Book of Genesis. Part II: From Noah to Abraham, Genesis VI9-XI 32.* Jerusalem: Magnes Press, 1974.

Cohen, Arthur A. *The Tremendum: A Theological Interpretation of the Holocaust.* New York: Crossroad, 1981.

Cohen, Avner. "*Kiddush Hashem* on Sabbaths and Holidays in the Holocaust." *I Will Be Sanctified: Religious Responses to the Holocaust.* Ed. Rabbi Yehezkel Fogel. Trans. Edward Levin. Northvale, New Jersey: Jason Aronson, 1998; 61–82.

Bibliography

Cohen, Jeffrey M. "Consequences of the Akedah." *Jewish Bible Quarterly* 24 (1995): 241–6.

Cohen, Norman. *Noah's Flood: The Genesis Story in Western Thought.* New Haven: Yale University Press, 1996.

Cohen, Norman J. *Self, Struggle, and Change: Family Conflict Stories in Genesis and Their Healing Insights for Our Lives.* Woodstock, Vermont: Jewish Lights, 1995.

Dawidowicz, Lucy S., ed. *The Golden Tradition: Jewish Life and Thought in Eastern Europe.* New York: Holt, 1966.

_____. *The War Against the Jews: 1933–1945.* New York: Holt, 1975.

Des Pres, Terrence. *The Survivor: An Anatomy of Life in the Death Camps.* Oxford: Oxford University Press, 1976.

DiCicco, Mario, O.F.M. "God Remembered Noah." *The Bible Today* 35 (1997): 16–21.

Dubner, Stephen J. *Turbulent Souls: A Catholic Son's Return to His Jewish Family.* New York: Morrow, 1998.

Eakin, Paul John. *Touching the World: References in Autobiography.* Princeton: Princeton University Press, 1992.

Eckstein, Yechiel. *How Firm a Foundation: A Gift of Jewish Wisdom for Christians and Jews.* Brewster, Massachusetts: Paraclete, 1997.

Eisendstadt, S.N. *Jewish Civilization: The Jewish Historical Experience in a Comparative Perspective.* Albany: State University of New York Press, 1992.

Eitinger, L. "On Being a Psychiatrist and a Survivor." *Confronting the Holocaust: The Impact of Elie Wiesel.* Ed. Alvin H. Rosenberg and Irving Greenberg. Bloomington: Indiana University Press, 1978: 186–99.

Elbogen, Ismar. *A Century of Jewish Life.* Trans. Moses Hadas. Philadelphia: Jewish Publication Society, 1946.

Eliach, Yaffa. *Hasidic Tales of the Holocaust.* New York: Vintage, 1988.

Eliot, T.S. "Tradition and the Individual Talent." *The Critical Tradition: Classic Texts and Contemporary Trends.* Ed. David H. Richter. New York: St. Martin's, 1989; 466–71.

Epstein, Adam. "Primo Levi and the Language of Atrocity." *Bulletin of the Society for Italian Studies* 20 (1987): 31–8.

Ettin, Andrew Vogel. *Speaking Silences: Stillness and Voice in Modern Thought and Jewish Tradition.* Charlottesville: University Press of Virginia, 1994.

Ezrahi, Sidra DeKoven. *By Words Alone: The Holocaust in Literature.* Chicago: University of Chicago Press, 1980.

Facing Hate: Elie Wiesel with Bill Moyers. A Mystic Fire Video (cassette). 1991.

Fackenheim, Emil L. *God's Presence in History: Jewish Affirmations and Philosophical Reflections.* New York: New York University Press, 1970.

_____. "The Human Condition After Auschwitz: A Jewish Testimony a Generation After." The B.G. Rudolph Lecture in Jewish Studies. Syracuse: Syracuse University Press, 1971.

_____. "Jewish Existence and the Living God: The Religious Duty of Survival." *Arguments and Doctrines: A Reader of Jewish Thinking in the Aftermath of the Holocaust.* Ed. Arthur A. Cohen. New York: Harper and Row, 1970.

Fass, David E. "Jacob's Limp?" *Judaism* 38 (Spring 1989): 143–50.

Feld, Edward. *The Spirit of Renewal: Finding Faith After the Holocaust.* Woodstock, Vermont: Jewish Lights, 1991.

Fest, Joachim C. *Hitler.* Trans. Richard and Clara Winston. New York: Harcourt, 1974.

Foley, Barbara. "Fact, Fiction, Fascism: Testimony and Nemesis in Holocaust Narratives." *Comparative Literature* 34 (Fall 1982): 330–60.

Bibliography

Fox, Marvin. "Kierkegaard and Rabbinic Judaism." *Judaism* 2 (1953): 160–9.

Friedländer, Saul. *Nazi Germany and the Jews, Vol. I: The Years of Persecution, 1933–1939.* New York: Harper Collins, 1997.

———. *Reflections of Nazism: An Essay on Kitsch and Death.* Trans. Thomas Weyr. Bloomington: Indiana University Press, 1993.

Frontline: Memory of the Camps. Videocassette. Prod. Sergei Nolbandov. PBS. 1985. 60 minutes.

Gates of Repentance: The New Union Prayerbook for the Days of Awe. New York: Central Conference of American Rabbis, 1978.

Gellman, Jerome I. *The Fear, the Trembling, and the Fire: Kierkegaard and Hasidic Masters on the Binding of Isaac.* Lanham, Maryland: University Press of America, 1994.

Genesis. *The Torah: A Modern Commentary.* Ed. W. Gunther Plaut. New York: Union of American Hebrew Congregations, 1974.

Genesis Rabbah: The Judaic Commentary to the Book of Genesis. Ed. Jacob Neusner. 3 vols. 1985.

Gilbert, Martin. *Atlas of the Holocaust.* New York: William Morrow, 1993.

Glatstein, Jacob. *I Keep Recalling: The Holocaust Poems of Jacob Glatstein.* Trans. Barnett Zumoff. Jersey City: Ktav Publishing House, 1993.

———. *The Selected Poems of Jacob Glatstein.* Trans. Ruth Whitman. New York: October House, 1972.

Goldberg, Edwin C. *Midrash for Beginners.* Northvale, New Jersey: Jason Aronson, 1996.

Goldberg, Michael. *Why Should the Jews Survive? Looking Past the Holocaust toward a Jewish Future.* New York: Oxford University Press, 1995.

Goldhagen, Daniel. *Hitler's Willing Executioners: Ordinary Germans and the Holocaust.* New York: Knopf, 1996.

Goldsmith, Emanuel S. "Introduction." *I Keep Recalling: The Holocaust Poems of Jacob Glatstein.* Trans. Barnett Zumoff. Jersey City: Ktav Publishing House, 1993; xxiii–xv.

Greenberg, Irving. "Voluntary Covenant." New York: National Jewish Resources Center, 1982.

Grunberger, Richard. *The 12-Year Reich: A Social History of Nazi Germany, 1933–1945.* New York: Holt, 1971.

Halevi, Jacob L. "Kierkegaard and the Midrash." *Judaism* 4 (1955): 13–28.

Halperin, Irving. *Messengers from the Dead: Literature of the Holocaust.* Philadelphia: Westminster, 1970.

Harries, Richard. *After the Evil: Christianity and Judaism in the Shadow of the Holocaust.* New York: Oxford University Press, 2003.

Hartman, Geoffrey H. "The Struggle for the Text." *Midrash and Literature.* Eds. Geoffrey H. Hartman and Sanford Budick. New Haven: Yale University Press, 1986; 3–18.

———, and Sanford Budick. "Introduction." *Midrash and Literature.* Eds. Geoffrey H. Hartman and Sanford Budick. New Haven: Yale University Press, 1986; ix–xiii.

Heschel, Abraham Joshua. *The Earth Is the Lord's: The Inner World of the Jew in Eastern Europe.* New York: Henry Schuman, 1950.

———. *God in Search of Man: A Philosophy of Judaism.* 1955. New York: Noonday Press, 1991.

Hitler, Adolf. *Mein Kampf.* Trans. Ralph Manheim. Boston: Houghton Mifflin, 1999.

Holtz, Barry W. "Introduction: On Reading Jewish Texts." *Back to the Sources.* Ed. Barry W. Holtz. New York: Summit, 1984; 11–29.

Bibliography

Houston, Walter J. "Misunderstanding of Midrash? The Prose of Appropriation of Poetic Material in The Hebrew Bible (Part I)." *Zeitschrift für die Alttestamentiche Wissenschaft* 109 (1997): 342–55.

Howe, Irving. "Writing and the Holocaust." *Writing and the Holocaust*. Ed. Berel Lang. New York: Holmes & Meier, 1988: 175–99.

Hyman, Naomi M. *Biblical Women in the Midrash: A Sourcebook*. Ed. Naomi M. Hyman. Northvale, NJ: Jason Aronson, 1997.

"Jewish Values in the Post-Holocaust Future: A Symposium." With Emil Fackenheim, George Steiner, Richard Popkin, and Elie Wiesel. *Judaism* 16 (1967): 266–99.

Jung, Carl. *The Basic Writings of C.G. Jung*. Ed. Violet S. deLaszlo. New York: Modern Library, 1959.

Kaplan, Harold. *Conscience and Memory: Meditations in a Museum of the Holocaust*. Chicago: University of Chicago Press, 1994.

Kaufman, Jonathan. *A Hole in the Heart of the World: Bring Jewish in Eastern Europe*. New York: Viking, 1997.

Kierkegaard, Søren. *Fear and Trembling/ Repetition*. Eds. and Trans. Howard V. Hong and Edna H. Hong. Princeton: Princeton UniversityPress, 1983.

Kodell, Jerome, O.S.B. "Jacob Wrestles with Esau (Gen 32:23–32)." *Biblical Theology Bulletin* 10 (April 1980): 65–70.

Lang, Berel, Ed. *Writing and the Holocaust*. New York: Holmes & Meier, 1998.

Langer, Lawrence L. *The Holocaust and the Literary Imagination*. New Haven: Yale University Press,1975.

_____. *Holocaust Testimonies:* New Haven: Yale University Press, 1991.

_____. *Preempting the Holocaust*. New Haven: Yale University Press, 1998.

_____. *Versions of Survival: The Holocaust and the Human Spirit*. Albany: State University of New York Press, 1982.

Laytner, Anson. *Arguing with God: A Jewish Tradition*. Northvale, New Jersey: Jason Aronson, 1990.

Lejeune, Philippe. *On Autobiography*. Trans. Katherine Leary. Minneapolis: University of Minnesota Press,1989.

Lenchak, Timothy A., S.V.D. "Puzzling Passages: Genesis 11:7." *The Bible Today* 35 (1997): 44.

Levine, Rabbi Aaron. *To Comfort the Bereaved: A Guide for Mourners and Those Who Visit Them*. Northvale, New Jersey: Jason Aronson, 1996.

The Long Way Home. Videocassette. Moriah Films, a division of the Simon Wiesenthal Center. 1998.

McMahon, Robert. "Autobiography as Text-Work: Augustine's Refiguring of Genesis 3 and Ovid's 'Narcissus' in his Conversion Account." *Exemplaria* 1 (October 1989): 337–66.

Montefiore, C. G., and H. Loewe, Eds. *A Rabbinic Anthology*. New York: Schocken, 1974.

Mosse, George L. *Nazi Culture: Intellectual, Cultural, and Social Life in the Third Reich*. Trans. Salvator Attanasio and others. New York: Grosset & Dunlap, 1966.

Moyers, Bill. *Genesis: A Living Conversation*. New York: Doubleday, 1996.

Namenyi, Ernest. *The Essence of Jewish Art*. Trans. Edouard Roditi. London: Thomas Yoseloff, 1957.

Neher, André. *Exile of the Word: From the Silence of the Bible to the Silence of Auschwitz*. Trans. David Maisel. Philadelphia: Jewish Publication Society of America, 5741; 1981.

Neusner, Jacob. *The Midrash: An Introduction*. Northvale, New Jersey: Jason Aronson, 1984.

_____. *What Is Midrash?* Philadelphia: Fortress, 1987.

Ofer, Dalia, and Lenore J. Weitzman, Eds. *Women in the Holocaust.* New Haven: Yale UniversityPress, 1998.

Olney, James. *Metaphors of Self.* Princeton: Princeton University Press, 1972.

"One Survivor Remembers." Dir. Kary Antholis. Video. United States Holocaust Memorial Museum and HBO. 1995.

Ozsvath, Zsuzsanna, and Martha Satz. "The Audacity of Expressing the Inexpressible: The Relation Between Moral and Aesthetic Considerations in Holocaust Literature." *Judaism* 34 (Spring 1985): 197–210.

Packman, Rabbi C. David. Personal interview. 20 July 1998.

Paperclips. Dir. Elliot Berlin and Joe Fab. DVD. Johnson Group. 2006.

Patterson, David. "The Annihilation of Exists: The Problem of Liberation in the Holocaust Memoir." *Holocaust and Genocide Studies* 9 (Fall 1995): 208–30.

_____. *The Shriek of Silence: A Phenomenology of the Holocaust Novel.* Lexington: University of Kentucky Press, 1992.

_____. *Sun Turned to Darkness: Memory and Recovery in the Holocaust Memoir.* Syracuse: Syracuse University Press, 1998.

_____. "The Twilight of Memory: Reflections in Holocaust Memoirs, Past, Present, and Future." *Dimensions* 13 (1999): 19–24.

_____. *Wrestling with the Angel: Toward a Jewish Understanding of the Nazi Assault on the Name.* St. Paul: Paragon House, 2006.

Plaut, W. Gunther. *The Torah: A Modern Commentary.* Genesis. New York: Union of American Hebrew Congregations, 1974.

Polak, Frank H. "The Restful Waters of Noah." *Journal of the Ancient Near Eastern Society* 23 (1995): 69–74.

Porter, Gary G. *Understanding Rabbinic Midrash: Texts and Commentary.* Hoboken, New Jersey: Ktav, 1985.

Porter, Roger, and Daniel Reisberg. "Autobiography and Memory. "*a/b: Auto/Biography Studies* 13 (Spring 1998): 60–70.

Rabinowitz, Peter J. "Reader-Response Criticism and 'The Dead.'" James Joyce, *"The Dead": Case Studies in Contemporary Criticism.* Boston: Bedford Books, 1994; 137–49.

Rosenberg, David. "Introduction." *Testimony: Contemporary Writers Make the Holocaust Personal.* New York: Times, 1989; xiii–xxiii.

Rosenberg, Joel. "Bible: Biblical Narrative." *Back to the Sources.* Ed. Barry W. Holtz. New York; Summit, 1984; 31–81.

Rosenblatt, Naomi H., and Joshua Horwitz. *Wrestling with Angels: What Genesis Teaches Us About Our Spiritual Identity, Sexuality, and Personal Relationships.* New York: Delta, 1995.

Rosenfeld, Alvin H. "Reflections on Isaac." *Holocaust and Genocide Studies* 1 (1986): 241–8.

Roskies, David G. Lecture. Jack and Anita Hess Faculty Seminar. United States Holocaust Memorial Museum, Washington, D.C.: 8 January 2007.

Rubenstein, Richard L. *After Auschwitz: Radical Theology and Contemporary Judaism.* Indianapolis: Bobbs-Merill, 1966.

Sarna, Nahum M. *Understanding Genesis.* New York: Schocken, 1972.

Schiff, Hilda. Ed. *Holocaust Poetry.* New York: St. Martin's Griffin, 1995.

Schindler's List. Film. Dir. Steven Spielberg. With Liam Neesin and Ben Kingsley. Universal, 1993.

Bibliography

Sherwin, Byron L. "Wiesel's Midrash: The Writings of Elie Wiesel and Their Relationship to Jewish Tradition." *Confronting the Holocaust: The Impact of Elie Wiesel*. Eds. Alvin H. Rosenfeld and Irving Greenberg. Bloomington: Indiana University Press, 1978; 117-32.

Sisson, Larry. "The Art and Illusion of Spiritual Autobiography." *True Relations: Essays on Autobiography and the Postmodern*. Eds. G. Thomas Couser and Joseph Fichtelberg. Westport, Connecticut: Greenwood, 1998; 97-108.

Smith, Sidonie, and Julia Watson, Eds. Introduction. *Everyday Uses of Autobiography*. Minneapolis: University of Minnesota Press, 1996: 1-24.

Speiser, E.A., Trans. *Genesis: Anchor Bible*. Garden City, New York: Doubleday, 1964.

Spiegel, Shalom. *The Last Trial: On the Legends and Lore of the Command to Abraham to Offer Isaac as a Sacrifice*. Trans. Judah Goldin. Woodstock, Vermont: Jewish Lights, 1993.

Steinberg, Milton. "Kierkegaard and the Jews." *Anatomy of Faith*. Ed. Arthur A. Cohen. New York: Harcourt Brace, 1960; 130-152.

Steiner, George. *In Bluebeard's Castle: Some Notes Towards the Redefinition of Culture*. New Haven: Yale University Press, 1971.

_____. "A Kind of Survivor: To Elie Wiesel." *Language and Silence: Essays on Language, Literature, and the Inhuman*. New York: Atheneum, 1967; 140-54.

Stille, Alexander. Forward. *At the Mind's Limits: Contemplations by a Survivor on Auschwitz and Its Realities*. By Jean Améry. 1980. New York: Schocken, 1990; vii-xvi.

Tanay, Emmanuel. "On Being a Survivor." *Bearing Witness to the Holocaust. 1939-1989*. Ed. Alan L. Berger, Symposium Series Vol. 31. Lewiston, New York: Edwin Mellen Press, 1991; 17-31.

Telushkin, Joseph. *Jewish Literacy: The Most Important Things to Know about the Jewish Religion, Its People and Its History*. New York: Morrow; 1991.

Tokudome, Kinue. *Courage to Remember: Interviews on the Holocaust*. London: Paragon, 1999.

Tos, Aldo J. *Approaches to the Bible: The Old Testament*. Englewood Cliffs, New Jersey: Prentice-Hall, 1963.

Weis, Richard D. "Lessons on Wrestling with the Unseen: Jacob at the Jabbok." *The Reformed Review* (Winter 1988): 96-112.

Wiesel, Elie. *Against Silence: The Voice and Vision of Elie Wiesel*. 3 vols. Ed. Irving Abrahamson. New York: Holocaust Library, 1985.

_____. "Noah's Warning." *Religion and Literature* 16 (Winter 1984): 3-20.

_____. "We Are All Witnesses: An Interview with Elie Wiesel." *Parabola* 10 (May 1985): 26-33.

Wiesel, Elie (words), and Darius Milhaud (music). *Ani Maamin: A Song Lost and Found Again*. Trans. Marion Wiesel. New York: Random House, 1973.

Wiesel, Elie, and Philippe-Michael De Saint-Cheron. *Evil and Exile*. Trans. Jon Rothschild. Notre Dame: University of Notre Dame Press, 1990.

Wiesel, Elie, and Albert H. Friedlander. *The Six Days of Destruction: Meditations Toward Hope*. New York: Paulist, 1988.

Index

Abel *see* Cain and Abel
Abraham 14, 29, 32, 72, 73, 77, 83, 87, 99, 100–105, 107–110, 112–116, 119, 120, 124–127, 135, 139, 140, 170, 181
Adam 33, 172, 175–176; *see also* Adam and Eve
'*adam* 34
Adam and Eve 29, 31, 33, 34, 36, 37–38, 39, 40, 41, 44, 45, 46, 49, 54, 55, 71, 83, 99, 124, 137, 171–173, 179
Akeda 29, 99–104, 106–110, 112–116, 118–119, 124–127, 178
allusions, literary 6, 12, 13, 16
Alter, Robert 2, 34, 45, 83–84, 105, 168
Améry, Jean 90, 93, 134, 147, 151, 154–155
Appelfeld, Aharon 28
Appelman-Jurman, Alicia 82, 90
Arendt, Hannah 160
Arieti, Silvano 70–71, 73
Aryan 6, 49, 58, 77
Auerbach, Erich 108, 114
Augustine's *Confessions* 12
Auschwitz (concentration camp) 16, 22, 40, 41, 42, 43, 44, 47, 48, 64, 70, 74, 171, 178, 79, 80, 85, 89, 90, 95, 96, 101, 107, 110–113, 116, 119–121, 141, 142, 144, 148, 149, 151, 154, 156, 158, 161, 162, 172, 173
Auschwitz (term to signify entire extermination camp system) 44, 69, 79, 81, 88, 119, 128, 131, 155, 163, 164
autobiography (definition) 11

Baal Shem Tov 21, 29
Babel, Tower of 14, 29, 54, 55, 79, 80–84, 86–89, 92, 96–99, 126, 181
Bakhtin, Mikhail M. 3, 12–13, 116, 164
Bau, Joseph 16
Berenbaum, Michael 59–60
Bereshit (definition) 31; *see also* Genesis

Berg, Lena 65, 82, 161
Berg, Michal 151–152, 154; *see also* Donat, Alexander
Bergen-Belsen concentration camp 47, 48, 70, 170, 171
Berger, Alan L. 2
Berman, Louis 106
Bernstein, Sara Tuvel 31, 35–37, 43, 46, 59, 93
Bettelheim, Bruno 134
Birkenau concentration camp 81, 110, 113, 149
Bodoff, Lippman 125
Borowski, Tadeusz 134
Brown, Michael 125
Bruss, Elizabeth 2
Buber, Martin 2, 13, 19, 39–40, 85, 87, 125
Buchenwald concentration camp 113
Budick, Sanford 19

Cain 33, 175–177; *see also* Cain and Abel
Cain and Abel 30, 39, 54, 83, 166–179, 181
Carmy, Shalom 15
Cassuto, U. 83, 98
Christian theology 38–39, 59, 104, 108, 126–127, 147–148, 170, 176, 183
Cohen, Arthur A. 3, 122, 123
Cohen, Avner 119
Cohen, Jeffrey M. 115
Cohen, Norman J. 125
Cyprys, Ruth Altbeker 63, 64, 65

Dachau concentration camp 151
Dallas Holocaust Museum/Center for Education and Tolerance 64–65
Dante 6, 13, 47, 183
Dawidowicz, Lucy 2, 8, 23
death march 48, 111, 112

193

Index

Delbo, Charlotte 161
De-Nur, Yehiel *see* Ka-tzetnik 135633
Des Pres, Terrence 3, 28, 63
Deuteronomy 17, 19–20, 97, 162
DiCicco, Mario 67–68
Dilthey, Wilhelm 23
Donat, Alexander 10, 57, 132, 151–152, 162; *see also* Berg, Michal
Doré, Gustave 62
Dribben, Judith 49
Drix, Samuel, M.D. 48–49, 58–59, 94, 117–118
Dube, Alfred 16
Dubner, Stephen 165

Eakin, Paul John 2
Ecclesiastes 183
Eden *see* Garden of Eden; paradise
Eichengreen, Lucille 16, 130, 151, 152–153
Eichmann, Adolf 159–160, 176
Eitinger, L. 89
Eliach, Yaffa 22, 146
Elijah 183
Eliot, T.S. 3, 14, 18
Epstein, Adam 93
Esther 7, 25
The Eternal Jew 60
Ettin, Andrew Vogel 3, 9, 97, 102
Eve 42, 43, 167, 179; *see also* Adam and Eve
Exodus 69, 87, 182

"Facing Hate" 29, 77, 97
Fackenheim, Emil 2, 3, 18, 25, 26, 32, 33
Fass, David E. 140, 157
Faulhaber, Michael Cardinal von 127
Feld, Edward 60, 92
Ferderber-Salz, Bertha 47, 48, 132
Fest, Joachim 2, 61
Flood 14
Frank, Anne 3, 23
Frankl, Viktor E. 149
Fratricide 166, 167, 175, 176
Freud, Sigmund 20
Friedländer, Saul 2, 3, 27, 54–55, 100–101, 146, 151, 155–157, 163

Garden of Eden 33, 34, 35, 42, 45, 48, 49, 137, 172; *see also* paradise
Gates of Repentance 126
Gellman, Jerome I. 124–125
Genesis 5, 6–10, 18, 31, 33, 34, 36–39, 44, 51–54, 67–68, 73–75, 79, 83, 99, 100–104, 108–110, 114–116, 124, 126–127, 131, 135–137, 139, 143, 165–168, 171–173, 175, 176, 177, 180, 181, 182, 183
Genesis Rabbah 17, 72, 74, 87, 97, 98, 126
Gilbert, Martin 134
Gilligan, Carol 69
Glatstein, Jacob 92, 117, 129
Goebbels, Joseph 60
Goëthe, Johann Wolfgang von 6, 13, 90, 183
Goldberg, Edwin C. 3, 17
Goldberg, Michael 182
Goldhagen, Daniel 27
Goldsmith, Emanuel S. 92
golem 183
Grese, Irma 122
Grunberg, Richard 2, 127
Gusdorf, Georges 2

Haman 7, 25
Harries, Richard 121
Hart, Kitty 149, 163
Hartman, Geoffrey H. 3, 19, 137, 139, 162, 165
Heiden, Konrad 2
Heimler, Eugene 79, 80, 118, 160–161
Herzberg, Abel J. 169–171, 173–175, 177
Heschel, Rabbi Abraham Joshua 3, 13, 19, 25–27
heteroglossia 12–14, 15
Hillman, Laura 43, 46–47
Himmler, Heinrich 90
Hitler, Adolf 1, 6, 7, 8, 9, 32, 47, 50, 56, 59, 60–61, 63, 66, 71, 73, 77, 88, 127, 128, 133, 134, 164, 166, 167, 170, 176, 178, 179, 181
Holocaust (definition) 8
Holtz, Barry W. 3, 19
Houston, Walter J. 18
Howe, Irving 3, 27, 28
hurban (definition) 9
Hyman, Naomi M. 16

Ibsen, Henrik 68
Illinois Holocaust Museum and Education Center 59, 65
intertextuality 11
Isaac 14, 29, 99–110, 114–116, 119, 120, 124, 126–128, 135, 170, 178, 181; *see also* Abraham; *Akeda*
Isaacson, Judith Magyar 41–42, 59, 64, 66, 82, 109–110, 149, 161

194

Index

Jackson, Livia E. Bitton 43, 44, 65–66, 80, 113, 114, 116, 133–134
Jacob 14, 109, 120, 131, 134–144, 146, 150, 157, 162–165, 170
Janowska concentration camp 48–49, 117
Jelinek, Estelle 2
Job 124, 183
Judenfrei 7
Judenrein 7, 48
Jung, Carl 138
Jungian 138, 140

Kaddish 16, 20, 77
Kafka, Franz 6, 183
Kaplan, Harold 2
Kaplan, Marion A. 56
Ka-tzetnik 135633 29, 94–95, 101, 118, 131, 134–135, 140–144, 146, 147, 150, 158–160, 163, 166, 177–180
Kierkegaard, Søren 108, 115, 119, 122, 124, 125
Klein, Gerda Weissmann 58, 73, 90
Kluger, Ruth 47, 76, 89
Kodell, Jerome, O.S.B. 137, 139, 140
Kushner, Rabbi Harold 108

Lang, Berel 27
Langer, Lawrence 3, 10, 14, 15, 86
Laytner, Anson 137–138
Leitner, Isabella 35, 48, 116, 162, 172–173
Lejeune, Philippe 3, 144–145, 150, 158
Lenchak, Timothy A. 98–99
Lengyel, Olga 65, 81, 95
Lerner, Lily Gluck 35, 47
Levi, Primo 5, 10, 15, 23, 24, 29, 64, 66, 79, 80, 81, 85–93, 95–96, 101–102, 111, 134, 147–148, 151, 173–174
Levine, Rabbi Aaron 121
Lewis, Helen 47, 62, 82, 93
lifewriting (definition) 11
The Long Way Home 130, 134

Maimonides 109, 125, 157
Majdanek concentration camp 128, 151
McMahon, Robert 12, 13
Mein Kampf 7, 60, 73
memoir (definition of term) 11
Mengele, Dr. Josef 109, 113
Midrash 2, 16–20, 26, 72, 86, 87, 97, 98, 140, 169, 175, 176, 181
Milhaud, Darius 109
Millu, Liana 80, 90
Milton, John 80

Moloch 13, 183
Montefiore and Loewe 62, 175–176
Moses 32, 69, 124, 128
Moshe (Moishe) the Beadle 119, 120, 129–130, 133
Mosse, George L. 2, 56, 57, 127
Moyers, Bill 69
Müller, Filip 7, 88, 116–117, 148–149, 182
Myth (definition) 33–34

Namenyi, Ernest 106
Neher, André 3, 30, 102, 112, 114, 121, 123, 124
Neusner, Jacob 3, 17, 72, 74
Night and Fog 9, 23, 24, 150
Noah/Noah's Ark 14, 29, 33, 50, 51–57, 62, 65–69, 71–78, 83, 85, 181
Nomberg-Przytyk, Sara 44, 48
Nyiszli, Dr. Miklos 173

Olney, James 2, 29
One Survivor Remembers 73
Orenstein, Henry 82, 91, 92

Packman, Rabbi A. David 19
Pagis, Dan 179–180
Paperclips 65
paradise 33, 34, 35, 36, 39, 44, 46, 47, 181; *see also* Adam and Eve
Pascal, Roy 2
Patterson, David 3, 21, 25, 116, 118, 119, 129, 140, 147, 150, 164
Plaut, W. Gunther 2, 34
Plaut *Commentary* 34, 38, 39, 67, 71–72, 76, 86, 98, 104, 105, 106, 114, 123, 125, 135, 140, 168–169, 171, 172, 175, 176; *see also* Plaut, W. Gunther
Polak, Frank H. 71
Porter, Gary G. 18
Porter, Roger 22
Procksch, Otto 98
Psalms 20, 67, 124

Rabbinic Anthology 62, 175–176
Rabinowitz, Peter J. 11
Ravensbrück concentration camp 43, 151
Rebekah 105–106, 135
Reisberg, Daniel 22
Renza, Louis 2
Rosenberg, Alvin H. 2
Rosenberg, Joel 84
Rosenblatt, Naomi H. 32
Rosenfeld, Alvin H. 114

195

Index

Roskies, David G. 74
Rubenstein, Richard L. 61
Rubinstein, Erna F. 149

Sachs, Nelly 96
Salsitz, Norman 55
Salton, George Lucius 40–41, 151, 153–154
Sarna, Nahum M. 3, 31, 33–34, 38, 58, 103, 136–138, 168, 169
Schiff, Hilda 96, 179
Schindler, Oskar 47
Schindler's List 169
Shakespeare, William 6, 13, 80, 183
Shema 15, 20, 119, 123, 147
Sherwin, Byron L. 18
Shoah (definition) 9
Shoah Foundations 9
Smith, Sidonie 2, 23
Speiser, E.A. 109
Spiegel, Shalom 104
Spielberg, Steven 9, 169
Spitzer, Esther 140
Steinberg, Milton 108
Steiner, George 3, 69–70, 119, 157
Stiffel, Frank 29, 51–52, 56–58, 64, 69, 70, 88, 161, 182
Stille, Alexander 154
Szalet, Leon 63–64

TaNaKH (definition) 16
Tanay, Emanuel 132
Telushkin, Rabbi Joseph 3, 18, 108, 147, 171, 176–177

Terezín (also Theresiendstadt) 47
Tokudome, Kinue 59
Toland, John 2
The Torah: A Modern Commentary 2, 37–38; *see also* Plaut Commentary
Tos, Aldo J. 84, 97
Treblinka concentration camp 113, 151

United States Holocaust Memorial Museum 59, 64, 74
University of Southern California 9

Vago, Linda Rosenfeld 41, 42–43

Wachtel, Shirley Russak 146–147
Wannsee Conference 61, 169
Watson, Julia 23
Wdowinski, David 134, 162, 163
Weis, Richard D. 137, 138, 140
Whirlwind (definition) 9
Wiesel, Elie 1, 6, 8, 10, 14, 24, 25, 28–29, 30, 35, 45, 49, 52, 55, 65, 68, 70, 71, 75–76, 77–78, 80, 90, 92, 96–97, 100–101, 103, 106–115, 117–122, 124, 128–130, 132, 133, 142, 147, 159, 163–164, 166, 171, 176, 181, 182, 183
Wilkomirski, Binjamin 145

Yale University 9
Yiddish 92, 93, 95, 117

Zelig, Dorothy F. 140

www.ingramcontent.com/pod-product-compliance
Lightning Source LLC
Chambersburg PA
CBHW032100300426
44116CB00007B/831